Contested Empire

Peter Skene Ogden, from a daguerreotype taken during a visit to New York, circa 1850. Oregon Historical Society neg. no. OrHi707.

Contested Empire

Peter Skene Ogden and the Snake River Expeditions

John Phillip Reid

Foreword by Martin Ridge

UNIVERSITY OF OKLAHOMA PRESS : NORMAN

ALSO BY JOHN PHILLIP REID

Patterns of Vengeance: Crosscultural Homicide in the North American Fur Trade
(Pasadena, Calif., 1999)
Policing the Elephant: Crime, Punishment, and Social Behavior on the Overland Trail
(San Marino, Calif., 1997)
Constitutional History of the American Revolution: Abridged Edition (Madison, 1995)
Constitutional History of the American Revolution, IV: The Authority of Law (Madison, 1993)

Published with the assistance of the National Endowment for the Humanities,
a federal agency which supports the study of such fields as history, philosophy,
literature, and language.

Library of Congress Cataloging-in-Publication Data

Reid, John Phillip.
    Contested empire : Peter Skene Ogden and the Snake River expeditions /
John Phillip Reid ; foreword by Martin Ridge
        p.   cm.
    Includes bibliographical references and index.
    ISBN 0–8061–3374–0 (hc : alk. paper)
    1. Ogden, Peter Skene, 1790–1854—Journeys—Snake River Valley (Wyo.-
Wash.)   2. Snake River Valley (Wyo.-Wash.)—Description and travel.   3.
Snake River Valley (Wyo.-Wash.)—Ethnic relations.   4. Ogden, Peter Skene,
1790–1854—Relations with Americans.   5. Ogden, Peter Skene, 1790–
1854— Relations with Indians.   6. Fur trade—Social aspects—Snake River
Valley (Wyo.-Wash.)—History—19th century.   7. Indians of North America— Snake River Valley (Wyo.-Wash.)—History—19th century.   8. Frontier
and pioneer life— Snake River Valley (Wyo.-Wash.)   9. Hudson's Bay Company—Biography. 10. Fur traders—Canada—Biography.   I. Title.

F752.S7 R46 2002
979.6'1—dc21

                                                                    2001052223

1   2   3   4   5   6   7   8   9   10

FOR

ANTHONY REID BUDD
SABRINA BUDD
REID ALEXANDER BUDD

Contents

List of Maps

Foreword

Readers unfamiliar with the writings of John Phillip Reid will doubtless
find this book intriguing because he seems to be telling one story within
another. This is true because he is neither a popularizer nor a traditional historian. He looks at the past in a different way, and he often
writes with the verve and passion of a lawyer making a case. This is natural; Reid is, in fact, a professor of law. But he is, also, a legal historian,
meticulous in his research and faithful in his re-creation of the lives of
people and of events. Reid's historical interests are wide-ranging. He
has written biographies of judges, several volumes on the American Revolution, studies of Indian law and interracial vengeance, and two books
on the Overland Trail to California, along with a score of articles dealing with the West. His interest in the West resulted in his traveling over
much of the region he writes about. As a result, he has a feel for the "lay
of the land" that gives his reader a sense of presence.

In this book Reid examines the fur trade from the British point of
view by dealing with one of the West's most familiar narratives: the great
fur-gathering expedition of Peter Skene Ogden in 1824–25. In Reid's
analysis, Ogden's expedition retains its sense of adventure, basic struc-
ture, and purpose. Ogden comes alive as a daring explorer and brigade
commander whose trials test his skills as a leader and diplomat. The
expedition from the British view is partly a quest for profit by the Hudson's Bay Company but primarily part of Great Britain's foreign policy
strategy. The Oregon country, what Reid calls the transboundary region,
was then under joint Anglo-American occupancy, and the British were
determined to hold the region north of the Columbia River by keeping
the Americans out. To implement this policy, Hudson's Bay Company
officers sought to strip every stream south of the Columbia River of its

beaver and other fur-bearing animals. Without the fur trade, the British believed, Americans would probably not try to settle beyond the Rockies for a generation, and only then south of the Columbia River. Their misconceptions and failure constitute an often-told tale.

For Reid, this is not the whole story. For example, his depiction of Peter Skene Ogden is not that of a man with an uncontrollable temper given to frequent fits of rage. Although a frontiersman by temperament, Ogden was a judge's son with a legal education. He knew the rules of society, which gave his leadership and diplomacy a special meaning. Because Reid asks new and deeper questions of the traditional narrative, he explains much that we did not understand about how the fur trade really worked. He describes a West where there were no government officials, no law enforcement agencies, no legislatures, no courts, and no lawyers to prosecute or defend miscreants. In the British Oregon country, under certain circumstances, even a Hudson's Bay Company local could act as judge and jury when dealing with Indians and mixed bloods, although not with whites.

In such circumstances, Reid asks, how did the fur hunters from the Hudson's Bay Company, and the Americans whom they encountered in the Snake River country, address such questions as property rights, personal contacts, self-interest, and homicide? How did men who represented different countries with conflicting interests carry on their business and interact with each other in a land they claimed, but which really belonged to Native Americans, some of whom were hostile to alien intrusion? How did they deal with their conflicting national interests and with the presence of Indians? Reid argues persuasively that the absence of formal legal machinery did not mean that the problems of an organized society were ignored or left unresolved. Reid's narrative explains that there was a rule of law among these men, perhaps made clearer because both groups came from the same legal tradition. His close analysis of the respect for the rule of law among the leading fur men, the employees of the competing companies, and even the free traders places the Anglo-American fur trade in a new light.

Traditionally, historians have dealt with the fur trade's competition as a zero-sum game, a war between two parties in which one side wins and takes all and the other loses. They have tended to view the story from the present: Americans take over what becomes the states of Oregon and

Washington, and the British retreat north of the forty-ninth parallel. Reid's story is more complicated. First, Americans were as destructive of fur-bearing animals as the Bay Company's brigades. Second, there were more than two players. And third, contrary to the idea that it was a war to the knife, as in a zero-sum game between two competing parties, there was a good deal of cooperation and mutual understanding among the fur men when they had to resolve problems. Therefore, instead of focusing on the dangers and threats of conflict at the international level as the traditional narrative does, Reid analyzes at a local level the methods of conflict resolution regarding facets of the trade that are frequently passed over and yet involved the everyday life of the fur men. In the end, Reid finds that the rule of law in the trade, so deeply ingrained in the major participants, resulted in not a zero-sum game with an American triumph but in an equilibrium in which each side achieved enough of its goals to be satisfied.

A careful reading of Reid's intriguing book thus enhances our understanding of a remarkable expedition and sheds much new light on the Anglo-American frontier experience.

MARTIN RIDGE

Contested Empire

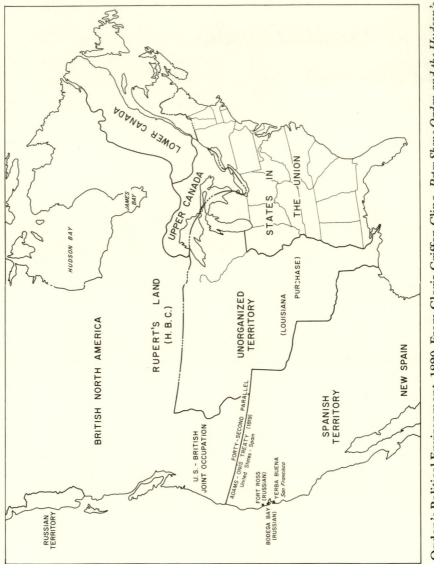

Ogden's Political Environment, 1820. From Gloria Griffen Cline, *Peter Skene Ogden and the Hudson's Bay Company* (Norman: University of Oklahoma Press, 1974).

CHAPTER ONE

To Prevent Disputes and Differences

A recent book reviewer made a point. "The Rocky Mountain fur trade of the 1820s and 1830s is one of the most thoroughly examined topics in American history," he wrote. "Indeed it is fair to say that twentieth-century historians working in this area have outnumbered the actual nineteenth-century mountain men."[1] If the reviewer's facts are accurate, they lead to at least one obvious conclusion: little is left to say about the North American fur trade, perhaps nothing at all. With so many writers working on the history of the fur trade, every conceivable worthwhile topic must be exhausted. In fact, that conclusion would be wrong. There is much that still can be told of the social, institutional, and legal behavior of American and British fur traders and fur trappers. Until recently, scholars of the trade have paid scant attention to law, or to the legal behavior of the mountain men. Indeed, more than other historians, those of the North American West, and not just of the fur trade, generally have written as if law and legal questions did not exist. In the story of the westward movement, law has largely been ignored.

Although disregard of legal questions touches all aspects of fur-trade history, we might think that the part of the Far West once known as the Oregon country would be an exception. After all, that transboundary region between the Rocky Mountains and the Pacific Ocean is the only large area of North America ever governed by a treaty of joint occupancy between two sovereign nations, surely just the jurisdiction to attract the curiosity of legal historians. On reflection, however, it may not be puzzling that its legal history has been neglected. It might be concluded that there would be no law to study, for, in fact, there was no government in the Oregon country during the era of joint occupancy. All during the years that fur brigades traveled back and forth across the Snake country, neither of the two governments that claimed it, not the United Kingdom of Great Britain nor the United States, had a single official in any part of the Oregon country. It was a territory that by treaty was open to joint occupancy, but not administered by joint government.

It may seem an exaggeration to say that there was no positive or state-imposed law in the Oregon country under the treaty of joint occupancy. The fact is, however, that the domestic law in the territory, that is, law regulating the conduct of individuals, was the various domestic laws of the local Indian nations. But that law was not positive or state decreed. Like the international law of the European nations and the international law regulating conduct between the various Native American nations, tribes, and bands, Indian domestic law was custom, it was not state imposed.[2]

We should not expect that the treaty of joint occupation between Great Britain and the United States would pay much attention to domestic law regulating the conduct of private citizens. Its purpose was not to govern territory and people, but to proclaim sovereignty. The two governments were putting European nations, especially Russia and Spain, on official notice that they claimed sovereignty over the lands north of the Spanish Californias and south of British-held New Caledonia, today's British Columbia. The details of which of the two nations was sovereign over what parts of the jointly occupied country were left to be negotiated at a future date. The treaty was concerned with precluding future claims by either Spain or Russia. Some scholars of the twenty-first century protest that such an interpretation is too narrow, that the sovereignty of the Indian nations must also be taken into account. That is anachronism in the extreme. Native rights to territoriality were details of occupation, not considerations in the European definition of sovereignty.

It may be doubted that the treaty did not give some consideration to domestic police. The very fact that the governments of Great Britain and the United States both claimed sovereignty to the Oregon country, and took the trouble of acknowledging by formal agreement their mutual rights, at the very least implies that they made some provisions for maintaining law and order. Surely when the treaty was negotiated the drafters knew that their nationals, and even citizens from other nations, might make contact in the territory, and the result could be commercial competition and international violence. Even if they did not anticipate fur trappers from both countries meeting in the wilderness and quarreling over beaver grounds and pelts, they had to know that ships from Boston and London were plying harbors and inlets in search of seal skins and their captains trading with the natives. Perhaps they did not worry that aggressive British or American sea captains would commit violence against their competitors. But they should have realized that any of them could encounter resistance from the natives just by harvesting animals that local Indians considered their exclusive property. Even more serious was the risk of killing a native. It took only one accidental homicide to put in jeopardy the life of any white person entering the region. Of course, we would suppose the treaty provided for the apprehension and removal (or even punishment) of troublemakers. In fact, it did not. The treaty's relevant article is surprisingly brief and may be said to have provided almost nothing at all.

The treaty, which entered into force on 20 October 1818, contained six articles settling various disputes between the two nations. The first dealt with the rights of American fisherman to dry fish and to seek shelter on the coasts of Newfoundland and Labrador. Another set the western boundary of the countries—the northern boundary of the United States and "the southern boundary of the territories of his Britannic Majesty"—as far as the Rocky, then called the Stony, Mountains.[3] The third article is the one that interests us. It provided:

> It is agreed, that any country that may be claimed by either party on the northwest coast of America, westward of the Stony Mountains, shall, together with its habours, bays, and creeks, and the navigation of all rivers within the same, be free and open, for the term of ten years from the date of the signature of the present convention, to the vessels, citizens, and subjects, of the two powers: it being well understood, that this agreement is not to be construed to the prejudice of any claim which either of the two high contracting parties may have to any part of the said country, nor

shall be taken to affect the claim of any other power or state to any part of the said country; the only object of the high contracting parties, in that respect, being to prevent disputes and differences among themselves.[4]

That was all that was said. Nothing more. The extraordinarily limited reach of the treaty is evident from the final clause. The "only object of the high contracting parties," it provided, was "to prevent disputes and differences among themselves." That is, disputes and differences between the United States of America and the United Kingdom of Great Britain and Ireland, not disputes and differences arising between citizens of one country and citizens of the other. Private or nongovernmental disputes and differences were of no concern. No judicial machinery was created to resolve them. Yet, before the decade of the treaty's duration expired, British and American fur-trapping parties encountered one another in that part of the jointly occupied Oregon country that was called the Snake country. There in the vast isolation of mountains, valleys, snow, and endless rivers, fur trappers from two nations crossed each others' paths with no government to regulate competition, no police to check violence, and scant legislation to guide social, economic, or legal behavior.

There was not even process for remedying complaints when one of the countries believed that its national interests were being damaged. A tale related in the following chapters concerns the Hudson's Bay Company's program to denude the Snake country, destroying all the beaver and creating a "fur desert" so unappealing for trappers that American fur men would think the area not worth canvassing. If they stayed south of the Snake, the lands to the north—the Columbia River valleys, Puget Sound, Vancouver Island, and New Caledonia—might remain forever British. Had American trappers realized what was occurring, and had they told Washington, the government would have had a serious grievance. The British were not treating Americans as equal joint tenants but were blatantly acting against their interests. Even if the United States had tried to complain, the treaty provided no mechanism for registering objection. All that was available were the regular channels of diplomatic negotiations—as if the treaty did not exist.

Although first Spain and then Mexico also claimed parts of the Snake country, all the fur traders and fur trappers came either from Lower

Canada, Great Britain, or the United States. None were from Mexico. First to arrive on the British side were the beaver hunters of Montreal's North West Company. They were soon followed by men of the Hudson's Bay Company. They had crossed the Continental Divide from Rupert's Land, and established fur trading posts in New Caledonia, today's British Columbia, and farther south along the Columbia River, in today's Oregon and Washington, and even as far east as the Flathead nation, in today's Montana. Their competition—their "opposition" to use the word of Hudson's Bay officers—came from the fur traders and fur trappers of St. Louis, the men who were the first to tell the United States government about the importance of the South Pass, the possibility of the Oregon Trail, and the existence of the Great Salt Lake. These men were the first to follow the route of Lewis and Clark to the headwaters of the Missouri River, and then to go across the Continental Divide to trap rivers that now have such names as the Salmon, the Lemhi, the Umpqua, and the Ogden. The company men of Hudson's Bay and the "free" trappers from St. Louis met and interacted on the headwaters of the Missouri, in the Snake River country, and along the streams that flow east to the Mississippi and west to the Pacific.

The history of the Snake country expeditions of the Hudson's Bay Company has usually been told in terms of the personalities of leaders such as Peter Skene Ogden and John Work. Or it has been related as a tale of exploration, of where the brigades went and of who first saw what valley, who "discovered" which lake, and who named what mountain. There has also been some attention focused on the social history of beaver trapping, of life in the wilderness, and the ethnic groups that formed the companies of trappers. Fewer questions have been asked about the institutional history of the Snake country; about the organization of expeditions, the effectiveness of leadership, or the maintenance of discipline, order, and security. Nothing at all has been said of the legal history. The possibility that the conduct of the mountain men who trapped beaver and hunted buffalo in the Far West of North America was shaped by legal values does not seem to have occurred to their many chroniclers. To the extent that the notion may seem extreme, a cautionary explanation will be helpful.

We should not look for precise legalisms or technicalities. Positive, state-imposed law may help us to frame our questions; it cannot determine where we find our evidence. To seek the legal history of the early North American West, we must consider legal behaviorism more readily than we study rules of law. We will find probate practice without a law of probate, creditors' liens claimed by American as well as British fur companies, but not workers' liens on those companies, and implied contracts executed without mutuality, detriments suffered, or benefits conferred. It is lawmindedness that we must seek as much as legal understanding, the lawmindedness not only of the ordinary, faceless men who trapped beaver for British and American fur companies but also the lawmindedness of William H. Ashley of Missouri and Sir George Simpson of Scotland, the American William L. Sublette and the Canadian John Work, and the most memorable of all the beaver trappers who explored the North American Far West, Jedediah Strong Smith and Peter Skene Ogden. The stories of their courage, adventures, sufferings, and discoveries have been told and retold in countless forms and innumerable ways. What we have not been told are tales of their legal behavior: of how they shared or did not share perceived concepts of property interests and enforced legal responsibilities, of how much they respected the rights of other nationalities, as much as the rights of their fellow citizens, and of how they held others to mutually understood duties. Indeed, it has not even been noticed how much duties, rights, and concepts were mutually shared on the international frontier.

The idea of legal behavior—personal conduct determined by adherence to perceived legal concepts or values—is not often noticed in American histories and is, at best, somewhat ambiguous. Interestingly, some of the clearest examples of the phenomena have come from the early history of the Far West. The reason may be that there are well-recorded periods of western history when there was no governmental authority enforcing law, no police, no prosecuting attorneys, or judicial tribunals, and yet there was general order and a uniform obedience of what the uncoerced people thought was legal conduct.

A striking instance is the mining camps of the Sierra Nevada before California's government was promulgated and extended east into the mountains. There the miners organized themselves into districts, wrote *sui generis* rules of real estate law, labor law, water law, and association law, and enforced those rules in courts that they created and whose legitimacy was founded entirely on popular support.

In another instance, legal behaviorism leaps out at the historian from the diaries of ordinary people traveling the Overland Trail to Oregon and California. Three incidents occurring on the trail in 1849 and one in 1852 should be enough to illustrate the concept.[5]

The first happened during 1849 in Death Valley, one of the most perilous sections of the California part of the trail. A man named Hall, who had had the foresight or luck to possess "plenty" of water, would not share any with his desperate companions. "He even refused to give a lady some," one member of the party wrote. "He gave it to his oxen. Thereby plainly showing that He would rather see a man without water than his oxen."[6] The next day there was "Considerable ill feeling in camp owing to Mr. Hall on yesterday refusing to give a lady some water (which was very scarce during the travel over the 34 mile streach [*sic*] on which we were 36 hours without water). . . . Mr. Hall was very much sensured by all the train and left him no friends."[7]

Hall seems to have been alone. The other emigrants outnumbered him and they were armed. It does not take much imagination to conclude that they thought of him quite harshly. He mocked their Christian values, particularly the lesson of the Good Samaritan and Jesus' injunction to love thy neighbor as thyself. They must have been sorely tempted to seize some of his water, especially when he fed it to his oxen. They did not, however, and one explanation is property law. The water belonged to him and it was his to dispose as he saw fit.

The incident of 1852 occurred on the Oregon section of the trail. A man owned several wagons. He drove one himself and lent the remainder to emigrants needing transportation, "with this understanding, that the teams and wagons were to be turned over to him as his property when they arrived at their destination." One of these wagons had been bailed to a family. The father became sick, the children were too footsore to walk, and the mother drove. The owner, fearful the draft animals could not haul so much weight, repossessed the wagon. The family was evicted and father, mother, and children were left on the Oregon Trail beyond Fort Boise.[8] Other emigrants in the train said the owner's conduct was morally reprehensible. But except for taking the family into their own wagons, surely at great inconvenience to themselves, they did nothing. The man owned the wagon. As owner he had a legal right to do what was morally wrongful.

The third example is the behaviorism of J. Goldsborough Bruff, a '49er, who took a wrong turn on the Humboldt River and found himself trapped by mountain snow in that part of the California trail that was called Lassen's Cut-off. He and a companion were facing certain starvation when a third man arrived driving three oxen he had recently found wandering along the road. The stranger told them he was keeping two and offered them the third—which "we might kill and eat." The two men desperately needed food but doubts that the animal was the property of the possessor produced some astonishing legal behavior. Believing that the ox "might not be his," Bruff and his companion "desired him to shoot [it] himself, which he done."[9] They then accepted the gift and ate it. They were isolated on a forsaken section of the trail. They not only craved the meat, they needed it for survival, and had to realize that the person whom they understood was the "legal owner" of the ox had long since passed down the road or was dead. Yet they refused to convert it. The man who had possession might kill the ox, they would not. The act of conversion was his, not theirs.

Less than a month later Bruff was again starving when a pair of oxen wandered up to his camp. They were, he knew, the "property" of a man named Roberts, also trapped in the mountains. Because of the snow, the animals had had no feed, and were so emaciated they were useless for anything but food. Experience told Bruff it was futile to ask Roberts, a possessive man, to sell one. "[R]eally," he observed, "I think the meat of their oxen would be better appropriated to our benefit, than left, as it will be, for the benefit of grizzlers and wolves.—Who will assuredly nab them tonight." Bruff had a gun but could not bring himself to use it. "Roberts oxen are gone," he noted the next day, "doubtless devoured by this time."[10]

Making too little of these incidents would be a mistake. In each, the internalization of values was so strong that individuals refrained from taking steps that would have been in their own interests. Examples of legal behavior from the history of the Snake country are less unusual and certainly less puzzling than these from the history of the Overland Trail, but there were many instances where knowledge of legal rules and respect for what fur men understood to be property rights determined personal or corporate conduct. This behavior was noticeable not only around the trading posts where company culture and company supervision promoted shared interests and common outlooks but also in the isolated beaver hunts of the transmontane West. When the fur trappers of Hudson's Bay Company met their American rivals in the Snake country, both sides often demonstrated legal behaviorism. Instinctive respect for each other's rightful claims, helped both sides avoid conflict and violence in that vast expanse of unsettled territory where there was no government and there was no law.

Of course, matters were not always easily resolved and different notions of legal rights sometimes produced misunderstanding. The most famous confrontation of British against American in the Snake country was between Peter Skene Ogden of the Hudson's Bay Company and a party of St. Louis beaver hunters led by Johnson Gardner. An argument threatening violence arose from conflicting claims to ownership of horses, traps, and pelts that Ogden said belonged to his company but were possessed by (or had been trapped by) contractees of Hudson's Bay who were deserting their association with Hudson's Bay to join American trapping brigades. Ogden based his assertion of proprietorship to debts owed to Hudson's Bay by the contractees possessing those horses, traps, and pelts. Put in more technical language, he based his claim on what his legal education may have persuaded him was a lien on the goods. The men who possessed the horses, traps, and pelts, and who wanted to break their implied contractual agreements to Hudson's Bay and go over to the American fur parties, taking the property with them, based their claim on physical possession, and, perhaps, on knowing that if the property was destroyed or stolen the loss would have been theirs, not Hudson's Bay.

Few events in fur-trade history have been so extensively studied as the Ogden-Gardner fracas, yet much evidence has been missed. This book takes a different look at the incident, not asking again how close the British and Americans came to violence, but asking why violence did not occur. There are obvious answers that deserve the attention of western scholars. The trappers who deserted from Ogden's camp that day and took their beaver to the Americans for sale at Missouri prices are often depicted as repudiating their financial obligations. They left, it has been said, to avoid paying heavy debts owed to the Hudson's Bay Company. In fact, all the men who are on record acknowledged their debts and most, we know, eventually paid them. Some even settled with Ogden before deserting.

Conscientiousness in debt payment is a trait most stories of the trans-boundary mountain men do not dwell upon. It does not fit the stereo-type of the Hudson's Bay "freeman" or the American fur trapper. Of course, uncoerced payment of debts owes something to personal moral-ity or to moral behaviorism. But to some degree it was directed by respect for property rights and by the internalized value shared by most people in the nineteenth-century English-speaking world that financial obligations should be honored.

CHAPTER TWO

The Wild and Untrammelled Life

The initial major interaction between American and British fur men in the transboundary area west of the Rocky Mountains occurred at Astoria, near the mouth of the Columbia River, where the Pacific Fur Company of New York City had established the first trading post near the Pacific Ocean. When Great Britain sent a naval vessel to the Columbia during the War of 1812, the Americans—known in history as the Astorians—abandoned the area, leaving the future Oregon Territory and the country of the Snake River and its tributaries to the exclusive possession of Montreal's North West Company and to the local natives until the dawning of a new era in 1821 and 1822.[1]

In 1821 the North West Company of Montreal merged with the Hudson's Bay Company of London. The new concern was not only a monopoly in fact, it was a monopoly in law. The Parliament of Great Britain granted to it the exclusive right to purchase furs from the natives and to trap in Rupert's Land, New Caledonia, and the Oregon Territory. All competition was prohibited, with one exception. Under the provisions of the treaty of joint occupancy, neither Great Britain nor the United States could exclude people from the other nation nor legislate for them. The statute granting the new Hudson's Bay Company a commercial monopoly, therefore, provided that the grant was not to be "deemed or construed" as giving to Hudson's Bay any trading rights "to the Prejudice or Exclusion of any Citizens of the said United States."[2]

In 1822, the very next year after Parliament recodified the monopoly of the fur trade in British North America, the United States Congress ended any semblance of monopoly in the fur trade in the republic to the south. The American government's factory system of regulated Indian stores, which alone had been permitted to trade with the natives in the "Indian Country," were closed forever. As a result, fur trading was opened to all comers. That year John Jacob Astor, the entrepreneur who had sent the Astorians to the Columbia River eleven years before, opened an office in St. Louis. Also in St. Louis, William H. Ashley placed in the *Missouri Gazette* what has become the most famous advertisement in the history of the American fur trade. It solicited one hundred men who, as members of a beaver trapping expedition, were "to ascend the river Missouri to its source, there to be employed for one, two, or three years."[3] Some of those who answered that advertisement and joined the expedition up the Missouri, were destined to become legends among fur trappers, even in their own day. One transboundary mountain man would become the first American to encounter the Hudson's Bay expedition in the Snake country: Jedediah Strong Smith. The American return to the Columbia River was under way.

It was also a return to the Snake River country. Twelve years earlier, Andrew Henry, one of Ashley's partners in 1822, had been a member of the first expedition to hunt beaver in the three forks region of the upper Missouri River. The fur men from St. Louis had laid some traps but were allowed to do little else. Blackfoot warriors pinned them into their stockade and they did not dare go out even to inspect the catch. They had to retreat. Driven from the headwaters of the Missouri, Henry led a trapping party west across the Rockies to the Snake, where they worked a branch of the river now known as Henry's Fork and became the first Americans to bring pelts from the Snake country back to St. Louis.

In the decade after Henry abandoned Henry's Fork and returned to St. Louis, the Snake country was approached by fur traders only from the west. The North West Company operating from the Columbia conducted its business through small trading posts scattered about the interior, buying fur directly from the natives. Donald McKenzie persuaded his North West partners that trade could not be conducted that way in the Snake country. It was rich in beaver, but there was little chance of buying pelts. He had concluded that the local Indians had slight interest in manufactured products, not even trade tobacco, and could not be induced to bring furs to fixed posts to sell. If the North West Company wanted the beaver of the Snake River country, it would have to harvest them itself. And McKenzie proved that the job could be done. He led the first brigade of North West trappers from Fort Nez Perces, a post he established for that purpose near the mouth of the Walla Walla River, east to the Snake River, where they trapped beaver and then rode back to the Columbia with their pelts.

Donald McKenzie was perhaps the most memorable of the North Westers to command a Snake country expedition, but, unfortunately, he left few records. Though a man of boundless energy, great courage, and disciplined leadership, he was not a writer and apparently refused to keep a journal. The little we know of his exploits in the Snake country was written by his North West colleague, Alexander Ross, for whom McKenzie was a hero.[4] For students of the Snake country expeditions, Ross, too, is a bit of a hero. Without him, we would know little about the early years of fur trapping in the Snake country. He not only wrote accounts of the exploits of the early fur brigades led by McKenzie, Finan McDonald, and Michel Bourdon, he also kept the first journal of a Snake country expedition. In 1824 Ross led the first significant brigade sent out by the reformed Hudson's Bay Company. Unlike the North West Company, Hudson's Bay required that officers in charge of trading posts and fur or exploring expeditions keep journals. Ross's journal provides one of the most detailed and informative accounts of a Snake country expedition.

Ross was a fine writer. He published a history of the Red River settlement, the future Winnipeg, and the memoirs of his years on the Columbia with the Pacific Fur Company, the North West Company, and Hudson's Bay filled two printed volumes. He was not, however, an effective leader in the Snake country. He was, rather, quite inept. It is a close question whether he led his men or they led him. He had expected to go out again, leading the 1825 expedition, but when he returned with his brigade to Flathead Post in today's northwestern Montana, Ross was told that he would be replaced. George Simpson, the governor of Hudson's Bay for its North American operations, had lost all confidence in Ross. His own journals showed he was not a leader of men. At best, Ross was a labor negotiator, and that was exactly what a Snake country expedition did not need. Simpson knew a better man for the job. And he was right on hand, already on the West Coast, in Hudson's Bay Company's Spokane House, where Simpson was visiting at the moment. He was Peter Skene Ogden.

Ogden was different from most Hudson's Bay officers. As a general rule, they were Scottish. He was born in Quebec to American parents. Moreover, he had not gone into the wilderness to lift himself out of poverty and to make his fortune. He was neither a poor boy from the highlands nor the scion of an established but landless family. He was, in fact, the heir to a relatively distinguished lineage. His father, a loyalist who had left the rebelling American colonies for Quebec, was a puisne judge of the Court of King's Bench in Montreal.[5] His brother, Charles Richard, younger by only a year, would also have a distinguished legal career. In addition to serving several sessions as a representative for Trois-Rivières in the house of assembly for Lower Canada, he was a king's councilor, and was both solicitor general and attorney general of Lower Canada, and later attorney general of the Isle of Man.[6] It was truly said that Ogden "grew up in a family wedded to the law." Yet, "although Ogden seems to have received some tutoring in law, the legal profession evidently held few attractions for him."[7]

We should want to know why law did not interest Peter Ogden. The question matters because he is the one individual we have to understand if we are ever to reconstruct the story of the Snake country expeditions. Why did he turn his back on civilized comforts, the prestige of family, and a promising economic future for danger, hardship, and discomfort? If we knew, we might learn something of the elements of character and human drive that contributed to successful leadership in the Snake country.

Two theories explaining why Peter Skene Ogden thought himself not suited for the law are worth close consideration. They tell us a great deal about Ogden—at least why Ogden spurned law practice, not why he was drawn to the untamed, dangerous wilderness of the Saskatchewan River and places farther west. But the first question is almost as important as the second. Perhaps not for most mountain men, but certainly for Ogden, who gave up far more by abandoning eastern society than did almost any other fur trader we know of. On first impression, the two explanations appear to disagree, for they stress contrary aspects of those characteristics that shaped Ogden's behavior. Read a second time, how-ever, the two appraisals become more complementary when it is appre-ciated that both describe the same Peter Ogden. One was written in a memoir by a fellow trader, a colleague in the North West Company, who met Ogden briefly and greatly admired him. The second is by one of Ogden's twentieth-century biographers.

The first—the fur-trade colleague—was Ross Cox, who originally went to the Columbia River as an Astorian, and, when the Pacific Fur Com-pany was driven from the Columbia River by the British navy in the War of 1812, joined the North West Company. He worked for North West until 1817, when he left the fur trade forever, returning to his native Ireland, where he became a Dublin journalist and published one of the three his-torical memoirs that were written by participants in the early Pacific fur trade. (The other two were by Gabriel Franchère and Alexander Ross.) In his history, Cox tells of meeting Ogden as he was passing down the prairie rivers on his way to Montreal. The visit was relatively short, but Cox heard enough to believe he had met a man temperamentally unsuited for the law. Ogden, he thought, was a born adventurer who sooner or later would have found his way to the western frontier. "The study of provincial jurisprudence, and the seignorial subdivisions of Canadian property, had no charms for the mercurial temperament of Mr. Ogden," Cox explained; "and contrary to the wishes of his friends, he preferred the wild and untrammelled life of an Indian trader, to the 'law's delay,' and the wholesome restraints which are provided for the correction of overexuberant spirits in civilised society."[8] Cox does not quite say so, but it is clear he thought Ogden one of those "overexuberant spirits." At the moment of Cox's visit, Ogden was holding prisoner a large number of Hudson's Bay employees, and many members of the Hudson's Bay Com-pany had such a hatred for him they would have said he was an "overex-uberant spirit" whom even the law could not have corrected.

One of Ogden's twentieth-century biographers has a quite different explanation for Ogden's preference of "the wild and untrammelled life." He thought the call was at least as much physical as it was tem-peramental. Nature had not designed him for the practice of law.

> Even while he read law books to please his father, he knew that he
> was never intended for the law, where much depended on an

impressive appearance and resounding voice, and on patience which he did not have. Peter grew out rather than up, to be less than average height and more than average width, with something troll-like in his irregular features; and even after he had become a man his voice retained some of its boyish squeak. With an athletic appearance and manly voice he might have reconciled himself to the law, but his stubby frame and uncommanding voice must prove themselves among hardships in the wilderness.[9]

It is an odd assessment. Peter Ogden, one of the most memorable, toughest, and enterprising of the leaders of North American fur trappers, did not have the "athletic appearance and manly voice" needed to be a Quebec lawyer. He certainly had the intelligence to succeed at the bar, or at many other occupations, for that matter. It may be he lacked the temperament for the law or the patience for town living, but he was psychologically fitted for life in the wild.

Alexander Ross had not been successful leading the Snake country expedition of 1824. He had doubted whether anyone could lead it. Peter Skene Ogden would prove him wrong. He would not only lead the Snake country expedition, he would generally succeed in leading it where he wanted it to go, and he would make it an effective instrument for Hudson's Bay policy while ruthlessly denuding the land of beaver. He would fail in only one respect. He would not keep the Americans from the Oregon Territory. No leader of any Snake country expedition could have done that. No Hudson's Bay officer could have stemmed the American tide.

It does not do to ignore the failings. Ross Cox was undoubtedly right that Ogden "preferred the wild and untrammelled life of an Indian trader, to . . . the wholesome restraints which are provided for the correction of overexuberant spirits in civilised society." There was more to Ogden's makeup, however, than a preference for the wild, an explosive temperament, or an unprepossessing appearance. There was a tendency for violence that may have made Ogden unsuited for life in Montreal, Rivière-du-Loup, or even Trois-Pistoles. His instinct was to attack, to destroy, to beat down his opponent, even to kill. Had he remained in Lower Canada, who can say that the "wholesome restraints" of the law's "correction" would not have come down on him?

CHAPTER THREE

One of the Most Unprincipled Men

When he first entered the pages of recorded history, Ogden was what the North West Company called a "winterer." Usually the term referred to a partner. He was a clerk, not a partner, but he was expected to stay in the western woods and lakes during the winter, trading directly with the natives and—apparently more than most North Westers—competing against the Hudson's Bay Company. It is necessary to understand the nature of that competition. It provided much of the schooling that later made Ogden successful in the Snake country.

Ogden first went to the North American West to serve as a clerk at the North West Company's post at Ile-à-la-Crosse. There he was in "opposition" to a Hudson's Bay post. We cannot reconstruct the story from the North West Company's perspective. Its records have not survived. To learn anything about Ogden from the time he joined the North West Company in 1809 until it merged with Hudson's Bay in 1821, we have to rely on the writings of his enemies, officers of Hudson's Bay Company. It is not a flattering picture. The men of Hudson's Bay, one biographer has written, "generally did not see Ogden as a youthful, exuberant, competent competitor who was fond of coarse practical jokes, but an irritating, irresponsible individual who was capable of the most savage and cold-blooded crimes." During the years with the North West Company, another biographer agrees, "the young Ogden earned an unenviable reputation for violence."[1]

The competition was rooted in a rivalry that began when traders from Montreal first invaded the Hudson's Bay territory in western North America known as Rupert's Land, by moving beyond the Great Lakes, and penetrating the Saskatchewan country and Athabasca. Once fur buyers came west, the Honourable Company could no longer expect that the Indians would bring their furs to York factory, its headquarters on Hudson Bay. The company had to establish its own posts in the interior. Any trader who established a trading post at a fixed location was soon followed by rival traders, a partner of the North West Company (who died the year before Ogden was hired) explained. "Thus circumstanced, he, in turn, resorted to every means for securing to himself the preference of the Indians, and for injuring his competitor. This conduct provoked retaliation." "This jarring of interests," another North Wester wrote six years before Ogden joined the company, "keeps up continual misunderstandings, and occasions frequent broils between the contending parties; and to such a height has their enmity risen, that it has, in several instances, occasioned blood shed." He was upset that "murderers" escaped punishment, because British law did not run in the wilderness. He had heard, however, that legislation was being planned. "If something should not be done soon," he concluded, "I fear many of us may lose our lives."[2]

That North Wester was writing about violence committed by the XY Company, not by Hudson's Bay. That is, violence of Canadian Scot against Canadian Scot, not Canadian against British. When the competition did involve Canadian company against British company, Alexander Ross, a North Wester, freely admitted that the violence was on the Canadian side.

> The North-Westers had of late years penetrated through the very heart of the Hudson's Bay Company's territories as far as the Atlantic, which was of Hudson's Bay, and set at defiance every legal restriction or moral obligation. Their servants pillaged their opponents, destroyed their forts and trading establishments as suited their views, and not unfrequently kept armed parties marauding from post to post, menacing with destruction and death every one that presumed to check their career, till at last, party spirit and rivalry in trade had convulsed and changed the whole social order of things, into a state of open hostility.[3]

Soon after arriving at Ile-à-la-Crosse, Peter Ogden was in the front lines of these battles. More aggressive than most of his colleagues, and even provocative, he may not have set the pattern, but he certainly followed it. In almost all of the confrontations between North Westers and Hudson's Bay officers in which he participated, at least those that we know about—and remember, all our information comes from Hudson's Bay officers—the Canadians were clearly the bullies and the Hudson's Bay people the cringing victims. Historians of the Canadian West have attributed the difference between the two companies to ethnic background of their officers. "The only explanation I can offer to myself," Arthur S. Morton wrote of the North Westers, "is that they were Highlanders—McTavishes, M'Gillivrays, Mackenzies, McLeods, MacDonalds, Campbells, Camerons, and Frasers—whose ancestors but two generations back had gloried in their deeds as plunderers. Though the MacDonalds and the Campbells and the rest of them were the bitterest of foes in the old land, all their enmities were sunk in the new clan, the North West Company, and everything was, as of old, justifiable, done in the interest and for the glory of the clan. This would account for the blend of greed and sport, not to say cruelty, which characterized the raids of the Northwesters on the men of Hudson's Bay Company."[4]

The ethnic explanation may seem a bit farfetched, but Paul Chrisler Phillips said much the same after examining the evidence from the opposite perspective, that of Hudson's Bay officers. "As products of London charity schools and homes for poor children," he explained, "they lacked the vigour and resourcefulness to withstand the hardy and experienced Scotch, French, and American traders, who had grown up on the frontier. Many Hudson's Bay men feared the wilderness, feared the Indians, and, most of all, feared the Nor-Westers."[5] To read some Hudson's Bay journals, it would seem they feared Peter Skene Ogden most of all.

Only two other North Westers aroused the anger of Hudson's Bay traders as Ogden did. They were Cuthbert Grant, leader of the *métis* in their violent opposition to the Red River settlement at the junction of the Assiniboine and Red Rivers, hundreds of miles east of where Ogden was posted, and Samuel Black who became Ogden's closest associate and best friend in the fur trade. Black was described by the biographer of Peter Fidler, a leading officer of the Hudson's Bay Company, as "the cruelly effective Samuel Black." Fidler himself referred to Black as "the

most malicious and imprudent man I ever saw." Hudson's Bay sent Fidler
to oppose him at Lake Athabasca and within two years Black drove him
and his men from the area.[6]

Black was at Ile-à-la-Crosse in today's northwestern Saskatchewan
when Ogden arrived there in September 1810, his first station with the
North West Company. Ile-à-la-Crosse was a vital location in Hudson's
Bay's plans to move into territory where the North West Company was
doing business. The company again sent Peter Fidler to oppose Black
and he was serving as postmaster of the nearby Hudson's Bay house
when Ogden joined Black. Immediately, they began a program of harassment. On 12 October, for example, just as Hudson's Bay workers had
finished building stockades about their post, Black and Ogden showed
their contempt by climbing over them. They then proceeded to strut
through the post, "armed with Pistols & Daggers."[7] Thirteen days later
Fidler, in his post journal, indicated how easily Hudson's Bay men were
intimidated, even though they far outnumbered the two North Westers:

> Mr. Black and Ogden came to our Gates this morning & in the
> evening they both came into our yard at the East Gates to pass thro
> it—Mr. Black with a loaded Gun & 2 Pistols & Ogden with his Dag-
> ger. . . . I told them both to return the way they came & that they
> should not pass thro' our yard in the Insulting Manner they
> intended—I told one of our men to shut the West Gates—which
> was at last done—they persevered in passing, when I struck Mr.
> Black with a stick two or 3 times. Ogden immediately drew his dag-
> ger & cut 2 large holes in the Side & Back of my coat & pricked
> my body—but no further—Mr. Black then took up part of the stick
> I had broken over him & struck me on the Thumb close to the
> upper end of the nail & smashed it to pieces. Ogden also struck
> me twice with a stick. All our Men looking on the whole time with-
> out giving me any assistance. Mr. Black & Ogden then followed
> me to my room with their Gun & Dagger & abused me very much
> whilst my Thumb was dressing. They then went & opened the West
> Gate & went away saying that we all should lead a very miserable
> & unhappy winter.[8]

It is safe to guess that Fidler spent a miserable and unhappy winter
knowing Ogden would be back again when the weather was warmer.

And he was. One of Ogden's biographers says that "he returned to the newfound pleasure of harassing serious and often humorless Peter Fidler and the Hudson's Bay Company."[9] Humorless Fidler may have been, but he also was observant and in his post journal kept a running account of what was happening. It told a story that made Ogden infamous at Hudson's Bay headquarters, and became a record that company would use against him. "Some people in reading this Journal might very naturally suppose, that many of the ill actions that has been done was by people in a state of inebriety," Fidler observed, "but they are very sober people—it is a systematic plan that has been laid at the Grand Portage to harass & distress us & determined to expel us from these parts of the Country where they get the greater part of their very prime furs at very little expense." Grand Portage was the location of Fort William, the western headquarters of the North West Company, and Fidler was asserting that the harassment was official company policy. One reason he thought so was that Samuel Black swore to him Hudson's Bay "shall not get a single skin at the Ile à la Crosse—& that this is the resolve of their Company."[10] At Ile-à-la-Crosse, Ogden and Black "so badgered Fidler and his men that they departed within a year." His post was then burnt by the North Westers.[11]

After his service at Ile-à-la-Crosse, Ogden was made master of a post at Green Lake. Now, without any superior to report to, he became more bold and more menacing. There is no need to follow the details of his harassment.[12] The Hudson's Bay Company watched him closely and continued to keep a record of what he was doing. It was the strong hatred that Hudson's Bay officers developed for him during this time that would come close to ending his career in the fur trade. When the two companies merged in 1821, it was the Hudson's Bay people who would deny him a place in the new organization.

James Bird was in charge of Hudson's Bay inland trade when Ogden first went to the Saskatchewan region for the North West Company. It was he who kept company headquarters informed of Ogden's activities. "Nothing worthy of particular notice has occurred within the District this year except the violent and illegal Conduct of a Mr. Ogden (master of a House at Green Lake)," Bird wrote in his annual report for 1815. He had already recorded some of the incidents in his own post journal, which also was sent to headquarters to be read by the people in charge.

In one affair, an employee of Hudson's Bay named James Spencer and an Indian were sent to deliver letters destined for Ile-à-la-Crosse. They were stopped by Ogden and some of his men, who "so terrified" the two messengers, according to Bird, "that they returned to Paint River without accomplishing the object of their Journey. Mr. Ogden it is said drew a Pistol from his pocket and swore that if they did not return immediately to Paint River he would kill the Indian and their Horses and take every thing that James Spencer had from him."[13]

Meeting another Hudson's Bay party, Ogden ordered his men to strip and to challenge the Hudson's Bay employees. When all but one of the Hudson's Bay people refused to fight, Ogden physically attacked the officer on the other side. With that action Odgen raised intercompany violence in the Saskatchewan district to a higher level. He tried to intimidate the HBC workers and when they still would not fight, he, a clerk for the North West Company, deliberately assaulted an officer of Hudson's Bay. Bird concluded that the situation was becoming too dangerous and that Hudson's Bay had to take defensive action, if not move to the offensive. First, in the hope he might have an opportunity to prosecute Ogden in Lower Canada, he began to gather evidence. He collected "Depositions from the men themselves that if possible the villain who would dare to assault men who were peacefully doing their Duty may be brought to punishment."[14]

Second, Bird undertook to defend his people. The next time Bird sent a messenger through Green Lake, he arranged for a strong escort. It was formed by two officers and three men who "all volunteered for this service," Bird wrote, "and will I think repel with becoming resolution any violence that may be offered them." It may have been unprecedented for Hudson's Bay to recruit volunteers to guard its messengers from rival fur traders. At least that is the impression that Bird gave by lavishing praise on the men and giving them unusually detailed instructions. "The indignation you have expressed at Ogdens conduct and the voluntary office you [and the other men] have made for this service," Bird told one of the officers, "is as gratifying to me as credible to yourselves and renders it unnecessary for me to add any thing further than a desire that you conduct yourself with coolness and discretion and bear in mind that you are not sent to provoke insult, but to reject with spirit and firmness any violence that may be offered you." Put another way,

Bird did not want his men to start trouble. Ogden would do that and, once he did, they were free to meet force with force. "[B]ut if the occasion will admit of such a measure I could desire that you seize the contemptible Villain and carry him a prisoner to Mr. Howse or Paint River as you may find most expedient."[15]

The officer, John Stewart McFarlane, was overzealous. He encountered Ogden by the gates of his trading post "when he had only a single Man at home." McFarlane, even though he had not been harassed or even threatened, seized Ogden. We may assume he thought it an opportunity not to be missed. But it also could not be ignored by the North West Company. The master of Fort Augustus, the North West post nearest to Bird's Edmonton House, protested "the way Ogden was taken and declared his determination to attempt to rescue him by force." Bird faced a difficult predicament. On one hand, Ogden and Samuel Black were certainly the most serious troublemakers on the North West side in the Saskatchewan country and they were the two that Hudson's Bay officers most wanted to have prosecuted. On the other hand, there was little violence in most of the locations where the two companies competed, and none at all between Fort Augustus and Edmonton House. Now his peaceful neighbor was threatening retaliation, and Bird concluded it was more valuable to preserve good relations with the neighbor than to punish Ogden.

> I replied that it had not been my desire for Mr. McFarlane to seize Mr. Ogden unless Mr. McFarlane and party should themselves be interrupted or insulted by him, and that if the affair was as Mr Ogden represented it, I would order him to be released immediately: but that if it should prove that Mr Ogden had been taken in the act of attempting to interrupt our people I would by no means release him till he was carried before a proper tribunal. I ad[d]ed that I consented the more readily to release Ogden from a desire to prevent the effect of quarrels originating in another Department extending to this river and destroying that good understanding which had so long subsisted between us and which had been productive of so much benefit to both concerns, and of so much comfort to ourselves.[16]

Bird sent one of his officers to investigate. Less than a day out, the officer met a Hudson's Bay party bringing Ogden as a prisoner to

Edmonton House. The group had a letter from McFarlane explaining how Ogden had been seized, as well as an eyewitness to the capture. Both said that Ogden had been seized without any provocation on his part. The officer "gave up the prisoner," and Ogden returned to Green Lake.[17]

Ogden may have known enough law to realize that even as McFarlane's prisoner he was not in serious legal jeopardy. Hudson's Bay might have been willing to expend the resources needed to get him before a magistrate, but it is doubtful if he could have been held. Hudson's Bay might not have sent to Lower Canada the witnesses needed to obtain an indictment and to put him on trial. They were all officers or *engagés* who would have been lost to the company's service for months, if not for a year or two. It is quite likely Hudson's Bay would not have been able to pay that high a price.

It may be, however, that McFarlane had taken some of the fight out of Ogden. At least the records Bird kept for the Saskatchewan department raised no new charges against Ogden for about a year afterward. Then the worst happened. Ogden not only "crossed the boundary between physical assault . . . and killing," he may have put some Hudson's Bay people in danger.[18]

In May 1816, Ogden was still postmaster at Green Lake when two of his men confronted an Indian named Buffalo and tried to force him to go to the North West post. It is unclear why. At first, Bird believed it was because the North Westers became suspicious of Buffalo's movements. Later the Hudson's Bay story changed, for HBC people claimed that Buffalo had been coming to their house to trade, that he had wanted to trade with them, and had not wanted to trade with Ogden. Whatever the reasons or intentions of the two North West *engagés*, Buffalo refused to follow them. When they persisted, he "fired his gun at them but (perhaps intentionally) missed them." They dashed off to tell Ogden and Buffalo ran to the nearby Hudson's Bay house for refuge. Ogden and his men followed and demanded that the Hudson's Bay postmaster surrender Buffalo. At first the Hudson's Bay clerk refused, but for some reason changed his mind and gave in. As James Bird wrote,

> the Indian was turned out of the House <u>unarmed</u> to the mercy of
> Ogden and his worthy companions. Ogden and his men, who were
> principally Half Breeds, dragged the Indian out in the Ice of the

Lake and there butchered him in a most cruel manner. They first fired two Balls into his Body, then a Canadian half-breed stabbed him in the belly with a Bayonet and his Bowels fell out: The Indian then requested a gun that he might have a chance of revenging himself before he died; to which Ogden replied by ordering a Canadian to knock him down with an Axe. Still the Indian continued on his Feet till Ogden enraged tripped him, and when he was down he stabbed him with his Dirk, after which a half-breed literally cut him to pieces in revenge for the difficulty they had in killing him.[19]

Bird's account, one of Ogden's biographers has charged, was "very biased" and "unbelievable in many respects."[20] Even if that supposition were correct, the account is worth our consideration for showing what Hudson's Bay officers thought Ogden capable of doing, or, if Bird was deliberately stretching facts, what he thought other officers would believe about Ogden. One point that Bird may not have noticed: by dragging Buffalo out on the ice immediately from the Hudson's Bay house, Ogden made the Hudson's Bay clerk a party to the killing, at least by the general principles of some Indian law. By surrendering Buffalo, the Hudson's Bay clerk became a cause of his death. Of course, he was not a cause to the same degree as Ogden, but he was a cause and could be held liable under the general principles of the North American Indian international law of vengeance.[21]

By 1817 Bird was filling several pages of his journal with depositions and other accounts of violence or alleged violence committed against Hudson's Bay Company by North Westers. One man told of how, on 11 February, he and two other Hudson's Bay employees "were assaulted by Peter Skene Ogden, a clerk of the North West Company, and five armed Canadians, who took from them their Sledges containing their bedding and a Packet of Letters," and then forced them into a North West post "where they were forcibly detained several days." That story spurred Bird to act against Ogden, "for the apprehension of whom I drew out a Warrant and delivered it to John McDougald (who was sworn in a constable of the Northern Department) to be by him executed . . . the first favourable opportunity."[22]

Bird had his chance to get Ogden a month and a half later when some members of the Cree nation suggested that "if I would send two or three of the officers of this place at their head, they would raise a party and take Ogden and his men prisoners." Bird appears to have been tempted, but once again worried about North West retaliation:

> I did not however think it prudent to accept of their offer at present from a consideration that such a step, even if attended with complete success, would not effectually reestablish our affairs, while the adoption of retaliation measures on our part would not fail to render the violent proceedings of the North West Company less striking, less calculated to excite general indignation, and consequently more unlikely to draw forth speedily on the authors of them the punishment they so richly deserve.[23]

Bird must have been thinking of the British colonial officials in the Canadas, not the British government at home. London was not as likely to appreciate what a dangerous, desperate measure it would be to employ Indians to settle a quarrel between the two fur companies. He may well have been right that the authorities in Montreal would have lost whatever sympathy they had for Hudson's Bay, especially if anything went wrong and North Westers were killed when the Crees stormed into Ogden's post on Green Lake. The North West Company had its headquarters in Montreal, and its officers, who were local men of substantial social standing in the community, had far more influence there than did Hudson's Bay. Bird also had to consider the possibility that North West could retaliate by paying other Indians to attack the Crees. The two fur companies could become involved in an Indian war.[24]

Bird need not have worried about provoking North West Company. The level of violence was raised by Samuel Black without any provocation from Hudson's Bay. He seized the Hudson's Bay post at Ile-à-la-Crosse and then went to Green Lake to ransack the Hudson's Bay post there. At Green Lake he had a ready ally in Ogden, who was, a biographer says, "pleased to hear" what had been done at Ile-à-la-Crosse and "exhilarated" at the idea of attacking the post at Green Lake.[25] He readily joined Black, and they and their men invaded the nearby Hudson's Bay post, plundered the place of its furs, rounded up all the Hudson's Bay people there, and took all of them to Ile-à-la-Crosse.[26]

It has been asserted by some students of the fur trade that Black acted under color of law or, at least, claimed to do so. One of the North West officers at Ile-à-la-Crosse was a justice of the peace who issued warrants to Black. And at least one other member of the company that attacked the two Hudson's Bay posts was sworn in as constable. Then, when his actions were challenged, Black, it is said, could claim that he was acting under the authority of a justice's warrant and was accompanied by a constable.[27] The warrant may have persuaded some of the Hudson's Bay people not to fight back, but it had no legal substance. The attacks on the Hudson's Bay posts at Ile-à-la-Crosse and Green Lake were criminal, pure and simple.

By now London headquarters of the Hudson's Bay Company had become all too familiar with the names of Samuel Black and Peter Skene Ogden. Something had to be done. Governor Joseph Berens was especially enraged against Ogden. Among other things, he had been told that Ogden had killed the Indian, Buffalo, at Green Lake because Buffalo insisted on trading with the Hudson's Bay post at Green Lake and would not trade at Ogden's post. Berens wrote Lord Bathhurst, secretary of state for war and the colonies, asking him to take official action. Ogden's crimes were particularly offensive, Berens argued, for like most of the North West Company's offenses, they were

> by no means confined to ignorant and half-breed Indians, but they are committed by persons who have generally received a good education, such at least as regularly to qualify them for commercial or mercantile concerns. Ogden a principal clerk of the North West Company, the son of one of the Judges at Montreal, cannot surely shelter himself under the plea of not knowing right from wrong, or grounding thereupon an excuse for murdering an Indian in cold blood, merely because the Indian was attempting to trade with British subjects not associated with himself or his employers.[28]

It is a strikingly unexpected argument. The governor of Hudson's Bay Company claimed that Ogden was especially culpable because of his family background and education. How Ogden would have answered Berens will never be known, but Ross Cox may have left us a good indication of what Ogden thought at the time. On his way home to Ireland from the Columbia River, Cox had stopped at Ile-à-la-Crosse just after Samuel Black had attacked the Hudson's Bay post there and the one at Green Lake. Ogden apparently bragged to him about how he had harassed his commercial opponents. "His accounts of his various rencontres with Orkney men and Indians would have filled a moderate-sized octavo," Cox recalled, "and if reduced to writing would undoubtedly stagger the credulity of any person unacquainted with the Indian country; and although some of his statements were slightly tinctured with the prevalent failing of *La Guienne*, there was *vraisemblance* enough throughout to command our belief in their general accuracy."[29]

Cox took strongly to Ogden's stories of violence. Even more, his imagination was captivated by "the humorous, honest, eccentric, law-defying Peter Ogden, the terror of Indians, and the delight of all gay fellows."[30] Particularly important to us is the fact that the words Cox wrote down are the closest we will ever come to hearing Ogden defend himself. The words are authentic. They not only sound like what Ogden would have said, they show evidence of the legal training that he supposedly received in his youth.

> In a country . . . in which there is no legal tribunal to appeal to, and into which the "King's writ does not run," many acts must be committed that would not stand a strict investigation in *Banco Regis*. "My legal primer," said Ogden, "says that necessity has no law; and in this place, where the custom of the country, or as lawyers say, the Les [*sic*] *non scripta* is our only guide, we must, in our acts of summary legislation, sometimes perform the part of judge, jury, sheriff, hangman, gallows and all."[31]

These words may be genuinely Ogden's, but they say nothing that is original and little that is surprising. Anyone would have pleaded necessity. More puzzling is what he meant by "the custom of the country." Because Hudson's Bay people had been mostly passive, not even fighting back on most occasions, it was Ogden himself who had determined the course of events. In other words, if there was any "custom of the country," it was custom he created. He was correct about being the legislature. He promulgated the rules and then executed the policy. There was no necessity determining Ogden's actions. What determined them, rather, was his and Samuel Black's willingness to use force. Hudson's Bay, not Peter Ogden, had the law on its side.

An indictment for murder was returned in Lower Canada against Ogden. Hudson's Bay easily found men to serve it. The North West

Company moved more quickly. By the time the arresting party arrived at Ile-à-la-Crosse, Ogden had been ordered west to the Columbia River district. "[T]hat vagabond Ogden," the leader of the arresting force reported, had "gone across the mountains," and was beyond the reach of Hudson's Bay and British law.[32]

Very little is known of Ogden's service with the North West Company on the Columbia River. At first he was stationed briefly at Fort George, the old American post formerly called Astoria, near the mouth of the river. While there, he was ordered to investigate the killing of an eastern Indian, said to have been an Iroquois, by a Cowlitz. He took a party of thirty to forty men with him to the Cowlitz village, should he need support in punishing the supposed killer or killers. Unfortunately, most of his men were eastern Indians, probably Iroquois. They went on a rampage, killing twelve Cowlitz Indians and scalping at least three. Ogden attempted to stop them and he may not have been to blame, but the incident did not help his reputation. After that, he went north, to New Caledonia, where he took charge of Fort Thompson, a post that traded mainly with the Shuswaps. While there, he was notified that he had been made a partner of the North West Company.[33] Then his world came crashing down about him.

Partly because of the violence between the two companies, the British government forced a merger of Hudson's Bay with North West. There was a general amnesty and the officers of both companies were admitted into the new organization with only a few exceptions. The most notable were Samuel Black, Peter Skene Ogden, and Cuthbert Grant, an especially violent North Wester who had led the *métis* and Indians in the infamous "Battle of Seven Oaks" and there had shot Robert Semple, the governor of Hudson's Bay's Assiniboia district. Although fear that he might go into opposition made a few members of the old Hudson's Bay Company willing to admit Ogden, most insisted that he be kept out. As far as the new company was concerned, Ogden was finished as a fur trader.[34]

Ogden did not want to leave the fur trade. To win back his position, he took a bold, dramatic step. He left the Pacific Coast and traveled back through the rivers of his enemies and even into the jurisdiction where an indictment against him was still outstanding. He went over the mountains, the length of Rupert's Land, through Upper and Lower Canada, and across the ocean to plead his case at the London headquarters of the new Hudson's Bay Company. The trip certainly helped Ogden to present his case, but the decision was not made in London. It was made by the North American governor of the new company, George Simpson. London headquarters accepted his recommendation that Ogden and Black both be admitted to Hudson's Bay. "This has been done in great measure in consequence of your recommendation & from your representing that they had been rather the instruments than the contrivers of the mischief," the British governor wrote Simpson. "Whatever might have been their delinquency they were not a bit worse than many who had been in the first arrangements."[35]

If Simpson really told London headquarters that Ogden was not a contriver and not a worse offender than other North Westers, he was stretching the facts to find some excuse for bringing Ogden into the new company. Ogden and Black had been as much the instigators as they were the instruments of North West violence. Of course, we cannot be certain, but from the little evidence available they seem to have commenced their acts of harassment on their own authority and volition. Even as "instruments," they certainly were more to blame than almost any of the officers who had become members of the new company "in the first arrangements." Surely Simpson did not think they had been treated unfairly. He cared nothing about fairness. What concerned him was competition. By going to London, Ogden dramatically demonstrated his determination to remain in the fur trade. If he was not part of Hudson's Bay Company, he most likely would go into opposition. But how? Hudson's Bay Company was a statutory monopoly. Competition was prohibited by law. No one else could buy fur from the natives. The one possibility has to be that Simpson feared Ogden would join an American trading and trapping company. If he ever did join an American outfit, Ogden certainly would head directly for Oregon and the Snake country. If we can measure Simpson's concerns by his actions—by the fact that he will order that the Snake country be denuded of all its beaver to make it unattractive for Americans—then it is safe to say the very last thing that Simpson wanted to see in 1823 was Americans in Oregon.

In July 1823, at a council meeting at York Factory, Peter Ogden was voted into the Hudson's Bay Company. A resolution was passed appointing him "to fit out a Trapping expedition next spring for the Snake country, for which 8 additional hired Servants to the present establish-ment, will be provided him, and that said expedition will be placed under the direction of Alexr. Ross Clerk." In other words, he was told to prepare the Snake country expedition of 1824 to be led by Alexander Ross and, remaining at Spokane House, to be the company's contact with the expedition while it was abroad. That was Ogden's introduction to the Snake country.[36]

"Ogden has gone to the Columbia and determined to do great things," George Simpson wrote London, "he does not want for ability."[37] It is possible that Simpson already knew how he would utilize that abil-ity. If not, he learned in just a few months when he followed Ogden west, making his first trip of inspection to the Columbia River department. After he had crossed the Rockies he decided that Alexander Ross would have to be replaced as leader of the Snake country expedition. He did not have to go outside of Spokane House to find a replacement. It is not known if he seriously considered other candidates. Probably not. Ogden was such an obvious choice.

Ogden's reputation followed him out into the Snake country and even into the history books. "Ogden's combative temperament was now to be given full reign" in the Snake country, one scholar has written. "Ogden's physical prowess as well as his alleged ability to outbrawl, outswear, and outjest any of his subordinates," a second historian agreed, "made him an excellent choice for the leadership of the Snake Coun-try Expedition."[38] Other historians have not agreed that Ogden was the best choice. "In appointing to the management of the Snake country a man whom he believed to be unscrupulous and addicted to violence, Simpson took upon himself a grave responsibility," John S. Galbraith has contended. "A collision between Ogden and the Americans might have serious consequences for Anglo-American relations, and Ogden was given no specific instructions on his conduct toward American par-ties or on the limitations of his area of operations." R. M. Patterson dis-agreed. He thought Ogden exactly the right Hudson's Bay officer to meet the Americans, and for exactly opposite reasons—not because he was violent but because he was educated. Noting that Simpson had sent Samuel Black, "who was best at playing a lone hand," to explore the Finlay-Stikine-Liard headwaters, and Ogden to confront the Americans in the Snake country, Patterson argued:

In these two men who had so distinguished themselves in the struggle between the Companies that they were specially excluded by the terms of the coalition, the Governor found, ready at his hand, two instruments that might have been specially designed to carry out his plans in the empty countries on the edges of the known lands. The Finlay and the Snake seemed, in their turn, to have been expressly created for the employment of those men of direct action—and into those territories, in the dawn of the Eighteen Twenties, the crippling paralysis of legalism, the curse of the Anglo-Saxon race, had not yet come. The Snake Country, with its possibilities for international conflict, was assigned to Ogden who, having some knowledge of the law, would be less likely to fall gratuitously foul of the American trappers.[39]

Certainly George Simpson never forgot Ogden's reputation. Few men served Simpson better than Ogden, and few contributed more to Simpson's successful management of Hudson's Bay Company. Over the years, Simpson's view of Ogden somewhat mellowed, but he never quite lost his mistrust of his former North West adversary.

Simpson kept a "Character Book" in which he recorded his thoughts and dislikes of his officers. His entry for Ogden was written after Ogden had completed his years of service in the Snake country, but before Simpson could bring himself to promote him to chief factor.

A keen, sharp off hand fellow of superior abilities to most of his colleagues, very hardy and active and not sparing of his personal labour. Has had the benefit of a good plain Education, both writes and speaks tolerably well, and has the address of a Man who has mixed a good deal in the World. Has been very Wild & thoughtless and is still fond of coarse practical jokes, but with all the appearance of thoughtlessness he is a very cool calculating fellow who is capable of doing any thing to gain his own ends. His ambition knows no bounds and his conduct and actions are not influenced or governed by any good or honourable principle. In fact, I consider him one of the most unprincipled Men in the Indian Country, who would soon get into the habits of dissipation if he were not restrained by the fear of those operating against his interests, and if he does indulge in that way madness to which he has a predisposition will follow as a matter of course.[40]

It was a harsh judgment by a harsh man, but probably more honest than most of the appraisals Simpson wrote in his "Character Book." It was also the judgment of a superior officer, who, although not violent, was in many respects not as good a person as Ogden. Simpson also knew how much he owed Ogden and that Ogden would have to be given his due. Ogden, he feared, was "likely to be exceedingly troublesome if advanced to the 1st Class" of the trade, that is, promoted to the office of chief factor. "[B]ut," Simpson added, "his Services have been so conspicious for several years past, that I think he has strong claims to advancement."[41] He was referring to Ogden's services in the Snake country.

CHAPTER FOUR

We Hold This Country by So Slight a Tenure

It would be wrong to make too much of Ogden's "combative temperament."[1] In truth, Ogden brought far more to the Snake country than his fists. He brought an outstanding intelligence, a keen appreciation of harvesting the resources of the land, and an insatiable drive to explore the countryside so he could report to the world what lay beyond the valleys and the mountains that already were known.

Ogden gave the Snake country the descriptive definition that almost everyone since has used. He made it a much wider area than the land drained by the Snake River. "The Snake Country," he wrote, "is bounded on the North by the Columbia Waters[,] On the South by the Missourie, On the West by the Spanish Territo[ries] and the East by the Saskatchewan Tribes." The geography was not precisely accurate, but it served his purposes and seems to have satisfied most historians since.[2] The Saskatchewan tribes were the four nations of the Blackfoot confederacy: the Blackfoot, the Piegan, the Blood, and the Gros Ventre of the Plains. Also called "the War Tribes" by Ogden, they were the peoples who made it necessary that expeditions going toward the northeast be larger and move more cautiously than those going to other sections of the Snake country. The "general rendezvous" of the Blackfoot nations was "without exception the most dangerous part of the Snake Country," Ogden warned, "and we already know from the different Trapping Expeditions who have attempted reaching it, that they have been obliged to retreat not only with the loss of many lives, but also property."[3]

A striking feature of the Snake country when Ogden first went there, was that it contained no trading posts. Very early in the history of trans-montane fur trading, the Pacific Fur Company, that is, the Astorians, had constructed a post on the Boise River. It had been annihilated by a Shoshone band. Later, Donald McKenzie of the North West Company "made another Establishment there, but the want of means to support the party and the natives being hostilely inclined they were soon obliged to abandon it, [and] none has been made since nor," Ogden believed, "would any benefit or advantage arise from one being made." Warfare was too prevalent in the Snake country, leaving nations like the Bannocks with little time to hunt. "They live in a constant state of dread and apprehension of being attacked by the Saskatchewan Tribes, and many of them are killed." Besides, the most populous inhabitants of the country, the Snakes, showed no interest in trading. "On our goods with the exception of Knives they set little or no value and the few Beaver they kill, I am of opinion, they singe. Our trade with them is very trifling not amounting to 20 Skins."[4]

Ogden's expeditions took him to all sections of the Snake country, and beyond. He not only traveled the length of the Oregon Territory but also into American jurisdiction, as far as the headwaters of the Missouri in today's Montana. He went into present-day Utah and just missed discovering the Great Salt Lake; into the incredibly dry, hot Humboldt River desert; to the domains of the Klamath nation, and deep into Mexico's Alta California. The heart of the Snake country, however, was the land drained by the Snake River itself. It was a terrain that stunned Alexander Ross. He had grown up in Scotland, and, until he came to the Columbia River with the Astorians, had not imagined the extent of lakes and forests in the North American West. Ross attempted to describe the splendor of the Snake River basin, but could not.

> The general features of the Snake country presents a scene incomparably grateful to a mind that delights in varied beauties of landscape and the manifold work of nature. The soft Blue Mountains whose summits are above the clouds and the wide extending plains

with the majestic waters in endless sinuosities fertilizing with their tributary streams, a spacious land of green meadows. The towering hills and deep vallies, with their endless creeks and smiling banks, convey an idea that baffles all description.[5]

George Simpson planned Ogden's first expedition. He was implementing the suggestions of Alexander Ross and Chief Factor Alexander Kennedy. The year before, Simpson had ordered Ross to begin the Snake country expedition from the Flathead Post in the shadows of the Rocky Mountains during February and to return to the Flatheads the following November. Once in the field, Ross realized that this schedule meant the expedition would be away from the beaver during the best trapping season, when fur was thickest and the females were not carrying their young. He complained bitterly and Simpson listened. Dates were changed, and Ogden was ordered to leave in November, as soon as he possibly could after Ross's return to the Flatheads with the trappers. If all went well, that starting date would permit Ogden to have the expedition in the beaver grounds at prime hunting time. It also meant that the freemen—the trappers who were members of the expedition but were not employees of the Hudson's Bay Company—would not be idle for four winter months, hanging about Flathead Post or Spokane House, where, at best, the company might have to support them, and, at worst, they could make trouble with the local Indians.

Simpson also listened to Ross's complaints about having to return to Flathead Post at the end of the expedition. It was the wrong terminus for a Snake country expedition. Any place on the Columbia was a good deal closer to the beaver fields, and far less dangerous to reach. Depending on where one went, the roads to the Columbia led through the Nez Perce, the Cayuse, or some of the smaller nations that generally maintained trading relations with the fur companies and had never attacked trapping expeditions. The road to Flathead Post lay near enough to the Piegans to pose some hazard. Simpson agreed to change the route, but wanted Ogden to return much farther down the river than Ross recommended. The reason was that the road to Fort Nez Perces ran right through the powerful Nez Perce nation. The Indians might be peaceful, but he could not trust the freemen. He thought it too risky for the unruly freemen to pass through so large a nation.

[O]ur Freemen are composed of Europeans, Canadians, Americans, Iroquois, half breeds of all the different Nations on the East side of the Mountain and the Women are Natives of every tribe on both sides; such a motley congregation it is quite impossible to keep under any controul or restraint; they would be constantly gambling buying chopping & changing of Women Slaves Horses & Dogs with the Natives, quarrels would follow as a matter of course and the consequences might be fatal both to the Establishment [*i.e.*, Fort Nez Perces] and Expedition. I therefore conceive that the less intercourse we have with the Nez Percés beyond what is absolutely necessary the better; and I am decidedly of opinion that the only way in which we are likely to turn the Snake Expedition to advantage is that which I have already settled on with Mr Ogden, viz.:—to outfit them this season at the Flat Head Post   take them at once to their hunting Grounds in the heart of the Snake Country   pass the Winter & Spring there   come round hunting their way either by land or Water to the Umpqua River, across the Mountains that divide it from the Walhamot [Willamette] River, down the last and thence direct to Fort George with their returns, there enjoy themselves for a Fortnight or 20 Days   re-equip them from thence and send them back to pass the Winter in the Hunting Grounds from whence they came but on no consideration to visit any Establishment throughout the year except Fort George. Thus will their time be fully and usefully occupied; we shall . . . avoid the risk of quarrels with the Natives and the people will have an opportunity of Spending their money to their satisfaction.[6]

Purposes and policies in the Snake country were not always what they seemed to be. If anything should be obvious, it is that Hudson's Bay sent Peter Ogden's expeditions into the Snake country to make money by hunting beaver. That is true, but it is not the whole story. Ogden was sent to the Snake country to turn back the American trappers, not by violence, but by trapping the land bare of beaver. "If properly managed," Simpson explained to London about the Snake country, "no question exists that it would yield handsome profits as we have convincing proof that the country is a rich preserve of Beaver and which for political reasons we should endeavour to destroy as fast as possible."[7]

At a time when Peter Ogden was out in the field, leading his second expedition to the Snake country, Governor Simpson explained how his program of destruction was expected to work. "It is intended that a strong Trapping Expedition be kept up to hunt the country to the south-ward of the Columbia," he wrote to John McLoughlin, his superin-tendent for the Columbia department, "as while we have access thereto it is in our interest to reap all the advantage we can for ourselves, and leave it in as bad a state as possible for our successors." He was saying that Hudson's Bay trapping expeditions would destroy the beaver pop-ulation of the Snake country and of the area south of the Columbia River, so that should those parts of the Oregon Territory be ceded to the United States, they would be worthless in fur. Then the Americans might be slow to enter them, putting much less pressure on lands the British retained in the remainder of Oregon. "The opposition with which we are at present assailed all along the South side of the Colum-bia and at its entrance," Simpson told McLoughlin almost three years later, "renders our utmost exertions necessary for the protection of our own interests, and to prevent our rivals in trade from profiting by their encroachments. It is highly satisfactory to find that hitherto these important objects have been attained and if we do not relax there is lit-tle doubt we shall soon be left Masters of the Field." Simpson wrote these words after Ogden had made four expeditions. He was saying that the program was working.[8]

It must not be thought this was a program concocted in North Amer-ica and never heard of in Great Britain. London headquarters knew all about it and supported it fully. "[A]s you are already in possession of our views as far as regards the Americans," the company's governor and committee wrote to the chief factors of the Columbia department, "we have merely to observe that it will be advisable to work the southern portion of the Country as hard as possible, while it continues free to the subjects of both nations." Two years later they repeated these orders to Simpson. "[I]t is extremely desirable to hunt as bare as possible all the Country South of the Columbia and West of the Mountains," he was instructed. It was, of course, unnecessary to tell Simpson. No one summed up the policy in clearer words than he. "[A]n exhausted coun-try I conceive to be the best protection we can have from opposition." He meant exhausted of *all* beaver. There is much merit to Merrill Mattes's claim that beaver "caused more historical rumpus than any other North American native, except the Indian."[9]

Peter Ogden was vital to the program of destruction. It is simply wrong to think that "Ogden had the misfortune to receive command of the expedition just at the time that American traders were penetrating to the Snake country in some force." There was no misfortune. In fact, the Americans may have been Ogden's fortune. Simpson needed him to oppose the Americans. Indeed, the better view, as suggested by another historian, is that Simpson may have been thinking of the Snake country expeditions when he persuaded his superiors in London to forget past offenses and admit Ogden into the new Hudson's Bay Company.[10]

Ogden was to execute the program, but the theory was mostly Simpson's. "The plan of exhausting the frontier country of Beaver, and other Fur bearing animals we shall continue," he wrote in 1828, "and the consequence in the course of a few years I trust will be, that, the extended District of barren country seperating the Hon[ora]ble Company's Territories from opposition will protect us from its encroachments." The idea was that eventually Oregon would be divided between the United States and Great Britain, with the "north side" of the Columbia "falling into our share of a division." "[A]s we cannot expect to have a more Southern boundary than the Columbia in a Treaty with the Americans," he contended, "it will be desirable that the hunters should get as much out of the Snake Country as possible for the next few years." It also meant that Great Britain would "have something to give up on the South when the final arrangements come to be made."[11]

One student of Hudson's Bay history has suggested that Simpson reasoned syllogistically: "All American settlers will be traders and trappers; traders and trappers are interested in furs only; therefore, lay waste the fur country and there will be no American settlers." Actually, Simpson did not think the traders and trappers would be settlers. He expected the settlers would be farmers who would follow the route discovered and mapped by the fur trappers. If the trappers did not come, the farmers would not either. Hudson's Bay people believed Oregon was too distant to be colonized by sea. The trip around the Cape of Good Hope was too dangerous and too expensive. But discovery of South Pass—just at the time Simpson was formulating the denuding policy—meant that Americans could come by land. The existence of South Pass also meant

that they could come with wagons hauling household goods and farm
equipment, which would mean greater numbers than anyone would
have expected if there were no South Pass. That was Hudson's Bay's
greatest fear, settlement by substantial numbers of farmers with families. There was a theory prevalent among Hudson's Bay officers that the
company could not remain once the land was populated with people,
houses, and planted fields. McLoughlin explained the theory in a report
to the governor, deputy governor, and committee in London.

> An important point for consideration is Whether the trappers and
> Engaged Servants Who retire from the Service should be allowed
> to settle in the country or Not; and Whatever way we View it—it is
> attended with difficulties. Governor Simpson Writes me not to
> Allow any of our people to settle and of course I will obey the
> order. It is true I Know and Every One Knows who is acquainted
> with the Fur trade that as the country becomes settled the Fur
> trade Must Diminish and I therefore Discouraged our people
> from settling as long as I could without exciting ill Will towards
> the Company.[12]

The few old employees McLoughlin permitted to settle in the Willamette Valley had been joined by a few Americans in 1838 when James
Douglas, referring to the settlement as "the Colony," summed up Hudson's Bay's apprehension of emigration as concisely as it was ever done.
He was a leading officer in the Columbia department and, ironically,
future governor of British Columbia, a colony that would force Hudson's Bay Company to retreat even further. "The interests of the Colony,
and the Fur Trade will never harmonize," he wrote the governor and
committee in London, "the former can flourish only, through the protection of equal laws, the influence of free trade, the accession of respectable inhabitants; in short by establishing a new order of things, while
the fur Trade, must suffer by each innovation."[13]

Generally speaking, Hudson's Bay people had a word for the program of stripping the land of all its beaver. They used the verb *to denude*.
Ogden's instructions were to denude the Snake country. A Hudson's
Bay officer called it a policy of laying "waste the country." "[O]ur general
instructions recommend that every effort be made to lay waste the country," he wrote. Historians have referred to producing "a cordon *sanitaire*,"

creating "a buffer wasteland," making "a fur desert," a "fire guard," "a scorched-earth policy," and "a 'scorched stream' policy."[14]

Hudson's Bay had denuded fur in other districts where it had faced American competition. What made the Snake country unusual was that Ogden's denuding was not just aimed against a commercial competition, it was intended to promote the company's foreign policy.[15] In fact, officers were told that in the Snake country costs and profits were not the first consideration. "By attempting to make such expeditions too profitable the whole may be lost," the governor and committee warned Simpson. The London authorities said this, even though people at headquarters believed there was a way both to make money and diminish American competition.

> It would be more profitable and a more secure Trade, if we could bring the Country to produce four times its present returns which could easily be accomplished, and sell these returns at half the present price p. lb. The cost of obtaining that large quantity need not be more than what is paid for the present returns and the moderate price of Beaver would put an end to all substitutes for it, and tend to diminish the temptation to oppose us on the frontiers of our Country.[16]

Who knows if that strategy would have worked? The significant consideration to keep in mind, is that it was not tried, because London gave priority to stopping any potential American advance over a "more profitable and a more secure Trade."

It seems that no one in the company openly opposed denuding, but there were officers uncomfortable with it, and their objections were not what we might think—that denuding was anticommercial, that it was not profitable, or that it did not secure the trade. More troublesome was the fact that denuding violated Hudson's Bay's general conservation policy and the values of most company officers who served in the North American West. Denuding seems to have troubled even Ogden. He occasionally complained that American trappers were stripping the land bare. This was hypocritical, of course, but gives us a good indication of what he really thought of his denuding assignment. On his second expedition, for example, he complained of the "[A]merican Traders who are certainly from the number of Trappers and encouragement they give exerting themselves to ruin the Country as fast as they can and this they will soon effect." Later, on the Owyhee River during his fifth expedition, Ogden sadly noted that he and his trappers were creating a wasteland. "Our traps visited and produced only seventeen beaver," he lamented. "It is scarcely credible what a destruction of beaver by trapping at this season, within the last few days upwards of fifty females have been taken and on an average each with four young ready to litter. Did we not hold this country by so slight a tenure it would be most to our interest to trap only in the fall, and by this mode it would take many years to ruin it."[17]

Denuding went against the grain of conservation, and conservation was official company policy for Hudson's Bay officers. As with *denuding*, they had a word for it. The word was *nursing*. The descriptive term was "nursing the country."[18] Indians were encouraged to take only winter beaver, not summer, or cub beaver.[19] To protect beaver, a quota system was imposed on the heads of company districts located away from the American border.[20] They were ordered to inform Indians that they would not purchase pelts hunted out of season, and that they would pay more for the skins of other types of animals sold by Indians who did not trap beaver.[21] To encourage Indians to avoid killing beaver for food during times of hunger, trading posts were instructed to furnish them with fishing tackle, ammunition, and provisions "at a reduction in prices of 33⅓ per cent on the ordinary Sale Tariff."[22] There were even company attempts to ban steel traps and springs by forbidding both their sale and use.[23]

There was, of course, an exception to the conservation program. Several paragraphs are needed to explain it. It was stated clearly in the Hudson's Bay Company's "Standing Rules and Regulations." A resolution adopted in 1829 stated that the "nursing rule" (as it was officially called) "is meant to apply only to Districts of Country within the Hon. Company's Territories not exposed to opposition, but in frontier Districts it is recommended that every encouragement be afforded the Natives to hunt the country close, as by extirpating the Fur bearing race on the Frontiers, the home country will be effectually protected from the incursions of rival Traders." In fact, conservation in "the home country" may have spurred denuding in the Snake country. Nursing the land meant, of course, that fewer beaver were caught in the nursed districts, but fewer beaver in some districts did not have to mean fewer beaver overall. "[T]he deficiency," it was resolved in 1826, "might be made up by keeping all the frontier country hunted close, and by trapping expeditions in those countries likely to fall within the Boundary of the United States."[24]

When the company voted to keep "all frontier country hunted close," it had a very extensive area in mind. It may seem incredible, but California was part of "the frontier country." "It will be useful to give the Americans full occupation by active and well regulated opposition on the South of the river to prevent them advancing towards the North," the governor and committee instructed Simpson. Simpson gave the task to his superintendent of the Columbia department, John McLoughlin, who, as early as 1825, had sent a trapping party south under Finan McDonald.[25] About fifteen years after that date, he made an agreement with Mexican authorities permitting Hudson's Bay brigades to hunt and trap in California. By the end of five years, McLoughlin hoped, "we would have given the country such a hunting as would have left few Beaver remaining." It was, he said of California, "our interest to hunt the country as much as we can, and as quick as possible while it is in our power." His trappers certainly did a thorough job, for that very year General Mariani Vallejo realized that denuding was occurring. "The otter and beaver which abounded in California," he reported to Mexico City, "have been exterminated, the first by the Russians and the latter by the Columbians who still continue to trap them to the point of extinguishing the species."[26]

Considering the emphasis that Hudson's Bay put on conservation of beaver, perhaps the most surprising fact is that denuding extended even into New Caledonia. After all, the Columbia was being denuded in part to keep the American trappers from getting near New Caledonia. It should have been just the place for nursing, not denuding. Yet by 1841, when Ogden was in charge of Hudson's Bay operations in New Caledonia, he reported to Simpson a marked falling off of the quantity and quality of beaver. The decrease was, Simpson explained to London headquarters, due to "the double effect of benefitting by immediate results, and of rendering the country less inviting to the numerous United States trapping parties, who formerly threatened to overrun the whole of the accessible country on the west side of the Rocky Mountains."[27]

Amazingly, John McLoughlin even wanted to denude American territory. He must have been serious because he actually proposed a plan to Governor Simpson. He suggested sending a large trapping party from the Columbia, across the Rocky Mountains, to stay out for about three years, clearing the country in the direction of the Grand Tetons.

> If such a party was sent they ought to go direct to the Trois Tettons and hunt up that place, then turn North and hunt all the head branches of Missouries in the vicinity of where Mʳ Ogden was in Summer [of] 1825, in three years they would do this which would destroy the Inducements the American trappers from the other side have to push to the Head waters of the Columbia and by hunting the Head branches of the Missouries where I state diminish the inducements the Americans might have to equip hunting parties from this side of the Mountains and to interfere with our Saskatchewan trade sooner than they otherwise would.

What was McLoughlin thinking of? He might not have known that five years earlier, Hudson's Bay exploring parties had made extensive trips along the Bow and Red Deer Rivers, south of the Saskatchewan and north of the Missouri, and had found the area "almost destitute of beaver." With the Piegans, the Bloods, and the Blackfeet also roaming the region, it was unlikely Americans would enter Saskatchewan country from that direction. But when suggesting that the expedition go in the direction of the "head branches of Missouries," McLoughlin specifically mentioned that it was the place where Ogden had gone on his first Snake country expedition. He knew that London headquarters had reprimanded Ogden for trapping and hunting there and had warned Simpson to keep Snake country expeditions from crossing the mountains into United States territory.[28]

Americans certainly believed that Hudson's Bay was trapping in their territory. Most thought the British were getting the fur because they were nearer the western Indians, and could purchase as well as trap beaver.[29] Only a few complained that denuding was occurring. The British were not only killing beaver "of Six months old," they were destroying dams as well, the American secretary of war was warned. "At present the [American] trappers are only gleaning where the British have been reaping."[30] One man who had been to Oregon reported to the government that beaver were disappearing in the territory. His dates and numbers were quite a bit off, but he knew what was happening. "[S]ince 1828 a party of forty or fifty trappers (Canadians) with their women slaves &c generally amounting to 150 or 200 persons and 300 Horses," he reported, "go out from [Fort] Vancouver towards the south as far as 40 deg. North Lat. These parties search every stream and take every Beaver Skin they find regardless of the destruction of the young animals."[31]

Hudson's Bay Company's program of denuding the Snake country had two purposes. One was to take all possible profit from every part of the country Great Britain most likely would cede to the United States. "[T]he Tenure which the Company have of the South side of the Columbia is of that precarious nature," John McLoughlin explained, "that we are certain of being deprived of it when a Boundary line is run . . . and that it is the interest of the Company to make all they can out of it while it is in our power." The second objective was to keep American trappers from coming north. "In the present unsettled state of the boundary line," Simpson told London headquarters, "it would be impolitic to make any attempt to preserve or recruit this once valuable country, as it would attract the attention of the American trappers, so that there is little prospect of any amendment taking place in its affairs."[32] And, in fact, the beaver never returned to the Snake country in the numbers known before Ogden began his denuding campaign.

Just five years before the international boundary line was finally fixed, giving the Oregon country to the United States, George Simpson was satisfied. He believed that denuding had been successful. "There is not at present any organized trapping expedition belonging to the United States employed in the Snake country, although there are several straggling parties, the débris of former expeditions," he reported in 1841.

> [I]ndeed it is highly gratifying to be enabled to say that all opposition from citizens of the United States is now at an end, both in the interior and on the coast, and the want of success that has attended their endeavours of late years will I trust deter others from risking their lives and property in so hopeless an undertaking, as competition in the fur trade would at present be in that quarter.[33]

As an instrument of imperial policy, Peter Skene Ogden's Snake country expeditions would prove to have been effective.[34]

Ogden's expeditions would be effective, but only in part. He would do everything Simpson ordered him to do. The beaver would be killed* and many Americans would be driven from the fur business.[35] Denuding would not work as geopolitics, however. George Simpson had not understood the American threat. The Americans whom he knew were mostly fur traders or trappers, and he had contempt for them and their organizations. Because they were the first to travel the great rivers and the first to penetrate the forests of the west, Simpson assumed that they would be the vanguard of settlement. If they did not come to Oregon, the homesteaders might not follow.[36]

---

* No officer of Hudson's Bay Company seems to have given thought to the morality of denuding the land. It is not surprising that during the early nineteenth century company officials were not troubled by environmental questions. But it is well worthy of note that they did not consider either the impact of denuding on local natives or the reaction of the natives.

CHAPTER FIVE

They Are Too Lazy to Come In with Their Furs

Alexander Ross led the Snake country expedition of 1824 back to its home base at Flathead Post on the 26th of November. Peter Ogden, he noted, had arrived there "only a few hours before us." Next day Ogden handed Ross a letter from Governor Simpson appointing him postmaster at the Flatheads and giving him the news that "Mr. Ogden takes my place as chief of the Snake expedition."[1]

Simpson had wanted Ogden to start in November, but it took him over three weeks to re-equip the brigade. The trappers, including those who had just come in with Ross, had to be "supplied with Horses, Traps and other necessaries required for trapping beaver and feeding them-selves in [the] course of the voyage." It is unclear just how many men there were. William Kittson should have made the most reliable count for, as Ogden's second-in-command, he had to keep the accounts of individual trappers, recording what equipment they purchased from the company, and later readjusting their indebtedness as they handed in beaver pelts. He said that there were ten *engagés* and fifty-three free-men, with thirty-five children. But Alexander Ross, who helped equip the freemen, said that there were seventy-five "Men & Lads."[2]

The total of traps purchased fell well short of the number—ten per trapper—that Ross thought they should have,[3] and there was so much disappointment over the quality of the horses that Ross had trouble dis-tributing them. "The most equitable division could have not please[d] all," he wrote. "Those [purchased] from the Nez Percés were a shabby assortment of colts & unbroken in horses, not too well adapted for a Snake Expedition."[4] Most of the remainder of the equipment, however, was of high quality, and the arms and ammunition were ample enough for Kittson to suppose the brigade would be "able in all appearances to face any War party brought into the plains." All in all, Ross concluded, it was "A party the most formidable & best appointed of any that ever set out for" the Snake country. He is the only white man known to have seen them all.[5]

The horses were shoddy, but the men were worse. To appreciate some of the problems Ogden had managing them, they should be considered as two distinct groups, the *engagés*, salaried employees of Hudson's Bay, and the freemen, mostly *métis* or Iroquois trappers signed up for the expedition.

Besides the two officers, Ogden and Kittson, there were two interpreters, Charles McKay, who spoke Piegan and possibly translated for all the Blackfoot tribes, and François Rivir, Ogden's step father-in-law, who most likely spoke languages of the Columbia River country. Among the other engaged servants there may have been a hunter or two. The remainder were trappers. These men were Canadian *voyageurs* and were reckoned the most dependable members of the expedition. "These people are indispensable to the successful prosecution of the trade," the American fur trader, Ramsay Crooks, had written of them, "their places cannot be supplied by Americans who are for the most part . . . too independent to submit quietly to a proper controul." Certainly, the engaged servants were much less difficult to control than were the freemen.[6]

Probably no other Snake country partisan had as much trouble with freemen as Alexander Ross. He especially had difficulty with the Iroquois who made up a large percentage of his freemen. For him, the problems started at the very beginning, when the freemen signed on as members of the expedition.

> In the selection of men for a Snake expedition, it has always been customary, heretofore, to collect the refuse about the different establishments, merely with a view, it would appear, to make up numbers: —all the lazy, cross-grained, and objectionable among the engaged class; the superannuated, infirm, and backsliding

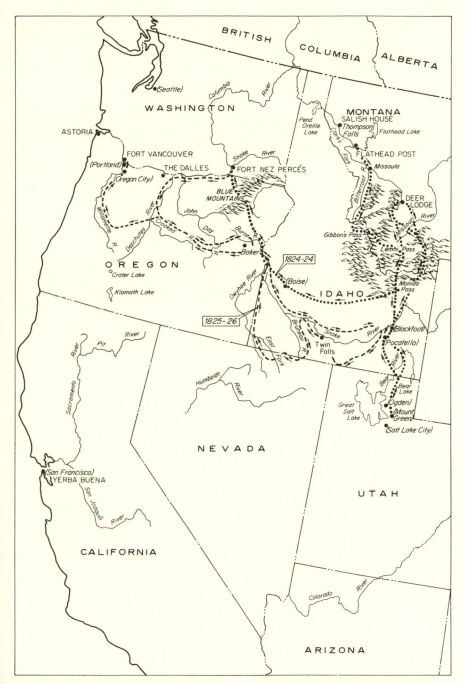

Snake Country Expeditions, 1824–25, 1825–26. From Gloria Griffen Cline, *Peter Skene Ogden and the Hudson's Bay Company* (Norman: University of Oklahoma Press, 1974).

freemen; the wayward half-breed, the ignorant native; and last of all, the worst of all, the plotting and faithless Iroquois: —taking it for granted that, if conducted by an experienced leader, all would go on well.[7]

Ross referred to the full-blood Indians as Iroquois, and so did just about every other officer of the Hudson's Bay Company. For fur traders in the North American West, especially those west of the Rocky Mountains, "Iroquois" was not the word we might think it was. As used by the mountain men, it did not necessarily mean a Mohawk, a Cayuga, or a member of the four other nations of the Iroquois league. It was a loose, generic term, applied to eastern Indians in general, no matter their nation or language family. They might be Algonquian-speaking, not necessarily Iroquoian. Their essential characteristic was that they were not native to the North American West, but were woodland Indians mostly from east of the Appalachians. As the records of the fur trade refer to them only as "Iroquois" that is how they will have to be identified in the following pages. The fur men wrote of them as Iroquois and their words cannot be changed.

Some twenty-first-century scholars have objected that these Indians are never identified as individuals. But few of them emerge from the journals and manifests of expeditions as identifiable personalities. We know of two or three only, such as John Grey and Old Pierre, who were Iroquois, but most are known only by name.[8] And even the names mean little in most cases, as Hudson's Bay clerks wrote imprecisely, using whatever spelling came into their heads at the moment. There was no consistency. It may be a comment on the values of the times that the Honourable Company saw no reason to record the identities or the precise nationalities of these eastern Indians. It is a comment on the correctness of our own times that a few of today's scholars object to that historical fact, but not to the fact that the French Canadian engaged servants and the Orkney Islanders are just as faceless. Few of them can be treated as individuals beyond their names and numbers.

Ross made a keen effort to weed out the worst from the freemen who applied to go on Ogden's expedition. No one knew their shortcomings better than he. At least three of the Iroquois who had gone out with him and had given him much trouble were "rejected as unfit for a Snake expedition." He hoped the expulsions would "have a good effect" on the other freemen. It is safe to say he wished he could have rejected even more, but he had to accept several whom he knew would be problems or Ogden would have had too few men.[9]

According to Kittson, the expedition started with ten *engagés* and fifty-three freemen. A historian of Oregon has said that those numbers put the brigade out of balance. "Too small a percentage of its trappers were *engagés*; too large a percentage were freemen," Frederick Merk observed. But why the imbalance? another historian asked. Governor Simpson, who detested the freemen, knew the risks inherent in taking them on expeditions, so why did he make it so difficult for Ogden by having him leave with a brigade that had five freemen for every company servant?[10]

The answer most frequently suggested is that Simpson was retrenching. The merger of the North West Company and Hudson's Bay had left him with a bloated organization, "two of everything"—two posts in locations needing only one, too many servants, even too many officers. The Columbia department was far too large, with approximately one-sixth of the total personnel employed by the company in North America. Simpson concluded that he should reduce operations by getting rid of 60 percent of the labor force. It was the need to retrench, it is said, that caused him to take the chance sending so many freemen on the Snake country expedition.[11] "He could let off engaged servants and thereby ease the payroll since the freemen were paid only according to their catch. He knew this would find favour in London and redound to his credit. Also he may have felt, as he afterwards openly stated, that . . . Ogden, with his experience and known success in handling Indians, would be able to keep the freemen in hand."[12]

Maybe, but there is a more persuasive explanation. The Snake country expedition was a social safety valve for Hudson's Bay, giving it some place to shuffle off the freemen who otherwise would be living around the trading posts which, if the situation became desperate, might have to feed them and their families, or who otherwise would be living among the natives where they might cause conflict, violence, and even commit homicide. That had happened in the Columbia department during North West Company times when Ogden led a party of Iroquois freemen to a local village where the Iroquois went on a rampage, killing defenseless people and scalping a few. And just two years before Ogden started on his expedition, in the area of Red River, the council for Hudson's Bay's Northern Department blamed freemen for provoking recent retaliatory homicides committed by Sioux.[13]

Every Hudson's Bay Company officer in the Columbia district had to worry about the explosive mixture of freemen and local Indians. After all, the Indians could not distinguish between freemen, *engagés*, and officers. Whether they thought of the fur men as "British," "white," or "Hudson's Bay," they were all one nationality to them. Hudson's Bay people could be collectively liable for what any freeman did, even while acting as a private individual. The killing of an Indian by a freeman, though an accident, and with the victim's nation understanding that it had been committed without intent or malice, could cause a crisis. At the least, the local Hudson's Bay post might have to pay some compensation, even if the manslayer had no connection with the place, and only lived somewhere in the vicinity. He would have been perceived as being of the same nation as Hudson's Bay officers and engaged servants, making all Hudson's Bay people collectively liable for the homicide, although only one would have to "pay" the blood debt. At the most, if no compensation was paid or other accommodation made, there could be a war between Hudson's Bay and the nation to which the victim of the homicide belonged.

Homicide, of course, was the most dramatic and drastic of potential offenses. There were many other actions that freemen could commit against Indians that might lead to international conflict, as Governor Simpson was painfully aware when planning Ogden's first Snake country expedition. Simpson gave Ogden instructions on many matters— when to leave for the Snake country, where to go once on Snake River, and what routes to take. On no issue concerning the freemen was he more motivated than the question of what trading post Ogden should return to. Alexander Ross had been ordered to end the Snake expedition of 1824 at Flathead Post. The brigade had started from there and Simpson wanted it to go back there so that the next expedition could also start from there.

Alexander Ross had raised very strong objections. Flathead Post was simply the wrong depot for the Snake country expeditions, he argued. Being so isolated, it was not easily furnished with the supplies an expedition had to have before it could depart for the Snake country. His most telling argument, however, concerned the route. It was just the wrong terminus for the Snake country expedition. Any place on the Columbia River was much closer to the beaver fields of the Snake country than was Flathead Post. This was an important consideration as Simpson wanted the expedition to trap at a time when furs were at their thickest. A Columbia destination allowed the trappers to remain in the beaver grounds for a longer time during the best trapping season. Moreover, the Columbia River was less dangerous to reach. Depending on where one went, the roads to the Columbia led through the Nez Perce, Cayuse, and some of the smaller nations that generally maintained trading relations with the fur companies, and had never attacked trapping expeditions. The path to Flathead Post lay near enough to the Piegans to pose some hazard, if not to be outright dangerous.

Ross's arguments were persuasive. Even Simpson, much as he might have wished to, could not ignore them. He agreed to change the route, but fear of freemen behavior when passing among Indian villages gave him pause. Ross wanted the expedition to return to Fort Nez Perces, the trading post closest to the trapping grounds. But that route meant that the expedition would pass through two relatively large nations, the Cayuse and Nez Perce. Simpson would not take the risk. Ogden's Snake country expedition could return to the Columbia rather than to Flathead Post, he agreed, but not to Fort Nez Perces. Simpson ordered Ogden to "come in" at Fort George, farther down the Columbia River than Fort Nez Perces. He had two reasons: to take advantage of the fact that the supply ship bringing trade goods from Britain and carrying the fur back to the London market, came to Fort George; and to keep the freemen away from the Nez Perces. He did not want the unruly freemen to pass through so large a nation. The risk for Hudson's Bay Company was too great.

It is important to understand just who the freemen were. Their status in relation to the Hudson's Bay Company is not easily defined as rules were changed and various officers whose ideas and interpretations differed from post to post attempted to apply what was never a uniform definition. In the Columbia River country during the 1820s there were basically two groups of freemen, separated by nationality and origin of service. One consisted of Iroquois. They were fur trappers who had been encouraged by the North West Company to migrate to the trapping of the Saskatchewan and its tributaries. After antagonizing the natives in that part of the West, many Iroquois had crossed the Rocky Mountains to trap the waters of the Columbia and Snake river basins.

The second group of freemen were more diverse ethnically, but collectively shared the fact of being French-speaking. A few were French Canadians who had either been released from the service of a fur company or preferred not to be under contract. Alexander Ross attempted to sum up their condition when he wrote that they were individuals "who have spent their better days in the quality of canoe men in the company's service, but who, deficient in provident sagacity to save part of their earnings for the contingencies of old age . . . and sooner than proceed to their own country to live by hard labour, resolve in passing the remainder of their days among the natives."[14]

Ross disliked freemen intensely[15] and in the statement just quoted was being very unfair. Idleness or the attractions of native life may have been why a few Canadians remained in the West after they were released by the North West Company, but it is a reasonable assumption that most stayed because they had Indian families.[16] And that was what gave rise to another group of non-Iroquois French-speaking freemen in the Columbia department. Although partly of French-Canadian descent, they were regarded by Hudson's Bay officers as a class apart from the French Canadians. They usually were offspring of French-Canadian *voyageurs* who had come west many years before, and, as there had been no French-Canadian women in the west for them to marry, they had had families with local native women. These freemen were *métis* who generally spoke both French and the language of their mothers. Quite often the mothers had been born in a Saskatchewan Indian nation and did not speak a language known west of the Rocky Mountains.

It is unnecessary to agree on a technical definition for the term *freeman*. A social definition will serve our needs just as well. Generally speaking, a freeman was a former trapper, blacksmith, *voyageur*, tailor, or other engaged servant below the rank of translator, usually of Canadian birth, who had completed his contract of service, or who had been discharged by a fur company, and who had remained in Rupert's Land or west of the Rocky Mountains, to survive the best he could, usually selling fur and meat to the local trading post. Or, a freeman was the son of a man, generally French-Canadian, who had been an officer or a servant of a fur company, and his native wife. Either way, he was called a "freeman" to distinguish him from the engaged servants or *engagés*, the men who worked under contract for Hudson's Bay.[17]

Simpson's retrenching following the merger of the two fur companies swelled the freemen population in the Columbia department. Whatever problems had existed before were compounded. And there had been very difficult problems. Now matters were worse, and, as a Hudson's Bay employee explained, something had to be done.

> It has become a matter of serious importance to determine on the most proper measures to be adopted with regard to the men who have large families and who must be discharged, and with the numerous halfbreed children whose parents have died or deserted them. These people form a burden which cannot be got rid of without expence, and, if allowed to remain in their present condition, they will become dangerous to the Peace of the Country and safety of the Trading Posts.[18]

There were not many solutions. One was to send the older Canadians with families to the Red River settlement. But that did not do for the young *métis* who had experienced only the Indian way of life and knew nothing about agriculture or commerce. For them, the obvious solution was employment, but the Hudson's Bay Company was the only employer in that part of British North America lying west of Upper Canada. For salaried servants, the company favored dependable Scots, especially Orkney islanders desperate for income. It had little work for freemen. Sometimes they would be hired by a local trading post on the Saskatchewan to hunt buffalo meat, and there could be occasional odd jobs, such as accompanying a messenger or herding the post's horses. It was that economic reality that gave the Snake country expeditions an unusual importance for Hudson's Bay officers serving in the Columbia department. The expeditions were just about the only source of regular employment the company was willing to provide freemen. Before the denuding program began, the main significance of the Snake country brigade was to give the freemen a source of income. In fact, the 1822 expedition, led by Michel Bourdon, had been sent out largely to take freemen away from the vicinity of Fort George, Spokane House, Fort Nez Perces, and Flathead Post.[19]

Very little is known of Bourdon's expedition except the problems that he had with the freemen. One difficulty was getting them to perform the routine daily tasks necessary on any expedition. Bourdon had so much trouble that his superior, Alexander Kennedy, realized that expeditions could not consist mainly of freemen as may have been the original plan. Hudson's Bay would have to send out some *engagés*, an expense Kennedy most likely had hoped to avoid.

> [F]rom the information received from Michel Bourdon last fall I have been induced to send a stronger Party along with the Freemen going to that quarter this Season, in hopes of being able to get out all the Skins that may be procured there as the freemen when left to themselves become so indolent and careless, that often after they have been at the trouble of procuring Furs at the risk of their Lives, they are too lazy to come in with them and the Consequence is that their Furs are either lost or damaged before they reach this place [Spokane House].[20]

Kennedy explained that at the time he was writing "there are Seven Hundred Skins remaining in the Snake Country." They had been "killed last spring by a party of Freemen who are heavily indebted to the Company, these fellows absolutely refused to come in with them, altho they are strongly pressed to do so by Michell Bourdon . . . he did everything in his Power to try and persuade them to accompany him to the Fort with their Furs, but his persuasion had no effect on them."[21]

Kennedy had a solution. On the next Snake country expedition, led by Finan McDonald, he sent both Bourdon and "five men with Horses &c to accompany the freemen."[22] After just a few days out on his first expedition, Peter Ogden could have told Kennedy that he had made a mistake. He should have provided McDonald with a much higher percentage of *engagés*.

A second problem with taking freemen to the Snake country, revealed by Bourdon's expedition, was the chance they might meet American traders. The freemen wanted someone besides Hudson's Bay to bid for their skins and there was no one else available to do so except American fur men. In fact, fourteen of Bourdon's freemen—four former Astorians and ten Iroquois—did not wait to meet Americans. They knew there was slight chance of seeing any in the Snake country during 1822.

So they deserted. They took the beaver that they had trapped, disappeared from Bourdon's camp, wintered with a band of Snakes, the next spring headed east for the Missouri, and went down that river to St. Louis to sell their pelts at American prices. The combination of freemen and American prices was to become Ogden's greatest challenge in 1825.[23]

Ogden would have been happier without freemen in his brigades. Even when he allowed them to separate, he had to worry about them. "Six men having volunteered to proceed down the river to trap I willingly gave my consent," he wrote while on his fourth expedition. "They promise fair, but Canadians always do so till fairly off, when they soon become negligent, disagree, separate, and nine times in ten lose their horses." Ogden could not depend on them. "But unfortunately, however fair Canadians promise, still they always will deviate from their instructions," he wrote during the same trip, "they ought never to be trusted alone when out of my sight."[24]

True, there were moments when Ogden felt for his freemen. They even had traits he admired, as, for example, their endurance. When sending six men to trap some distant rivers on his third expedition, he marvelled at sufferance.

> [I]t is certainly most harassing for the poor Trappers to Trap in such weather obliged to sleep out and two thirds without a Blanket to cover them   still not one complains but exert themselves to procure Beaver with all their *might & main* poor fellows   at times at least when I see them arrive which is too often the case in this rainy climate drenched in rain and shivering with cold feel most keenly for them   the life of a Trapper altho at times he has some idle hours which however does not often happen is certainly a most laborious one and one [that] in four years makes a young man look almost as if he had reached the advanced age of sixty   of this many convincing proofs are now amongst my party   the cold water which more or less they are wading in two thirds of the day ad[d]ed to the cold and sleeping often without fire and wet to the skin conduces to ruin their constitutions   well do they earn their 10 Shillings per Beaver   a convict in Botany Bay is a Gent living at his ease compared to them   still they are happy and amidst all their sufferings and privations if they take Beaver

all is well   thoughtless beings how much more comfortable and
with less labour could they earn an honest livelihood in their own
Country then they do in this and many are aware of this   but a
roving life pleases them and with nearly all it would be viewed
more as a punishment than a favour to send them to Canada.

Surely Ogden realized that in the last sentence he was writing about
himself, not just freemen. He too could live only "a roving life" and
Canada would have been as much a prison for him as for any freeman.
For he concluded: "God grant some *kind* Friend should succeed me and
I would most willingly steer my Course from whence I came altho I am
Canadian."[25]

There are puzzles concerning the freemen that are not always solved
by a close reading of Hudson's Bay records. Before Ogden's first expedition left Flathead Post, Ross reported that Ogden, in some way and
for some purpose that remain unclear, changed the status of some of
the men then at the Flatheads. "To day," he noted, "Mr. Ogden put several of the engaged men with families free, which will be a saving to the
company & make the Snake expedition ensuing campaign formidable."
Ross's text is written clearly in the journal, there is no mistaking his
words. But his meaning is ambiguous. Ogden apparently altered the status of those men, but in what way? Did several *engagés* ask to become
freemen, or did Ogden decree it against their will? Did the new freemen
have anything to say about the change? Ross seems to approve of what
was happening so it is unlikely the men asked to become free. He dis-
paraged anyone who did that. "There cannot be a better test for knowing a worthless and bad character in this country," he observed, "than
his wishing to become a freeman—it is the true sign of depravity, either
in a wayward youth or backsliding old man."[26]

If, in fact, Ogden changed the men's status by ordering them to be
freemen, he may have been acting under Governor Simpson's entrench-
ment program. Apparently, he could do it without their consent and
before their contracts of employment had expired. He undoubtedly
could not do it to Scots or Canadians without offering them transportation home, which may be why these particular men were selected
if the change of status was involuntary. Ross said they had families, so
Ogden may have known they would stay in the West and not ask to be

taken to Scotland or Montreal. But what did Ross mean that "putting" the men "free" would "be a saving to the company"? Obviously, the company saved money if it no longer paid their salaries, but it now had to pay for every beaver pelt they trapped. Ross may have been calculating that the low prices Hudson's Bay was then paying freemen for fur entailed no great outlay. Ogden would soon learn how economically oppressed the freemen felt. There was almost no chance they could get free of debt. When he returned from the expedition, Ogden persuaded the company to raise the prices it paid freemen for pelts, and lower the cost of the goods it sold to freemen. It is an important theme of this book that the freemen then became more content. The change in attitude may or may not be shown by François Payette, one of the most reliable and valued of the freemen. He refused to alter his status from that of freeman to engaged servant. Once the company began to pay ten shillings for a beaver or an otter, and charged lower prices for the supplies it sold him, Payette may have thought he could do better as a freeman than as an *engagé*.[27]

In 1825 the company was still charging exorbitant prices for the supplies that it sold to freemen. That may be why Ogden "put" the men "free" and why Ross said it would "be a saving to the company." These men had families. Their support would no longer be Hudson's Bay's responsibility. Even out on the expedition they had to find their own food and care for their privately owned horses, tents, traps, and other equipment. Moreover, everything that they purchased, either at Flathead Post or from Ogden when en route, was at higher prices than *engagés* paid.

It was the duty of Hudson's Bay officers to guard the company from the expense of supporting freemen. Two years before Ogden's first expedition, for example, the postmaster of Carlton House on the Saskatchewan granted a freeman and his family permission "to reside at the Fort." But there were conditions. They were not to become dependents. The man agreed to "find his own provisions and all other necessaries he may require like the rest of the freemen." The master of Carlton House was telling the freeman he was not to become a burden on the Hudson's Bay Company.[28]

CHAPTER SIX

No Money Would Induce Me to Risk Again

There is a question that has not been asked. The evidence is clear. The freemen did not readily obey orders. When they would not obey, what could the officers of Hudson's Bay Company do? Was there any way to discipline them? After all, they were not engaged servants. They were not under contract. They could not be penalized by docking their wages or sent out of the country by terminating their employment. Those sanctions could be applied against *engagés*, not freemen who had no wages to be docked and no employment to be terminated.

Perhaps the distinction can be clarified by considering the contrasting status of company servants and freeman among American trapping parties. The Americans also used the term *engagés* or, as a clerk for the Missouri Fur Company wrote it, "Engagees." These were the men, Washington Irving explained, who "have regular wages, and are furnished with weapons, horses, traps, and other requisites. These are under command, and bound to do every duty required of them connected with the service; such as hunting, trapping, loading and unloading the horses, mounting guard; and, in short, all the drudgery of the camp. These are the hired trappers." Ogden's *engagés* were in a similar condition of employment.[1]

What Americans meant by "freeman" is quite a bit less clear. John Ball defined "free trappers" as "men on their own hook."[2] Considering that Ball was a lawyer, we might have expected a more helpful definition.

Those words, however, are exactly how Thomas James, a freemen with the St. Louis Missouri Fur Company, described himself in 1809.[3] Robert Campbell, a famous American trapper as well as a fur company partner, described "free hunters," whom he contrasted with trappers hired by the company, as men "who lived entirely on what they killed." Benjamin Bonneville, who organized his own, not very successful fur company, and who hired many American freemen, was asked by Washington Irving to explain their status. He answered:

> They come and go when and where they please; provide their own horses, arms, and other equipments; trap and trade on their own account, and dispose of their skins and peltries to the highest bidder. Sometimes in a dangerous hunting ground, they attach themselves to the camp of some trader for protection. Here they come under some restrictions; they have to conform to the ordinary rules for trapping, and to submit to such restraints, and to take part in such general duties, as are established for the good order and safety of the camp.[4]

Bonneville seemed to think that freemen accepting protection with a larger party, incurred legal obligations as well as camp duties. "[T]hey are bound to dispose of all the beaver they take, to the trader who commands the camp," he claimed, "or, should they prefer seeking a market elsewhere, they are to make him an allowance, of from thirty to forty dollars for the whole hunt." Bonneville surely knew what he was taking about. We cannot be certain, but it seems reasonable to assume that he was describing the individual agreements he made with the free trappers who came to his camp for protection. There is, however, no evidence that obligations of this sort were a general, understood custom of the American fur trade.[5]

Most freeman who attached themselves to parties with which they had no agreements, usually did so to travel, not to trap. John K. Townshend was traveling with fur traders from St. Louis to the annual rendezvous of American trappers when the party reached the Laramie Fork of Platte River. "Here two of our 'free trappers' left us for a summer 'hunt,'" he explained. "These men joined our party at Independence, and have been travelling to this point with us for the benefit of our escort. Trading companies usually encourage the free trappers to join them, both for the strength which they add to the band, and that they may have the benefit of their generally good hunting qualities. Thus are both parties accommodated, and no obligations felt on either side."[6]

These last words—"no obligation felt on either side"—sum up the legal status of American freemen. It is also the condition of owing no legal obligations to a company that marks the difference between American freemen and the freemen of the Snake country expeditions.

In addition to freemen and company "engagees," Washington Irving told of a third status among American fur trappers. The legal conditions of these men, whom he called "skin trappers," closely matched the legal conditions of freemen in the Snake country.

> There is an inferior order, who, either from prudence or poverty, come to these dangerous hunting grounds without horses or accoutrements, and are furnished by the traders. These, like the hired trappers, are bound to exert themselves to the utmost in taking beavers, which, without skinning, they render in at the trader's lodge, where a stipulated price for each is placed to their credit. These, though generally included in the generic name of trappers, have the more specific title of skin trappers.[7]

Etienne Provost was an American trapper who owed William H. Ashley a debt obligation of the type Irving described.[8] It is doubtful, however, that Ashley thought he had any authority to discipline Provost, except to enforce the debt. Hudson's Bay Company officers acted on the premise that they had some power to coerce and sanction the freemen, but they seldom considered where that right came from and what the limits of punishment were. It is important to make another distinction between freemen and company servants. The company had a stronger disciplinary hold over its servants than over the freemen because its legal relationship with its servants was stronger. With the freemen the legal basis for discipline was debt. With the *engagés* the legal basis was contract. Whether it extended to corporal punishment was seldom considered. One of the few times that London headquarters gave the question attention occurred because a servant named William Brown was flogged at Fort Vancouver. He wrote his father that when he refused to return to his assigned post, Fort Langley, "they tied me to a cannon and flogged me, and treated me most cruelly and I had to turn back against my inclination for no cause."[9] Actually, Brown had been ordered back to Fort Langley because he had abandoned a child under twelve months and "it had been resolved, to prevent the departure of any Parent from the Country, unaccompanied by his children." He was whipped to persuade him to return and wait a year when it would be safer for the child to travel across the continent.[10]

After Brown's father complained to the governor in London, he and the governing committee, worried that the company might be sued, promulgated some rules. "We . . . have to impress on your mind that we cannot sanction violence or the infliction of Corporal Punishment on any of our Servants," they wrote James Douglas. John McLoughlin, who had ordered the flogging, was told, "The proper way to have dealt with that man, would have been to discharge him from the service on the spot, and not given him passage home which would have brought him to his senses; but the corporal punishment inflicted was decidedly illegal; and in order to guard against the consequences that might have arisen from an investigation of the case in a Court of Law, Governor Simpson, acting privately on your behalf, considered it expedient to compromise the matter by giving Brown a pecuniary consideration of £20, in full of all claims and demands whatsoever."[11]

If McLoughlin understood the limits of his authority after receiving this letter, what did he think three years later when the same governor and committee sent him instructions laying down different rules?

> When bad men are associated together, or mixed with the good, it will be impossible to preserve necessary discipline without having recourse sometimes to corporal punishment, but such punishment should never be inflicted under the influence of passion or caprice. To produce any good effect it should be administered with coolness temper and moderation, and at the same time with as much solemnity as circumstances will admit.

What McLoughlin made of these instructions is not known. Perhaps he weighed the possibility of lawsuits before inflicting physical correction. On the whole, one historian has concluded, even west of the mountains in New Caledonia the company did not always punish transgressors as harshly as it might have done.[12]

But what could the company do to coerce its engaged servants? Its most effective instrument of disciplining them was coercion of contract. "[A]cquaint all under Your Command that the Company expect their Servants shall go where their Commanding Officer shall please to send them, or they will forfeit their Gratuity and advance of Wages," the superintendent of the inland service on the Saskatchewan had instructed in 1777. It was an easy sanction to apply, and, if not actually utilized but just stated as a threat, could be effective. Governor Simpson made the threat when he suspected an employee of "carrying on Private Trade with the Indians." Simpson told the man, "that if I discover a single transaction of the kind on the part of any Officer or man in the Service, he shall forfeit whatever money is due to him in the hands of the Company."[13]

Engaged servants could be disciplined by fines. A fine would not be a financial penalty that the wrongdoer was ordered to pay. An assessment that the company had to collect would have been a clumsy way to do business in the wilderness. Fines that did not have to be paid in money, but were forfeitures of wages were more practical and certainly easier to administer. Not in all cases, however. It is said that the North West Company could not garnish the wages of its French employees because they were "generally in debt, and having neither good name, integrity, nor property to lose." But forfeiture of wages was "a sanction with real teeth" for the numerous Orkney men who worked for Hudson's Bay.[14] It all depended on the individuals and their financial expectations, especially if fines were backed up with threats of dismissal. The superintendent of the Saskatchewan department was on the way to York Factory in 1813 when he stopped at Carlton House.

> Mr. Pruden complains to me of the very ill Behaviors of John Mevice & Murdock Rose who refuse to perform their Duty to the reasonable Extent he desire them. I sent for and examined these Men before Mr. Pruden and as they were unable to assign any satisfactory reason for the non fulfillment of their duty I fined them in the sum of sixty shillings each and informed them that they were fined accordingly, telling them also that if they presumed again to disregard the orders Mr. Pruden might think proper to give them they would be fined in a much more considerable sum and dismissed from the service.[15]

Dismissal was not practical punishment for an engaged servant. Unless the dismissed man faced up to his predicament, begged forgiveness, and agreed to reform, the company either had to give him transportation out of the country, or the local trading post would be burdened with another, perhaps embittered, unruly freeman. That was a situation no Hudson's Bay officer in the West wanted to create. The preferred way of handling men like Mevice and Rose was not dismissal. Better to transfer them from the posts where they were troublesome to posts more isolated and where life was more harsh and punishing, or to one with a proven disciplinarian for a commanding officer.

John Peter Pruden, the master of Carlton House, got rid of a man "guilty of disobedience" by sending him up the Saskatchewan to Edmonton House "as a punishment." On a visit to Fort Nez Perces, Simpson learned that an interpreter was plotting with some Cayuse in a way that threatened the post. He could not arrest the man. That might enrage the Cayuse and endanger Fort Nez Perces. "[H]owever I have succeeded in enticing him away and he accompanies us under the impression that he is to return in the Fall, but while I am in the Country he may consider himself a Ruperts Land Man." In his own words, Simpson planned "to put him in Irons, bring him across the Mountain and fix him a few years at the Coast to keep him out of harms way."[16]

Simpson could have disciplined a freeman with much the same sanctions, but he was likely to be more cautious. Contract made a difference. It was not just that Hudson's Bay did not have the contractual leverage over freemen that it had over servants. The contractual relationship meant that the company had an obligation to provide transportation east or to York Factory and then across the Atlantic for a servant whose service was completed. Hence, if an *engagé* was ordered out of New Caledonia as punishment, and was escorted across the mountains and down the Saskatchewan by one or more of the brigades going east, the company did not incur extra expense. But Hudson's Bay owed no obligation to freemen. If an officer ordered a freeman to be transported east, he burdened the company with an unanticipated expenditure. That may explain why few freemen were transported east.

There is another possible explanation. Aside from a few French Canadians, the freemen were mostly *métis*. And a high percentage of those were at least one-half Indian. The problem does not seem to have been discussed, but it could have been dangerous to transport such a freeman near a nation that was enemy to his mother's nation, to transport a half-blood Cree, for example, from Rocky Mountain House to Edmonton House because the brigade might run into passing Piegan, Blood, or Blackfoot parties. The freeman could have been put in mortal danger and the brigade with which he was traveling would have faced some painful choices.

Another consideration was that the families of many engaged servants were in Scotland or Lower Canada. If an *engagé* was ordered out of the Columbia department, only one person had to be transported. Freemen had families in the West. Sentence a freeman to transportation and his family had to be sent as well, or the local trading post would have to support it.

Hudson's Bay Company and its officers had authority, granted by British legislation, to warn off and prohibit any unauthorized, non-native persons they found in Rupert's Land or New Caledonia, and to seize the furs that private individuals had purchased from the natives, and even to prosecute them in Upper Canada.[17] The power of prosecution was not exercised against freemen, however, in part because of the expense, and in part because there were other means of coercion more convenient and less costly.

The best weapon Hudson's Bay had to protect its monopoly to all the fur in the West was not its exclusive right, granted by Parliament, to buy furs from the natives. That grant meant nothing to freeman. What really was effective was the company's control of all the trading posts. After the merger with North West, it alone sold the ammunition and traps the freemen needed to hunt furs, or the blankets, knives, and other manufactured products needed for clandestine trade with the Indians. There was no place else where they could obtain supplies.

When passing between the Beaver and Athabasca Rivers in 1824, Simpson was told some freemen were planning "to go on a War Expedition against a poor helpless inoffensive tribe of Indians." He warned them if they did he would cut off their supply of ammunition "and that next Season they should be bundled down to Canada where starvation & misery should follow them." He was confident he had stopped the slaughter. "Those freemen are fully in our power," he boasted.[18]

Next month Simpson made the same boast. Preparing to cross the Continental Divide, he discovered that Jacco Findlay "and a band of followers (Freemen) were here watching the Shewhoppes in order that they might trade their Furs before they got to the Establishment [*i.e.*, Fort Thompson] and thereby make a profit on the hunts of these poor Indians, but I gave them notice that that practise must be discontinued." He wrote to the factors in the area, instructing them to sell Findlay and his men "no supplies of any description" if they "continue[d] this nefarious Traffick." Then the freemen "will soon be quite at our disposal as their very existence depends on us."[19]

The prohibition on freemen buying furs from the natives was one rule that Simpson knew every officer would enforce. Even with all the other anxieties that he faced in the Snake country, Ogden, when on expedition, watched the freemen to see if they purchased beaver from passing Indians. He was out on his third expedition when he discovered "that one of the Freemen had traded two Beaver Skins from an Indian[.] I lost no time in depriving him of them and forbid any from trading with the natives and if discovered they shall forf[e]it their hunts, they promise fair but I shall require to watch them narrowly—if the Freemen were allowed to trade with the natives they would soon place such value on their Furs we would never be enabled to trade with them so far as they lay sufficient value on them."[20] It was a simple law of monopoly economics that every officer seems to have believed. The monopoly would not make monopolistic profits if it did not protect its monopoly.[21]

To establish better control over the freemen, Alexander Kennedy suggested keeping them out of the Snake country altogether. He thought it might be done by closing Spokane House, moving its operations at least as far north as Kettle Falls, and keeping tight control over the supplies sold to freemen.

> It occurs to me that most of the Freemen would be much more advantageously employed up the Columbia near the Borders of the Rocky Mountains, where they would be more our Power [than in the Snake country], and the Furs are of a much better quality: if this Plan was approved of, we could adopt such measures as would induce them to go there next season, as by keeping Supplys

from them we could prevent their going to the Snake Country. A [missing word here] established at this end of the Rocky Mountain portage to supply their wants would enable them to explore a Country, that is but little known, and that is supposed to be rich in beaver.[22]

Kennedy thought the freemen could be controlled by manipulating supplies and closing or moving trading posts.[23] The company did not put his proposal to the test, however. His plan would have just moved the freemen problem to a new location, and, besides, freemen would be needed on Snake country expeditions if denuding was to be extensive. But consider the reverse situation. The power of supply could be used to force freemen into the Snake country even if they did not want to go, just the opposite of how Kennedy proposed using it. John Work was at Spokane House when Ogden was on the other side of the Rockies, returning from his first expedition. "Three of the freemen belonging to Mr. Ogdens party arrived here two days ago for supplies & say they were permitted to leave the party, to proceed across the mountains," Work reported. But the three men had no authority in writing from Ogden excusing them from the expedition, just notes specifying the state of their accounts with the company. That evidence was "not sufficient authority to give them any advances," Work decided, "and deeming it necessary to send them back to Mr. Ogden, so that he might keep his party as strong as possible, they were refused any advances but a little ammunition to take them back to where they would likely meet Mr. Ogden." He would not even sell supplies in exchange for the beaver that the men had with them. Instead, he took the pelts and gave them credit. They "have all money coming to them," he noted.[24]

Work does not say so, but withholding payment was surely as effective to keep freemen in line as withholding supplies. Those three men were owed money and, implicitly or explicitly, he told them they would not collect it unless they rejoined the Snake country expedition.

There are other instances of coercion that are less easy to explain or even to understand. Over three months later, Work ordered another freeman transferred from Flathead Post to Spokane House. "He denies that his engagement was only to be free as long as the Company thought proper and seemed unwilling to go," Work noted, "but on being told that he must comply he submitted, but with reluctance."[25] What the man's status was is not clear. Work speaks of the man being "free" at the pleasure of the company, but he does not indicate what being "free" meant, except that now that the man was no longer free, he could be ordered to Spokane House. Perhaps the man was an engaged servant who had arranged with the master of Spokane House to work for a time as a freeman, and was at Flathead Post hoping to join the next Snake country expedition. That is doubtful, however, as the company had not yet raised the prices it paid freemen for furs, and *engagés* were much better off financially than freemen. In any event, the argument appears to have been over contract, not over debt.

Just what coercive control the company had on the freemen when it had no financial hold over them is not disclosed by the records. Officers in charge of trading posts exercised some police power, especially the authority of permitting freemen to stay at the post or ordering them to leave, Also. in such small, closed societies, they felt they had the right to punish disruptive behavior, including immorality. The temporary master of Carlton House on the Saskatchewan "turned out of the house" a woman who was either a full-blood Indian or a *métisse*. She was, he claimed, "a bad example," with many faults. Specifically, she was a lover of the son of John Peter Pruden, the regular master who was on leave from Carlton House that season. Motivated by a theory of deterrence, the temporary master decided also to make a lesson of the younger Pruden, who undoubtedly was a *métis* since he was away with local Indians, probably his mother's people. "[T]he least punishment which in this instance I am disposed to adopt, that can have any effect in Deterring others from following the example of seduction and demoralization [is to] have him debarred from all Public amusement and while he remains at the Fort confined strictly to his own lodging." Three days later he "gave a horse whipping to the woman." She had been "in bed with Mr Prudens daughter Maria a girl between twelve and thirteen years old." Again his justification was deterrence. "[I]t was necessary to inflict some exemplary punishment on her as an example to others and I mistake much if it will not have the desired effect at least so far as to make them more secret."[26]

The most effective but rather costly punishment was to transport freemen out of the Columbia department or even out of Rupert's Land, that is, out of Hudson's Bay territory altogether. The authority was not always based on parliamentary legislation. When Alexander Ross was with the North West Company—which, unlike Hudson's Bay, had no statutory grant of monopoly—a freeman became quite unmanageable and went off to live with the local natives, with whom he was soon plotting trouble. "Our interest, our safety, our all, depended on our dissolving the dangerous union before it gathered strength," Ross wrote, in effect pleading necessity in justification for going out—at some risk to himself—to arrest the man. "On arriving at the fort, Jacob was locked up, ironed, and kept so until the autumn, when he was shipped on board of a vessel sailing for the Sandwich Islands." And, of course, he was not heard from again.[27]

Hudson's Bay officers could act with greater confidence in their authority, and carry freemen as prisoners from post to post. In 1833 John Rowand, the chief trader at Edmonton House, ordered the arrest of François Gardipie. "This man," it was explained, "has been very troublesome of late, and acting, since last spring, much against the benefit of the General Concern. On it being known of his drawing near us, measures were taken to secure him, this was effected in safety and to day he was put in Irons, in which situation he is to remain until further orders." Five months later, when Rowand left Edmonton House for the Bay with the annual catch in furs, he took with him, "F. Gardipie who is prisoner."[28]

Freemen on a Snake country expedition were much more difficult to discipline. Alexander Ross found the challenge beyond his ability. "What is the use of engagements or agreements if they are to be broken with impunity," he wrote on a day when several freemen rode away from his camp, deserting the expedition.

> [N]o person whatever can at all time have controul over such a medly of freemen in this distant part of the Country without being well backed: when he sees them act wrong his duty bids him speak out but his remonstrances are often derided, he then threatens them with a reprimand, fine, or punishment when they return to the fort, but this threat however just is never put in execution, therefore worthless persons take a footing upon it & the further they go the worse they get. A fine of 1, 2, 3 or 400 livres

for a transgression operating to the disadvantage of the expedition would if once put in force no doubt have a good effect or if a check in any other way could be put to the heedless & bad conduct of many of these people during these long voyages by a dread of punishment on returning to the fort: how much it would aid to the Success of the Undertaking, the interest of the Company, profit of the trapper and ease of the Conductor. But following the old plan let no man who has not to beg his bread ever come to such a Country with such a people.[29]

With Ogden now in command of the Snake country expedition, the "old plan" was reformed. Not only were three freeman whom Ross identified as unmanageable not permitted to join the brigade, five men whom Ross wanted to include, but who refused to return to the Snake country, were punished. They were not permitted to purchase "any supplies."[30] At least one of the freemen who made the most trouble for Ross was transported by force over the mountains to Rupert's Land. Simpson described him as "*Isaac* the Iroquois Chief (the leader of the Mutinous Dogs who were discharged from the Snake Expedition and one of those I had sentenced to transportation for Life from the Columbia for his uniform bad conduct)."[31] Simpson does not say how many other Snake country troublemakers he expelled from the Columbia department. They all were probably paraded at each post along the way so that their faces would be known and remembered. After being released somewhere in the area of the Red River, they would have no chance of going back up the Saskatchewan to return to the mountains. They would not get by the posts. Any other route would be dangerous, especially for Iroquois. That may be what Simpson meant when saying he had sentenced Isaac "for Life from the Columbia."

From what Ross said, he expected that punishment inflicted after an expedition would deter mutinous behavior on subsequent trips. If so, he was wrong. Nineteen years after Ross returned to Flathead Post, Michel Laframboise arrived at Fort Vancouver, having led a trapping expedition to Alta California. John McLoughlin asked him to lead another expedition. Laframboise refused. "I would not go again on any account," he explained. "[T]o save my life I had to bend, I could not command, I had to do as my men wished, I am come back alive, and no money would induce me to risk again." He said he returned from this expedition only because "I gave way to my men." Had he acted differently, "I would have been murdered by them."[32]

Even the strongest and most successful Snake country leaders, John Work and Peter Skene Ogden, could not force their wills when the freemen refused to go their way. "Work continues to follow the Freemen in one direction and Michael la Frambois in another," an officer wrote in 1833.[33] Ogden led one expedition to Fort George rather than to where he had been ordered to return because, he said, he had no choice. "[N]early one half of the Trappers are determined to return to Fort des Prairies . . . I must bend & Submit to the will of the party."[34]

On his first expedition Ogden was on a stream he called "the East Fork of the Missouri River," when he "proposed to the Freemen to go in the direction of Nez Percés which one half refused as they are determined on returning to the Saskatchewan this Fall, they said our losses have been too great in this Country to remain any longer." Ogden was writing not just to Governor Simpson but to all the higher officers, the chief factors and chief traders, of Hudson's Bay Company, and he wanted to be certain that they understood. "[I]t is not difficult Gentlemen to command but enforce obedience in the plains when at the mercy of Freemen it is the reverse."[35]

CHAPTER SEVEN

Let Rules Be Made They Will Soon Be Broken

Peter Skene Ogden departed from Flathead Post and commenced his first Snake country expedition on 20 December 1824, Or, as his second-in-command, William Kittson, expressed it, the brigade "[b]egan our long and dangerous journey." Peter Dease, a Hudson's Bay officer who rode out a few miles with Ogden, told Alexander Ross that the expedition had left "all in high spirits."[1]

As Ogden "bade adieu to the Flat Head Post," the very first entry in his Snake country journal strikingly presaged his problems with the freemen. There, at the first camp, were many local natives, who intended to travel east with the expedition. According to Ross, there were members from three different nations, "all [of] the Flatheads with part of the Kottannais & Pend d'Oreilles." He said that they were going across the Continental Divide for their annual buffalo hunt, intending to stay with the expedition for protection when it skirted Piegan territory, crossed the Rocky Mountains, and went into the plains where the smaller western nations had been hunting buffalo, ever since first buying guns from the fur traders. They had not needed the guns to hunt buffalo. They had needed them to defend against the Blackfoot who attacked anyone from the west who crossed the mountains to hunt buffalo.[2]

Ogden thought the Kootenais and Flatheads had other business in mind besides travel. When he arrived at the first camp, they were there, "waiting our arrival intending to raise Camp together," he noted, "but more with a view of trading with the Freemen & exchanging Horses in which I presume they [Kootenais and Flatheads] will not be disappointed altho' very injurious to themselves as they part with all their ammunition." He meant injurious to the freemen, not the Kutenais or Flatheads. The freemen would be the losers, the natives the winners. The exchanges had been a major problem for Ross on the Snake country expedition the year before. He accused the freemen, especially the Iroquois, of being compulsive buyers, purchasing everything they could get their hands on, paying exorbitant prices, for what Ross called "worthless" items. One problem for Ross, and now Ogden, was that the favored article of exchange was ammunition. Some freemen had traded away all their powder and balls, and Ross faced a double loss, both because he would have to furnish them new ammunition should they get near buffalo or Blackfoot, and because the ammunition the freemen bartered away had been purchased on credit from the company. They owed Hudson's Bay for it and, until it was paid for, the company thought the ammunition its own property, or, at best, property of the freemen on which it had a demand-right claim.[3]

Ogden had another reason to be concerned. Following the merger of the two fur companies, Governor Simpson had ordered economies, especially in the Columbia department where expenses were bloated. As mentioned before, the extravagance of the freemen gave the natives an exaggerated sense of value, especially concerning horses—exaggerated, at least, in relation to what Hudson's Bay wanted to pay for the animals. Recently *engagés* had been prohibited from trafficking with either freemen or Indians, and officers had been told to keep freemen from trading.[4] For a measure of how serious some officers thought the problem, consider that in October 1820, when the rivalry between Hudson's Bay and North West was at a height of intensity, the two companies negotiated a formal agreement. The eighth article provided "[t]hat both parties will discourage as much as possible the Freemen from carrying on any traffic with the Natives."[5] The companies might be warring, but they thought this problem so serious they momentarily laid their differences aside. They believed both could lower costs and increase profits, if freemen did not trade with Indians.

It is indicative of Ogden's problems as leader of the Snake country expedition that he could not just order the Kootenais or the Pend d'Oreilles out of the camp. They were too useful. They added armed strength to the brigade and made passage through the Snake country that much safer. Undoubtedly, the enemies of those Indian nations resented seeing them escorted by the fur trappers, but that would not cause them to attack. Flatheads and other Indians traveling with Snake country expeditions would not help to guard horses at night, but they were useful in other ways. Ogden even welcomed passing parties for the news they brought him. Flatheads and Nez Perces could always be counted on to tell of any Blackfoot or Snake war parties that they had seen. In fact, if Blackfeet or Piegans were nearby, Flatheads and Nez Perces sometimes sought safety by traveling close to the brigade. Ogden also expected that those returning west would report to the trading posts what they knew of the expedition. It was one way that John McLoughlin, at Fort George, could let company headquarters know what Ogden was doing and whether he had encountered difficulties. On the first of March, for example, three of the Flatheads who had traveled with the brigade to hunt buffalo east of the Rockies, returned to Flathead Post. "[T]hey told us that the Piegans had stolen 18 of Mr. Ogden's horses at the head waters of the Missouri river before he left them," Ross recorded. Next day "a Flathead chief Le Gros fried arrived & . . . confirmed the report of those yesterday respecting the stolen horses." Finally, on the sixth, all the Flatheads, Kootenais, Nez Perces, and Spokanes who had gone hunting on the plains came in. "The chiefs repeated the circumstances of the 1st Inst. & added that between dead & stolen our Snake party had lost 32 horses. They had letters from Mr. Ogden but these letters did not [mention] their loss in horses. Indian reports are often exaggerated."[6]

Despite exaggerations, traveling parties, especially the hunters who went directly home with their buffalo meat, kept the company somewhat informed of where the expedition had gone and even of how well it was faring. More important were the letters that they carried back from Ogden. The post master at the Flatheads who received the messages passed them on to John McLoughlin at Fort George, who sent them to Simpson at York Factory or Norway House.

Communication went two ways. On 12 February, when Ogden's brigade had been in the Snake country for fifty days, Ross received letters at Flathead Post that the sender at Fort George urgently wanted forwarded to

Ogden. Of course, Ross had no idea where Ogden was, but that posed no problem. There were men around—Indian, white, and *métis*—who could always find him. The difficulty was that few were dependable. Also, Ross wondered whether it was safe to send the letters from Flathead Post.

> The only possible means here, is to wait the arrival of the Flatheads, & by sending the letters with them they may reach Mr. Ogden in August. It is however very doubtful to me whether they will reach him at all, by this route. To send them by Iroquois is out of the question. The only practicable way is by Nez Percés Fort; & this is done by sending two white men off from there to the Snake falls in July   before the 10th or 15 of July it will not answer. Those deliver the letters to some of the Snake chiefs, they will reach Mr Ogden shortly after, without fail. Or a few Cayouse, with one white man will answer fully as well. This road is safe for two men.[7]

Two men could travel in relative safety from Fort Nez Perces to the Snake Falls, but not from Flathead Post. Because the road from the Flatheads to the Snake River lay closer to the Piegans, Ross would need a large party if he sent the letters from there. But he could not put one together. On the date he got the letters the local Indians, the Flatheads, were still away on their winter buffalo hunt. The men he had around the post were Iroquois, and Ross would not trust them on any mission. It would seem that he planned to send the letters to Fort Nez Perces, and have them taken out on that safer route by two men in time to reach the Falls around 10 to 15 July, when he knew the Snakes would come together to catch salmon. It was the annual gathering of the Snake nation. Ross had been there the year before. He was friendly with the headmen and it is most revealing that he felt he could rely on them to deliver the letters "without fail."

For some unexplained reason, the letters were not forwarded by the Nez Perce route. Ross still had them when a Flathead party again started for the Snake country. "Delivered the Governor's letters for Mr. Ogden to two Flathead chiefs," Ross reported, "& paid them, 2 Pistols, 200 Balls & powder and 2 lbs Tobacco. I am persuaded they will do their best to perform this business." They are probably the letters that Ogden received from Governor Simpson, delivered by "two of the Flat Heads & one of the Kootany chiefs." The messages were no longer of timely import, but had news to cheer up Ogden. "Thank God all well in the Columbia & doing well," he wrote, "I alone appear doomed to be unfortunate."[8]

The governor had written urging Ogden not to deviate from the route he had been instructed to take. He had been told to return to the Columbia at Fort George, not Fort Nez Perces, to keep the freemen away from the larger Indian nations. But circumstances would make it impractical for Ogden to travel from Bear River to Umpqua River, which, it was mistakenly believed, would have taken him to Fort George.

Simpson had remarkable control over the Hudson's Bay Company. He understood its business thoroughly and insisted on directing all aspects of its activities. Usually his management was successful, but occasionally he carried his supervision too far. That seems to be the case with Ogden's first Snake country expedition when Simpson undertook to plan the route and to lay out in detail where the brigade was to go and where it was not to go. In summary, his instructions to Ogden ordered the expedition to "proceed direct for the heart of the Snake country towards the Banks of the Spanish River or Rio Colorado[,] pass the Winter & Spring there and hunt their way out by the Umpqua and Wilhamet Rivers to Fort George next summer sufficiently early to send the returns home by the Ship." He explained why:

> By so doing we should be enabled to send your returns to market a full year earlier than otherwise, which is an object of material consideration—moreover it would save the heavy expense of sending your Outfit to the interior [that is, to send the supplies needed for the next expedition up the Columbia to Fort Nez Perces]. . . . You would furthermore by coming to the Depot [Fort George] have reinforcements of men and every thing that can be required for the Expedition without trouble or difficulty and have an opportunity of communicating direct with the chief Factor [John McLoughlin] superintending the Columbia Department which is essential to the good government of its service. All these advantages are lost sight of coming out at Walla Walla.[9]

By "Walla Walla" Simpson meant Fort Nez Perces. It had the disadvantages both that its road ran through the midst of the Nez Perce and Cayuse nations, and of being far from Fort George, where the annual ship from London docked. If Ogden "came out" of the Snake country at that place, his pelts would have to be carried down the Columbia before they could be sent to Great Britain. More drastic, because the vessel bringing trade goods to the Columbia department was unladen at Fort George, the supplies for the men of the next brigade would have to be carried up the river by canoe. That could not be done, Simpson insisted, "unless a Brigade of extra men were kept specially to take European Provisions from Fort George for their use which would eat up all the profits of the Expedition."[10]

The fact thst Simpson would have had to maintain extra hired men at Fort George to supply the Snake country expedition if it used Fort Nez Perces as its base of operations, tells us a great deal about what he thought of freemen. Like Ross at Flathead Post who would not employ Iroquois to carry the letters to Ogden, Simpson apparently gave no consideration to hiring Iroquois freemen as *voyageurs* to paddle the supplies up the Columbia against the current. Simpson was no different from other Hudson's Bay officers. They all stereotyped the Iroquois into a single class. All were undependable. Simpson would not trust them to do a routine job.

The main reason Simpson sent those letters to Ogden in the Snake country was to urge on him the importance of not changing his plans, no matter the problems he faced. He just did not want the expense of transporting supplies up the Columbia. If Ogden changed directions, he would "disorganize the whole system of the Department" and cause Hudson's Bay Company "most serious loss & inconvenience."[11] Circumstances, however, would make it impossible for Ogden to follow Simpson's instructions. He would not be able to trap the Colorado or to return to the Columbia by the Umpqua and the Willamette.

It is just as well that Ogden could not obey the instructions. Frederick Merk, however, exaggerated when he said that, had Ogden followed Simpson's route, "he would in all probability have led his party to destruction."[12] Ogden would have gotten through somehow. He always did. But he could not have traveled the road that Simpson wanted him to take. It did not exist. The year that Ogden led his first Snake country expedition out from Flathead Post, the officers of Hudson's Bay Company had only the most vague notion of the geography west of the Rocky Mountains. Several observant fur men had crossed the area—

Robert Stuart, Ramsay Crooks, Finan McDonald, Alexander Ross, and especially Donald McKenzie. They had reported their discoveries and there was a general understanding that certain rivers were out there and agreement about where they were located. The overall pattern of the land, however, was not known—how river systems interconnected, and where they flowed. Ogden had been instructed to go to Bear River, and, after following it downstream, to hunt the Colorado which, it was hoped, would be rich in beaver. McKenzie had been to the Bear and may have reported that it emptied into the Colorado. It seemed a reasonable conjecture because everyone knew the Colorado was in that general direction. But McKenzie had traveled only in the upper courses of the Bear. Ogden and his people would be the first to report going toward the lower reaches and to discover that the Bear was an independent river system, in a separate valley, unconnected with the Colorado. That was why Ogden never trapped the Colorado but trapped Mexican streams in today's Utah. He had been told to return by the Umpqua and Willamette because Hudson's Bay officers believed those rivers had their sources near the Bear. In fact, the Willamette flowed south to north, not from the west, and the Umpqua rose from a Pacific mountain range hundreds of miles from the Bear. Ogden was the explorer who straightened out this geography. It would be his most lasting service to the Hudson's Bay Company and, ironically, to the settlers who would be coming from the United States.

Americans, in fact, were another reason why Governor Simpson wanted the Snake country expeditions to return to Fort George. He hoped that traveling west to the Willamette would keep the freemen away from American fur traders. "The route now pursued," he wrote Ogden, referring to the road going to Flathead Post, "I fear will lead you into trouble in other respects as 'tis probable you may fall in with Americans in which case I am satisfied that more than half your people will desert."[13] He meant that the freemen, not the engaged servants, would desert.

The biographer of Ogden's Piegan translator formulated an apt descriptive analogy for the Snake country expedition of 1825. "The company more resembled an Indian village on the move than a business venture," he wrote. "The forty-six freemen were accompanied by their Indian families, thirty women and thirty-five children. There were twenty-two lodges and a horse herd soon to evaporate." There were at the start 268 horses, and the fact that those numbers would soon "evaporate" can in part be laid to Ogden's leadership. "Simpson could not have found a more capable, energetic and devoted leader than Ogden," two of Ogden's editors have written. "His field ability was unmatched. He knew how to manage the business of directing large expeditions of men, women and horses into wild, rough, and sometimes unknown country." There are good reasons for saying that. At times Ogden proved himself beyond compare. Yet there were issues on which his leadership was ineffectual. During the first weeks when the expedition moved toward the Snake River, Ogden was not always in command. Had he been able to manage the freemen as well as his admirers claim that he did, the brigade might not have lost so many horses.[14]

The expedition did not start well. "At day break I gave orders to raise Camp," Ogden wrote of the first morning away from Flathead Post, "but it was late ere we Collected all our Horses they being Scattered in all directions." Because of the horses the brigade did not go far that day. They had not been watched or hobbled, and had wandered so far afield time was spent looking for them that should have been spent traveling. Next day things did not improve. The evening before, Ogden had ordered that the horses be guarded. "[A] few of the Freemen joined us in that duty last night," Kittson noted in his journal. It must have been very few, as Ogden's journal entry for that day reveals. "Some of the Freemen decline keeping Watch there being No danger," he wrote, "but I fear ere long it will prove otherwise." It proved bad enough that day even without the danger of Indians. In the morning six of the horses were missing. "On the request of the Freemen," Kittson wrote, "Mr. Ogden decided on not raising Camp in order to give time for finding the lost horses." They were not brought into camp until the afternoon. As a consequence, they did not move at all that day.[15]

Less than a week out of Flathead Post, the Flatheads who accompanied the expedition decided to depart, at least temporarily. "[T]his I do not regret," Ogden noted, "as the Freemen will not refrain from trading with them, for a good race Horse, they will part with all their Supplies thoughtless wretches."[16] He does not say so, but behind the lines, Ogden is admitting that he was unable to stop trading. He was supposed to prevent it, and he had incentive to do so. All the freemen were in debt to the company. As far as Hudson's Bay was concerned, whatever property they exchanged with the Flatheads was property no longer securing debts. What they purchased, the company invariably considered valueless. What they sold was property that in most cases they had purchased on credit from the company and it thought of, at least until the debts were paid, either as its own or on which it had a claim.

During the third week of February, the expedition was leaving the headwaters of the Missouri where it had been hunting buffalo. Uncertain of the road ahead, Ogden sent the interpreter, Charles McKay, to scout the pass to Snake River. McKay returned to say there was no grass for the next three encampments and that as far as the eye could see the ground was covered with snow. Ogden decided to retrace his steps and take a route that Alexander Ross had traveled the year before. The freemen refused to go. They "gave in their word that as their horses were poor they would not consent to go the route purposed yesterday and that they were determined on remaining about here till their horses were in trim to start for Henrys forks (Snake River). Mr. Ogden had to give in." The day after that, the freemen prevented the expedition from moving at all. "According to the wishes of mostly all the party," Kittson reported, "we remained in this encamp[men]t in order to rest and recruit our poor horses, although the grass is not over good   yet is to be hoped that by rest and a little feeding they will be able in a few days to undertake the voyage from this to Snake River."[17]

The brigade was still on the American side of the Rocky Mountains, having crossed to the east to lay in a supply of buffalo meat. It was vital for the freemen to get meat then, for there were few buffalo west of the Continental Divide. Yet Ogden could not get them to work at what Hudson's Bay people called "making meat." They wanted the chase to be all sport and did not care for the bother of butchering the carcasses. When they saw buffalo they raced across the plains despite "the weak state of their horses," but they brought "little meat" back into camp. "It is the way of freemen," Kittson lamented, "they care little how hard they run their poor horses provided they have the pleasure of destroying animals the meat of which they leave to the wolves."[18]

Ogden was experiencing the same difficulties as Alexander Ross had. Ross had been unable to manage the freeman on the Snake country expedition of the year before. He could not get the freemen to spare their horses, and sometimes was delayed so those same horses could recover. He had even greater difficulty persuading them to keep a horse guard at night. So did Ogden, only his problem was worse as there were more Blackfoot warriors in the Snake River country in 1825 than Ross had encountered the year before. On the last day in January, on giving "the Call to raise Camp," Ogden learned that "26 Horses belonging to the Freemen were found missing & on Search being made tracks were discovered of thieves." They were Blackfoot and Blood warriors. Men sent in pursuit recovered nine animals. Getting back that many meant either that the horses recovered were too jaded to keep up with the others or that the raiding party had been too small to handle twenty-six horses in flight. It was a staggering loss, yet Ogden saw a bright side. "[T]hey have taken Some few Buffalo racers which I do not regret," he wrote, "& altho' the loss is heavy Still I am of opinion it will tend to have a good effect as the freemen will be more inclined to Watch at Night."[19]

He was right—for a few days. "[A]ll hands have Joined the Watch," he noted the next day, "which is divided into two so that 7 men are in the plains at one time, this makes it more secure, but I fear the Freemen will Soon relapse into their former Ways." And they did. Less than three months later, when trapping the Blackfoot River, twenty more horses were taken, this time by Bloods. "[T]hese belong to three men Old Pierre, Goddin & Geaudreau altho' the first lost everything last Summer nearly on the Same Spot & the last two Suffered this winter   Still they allow their horses full liberty." Kittson said that, because of the loss, six of the men had to proceed on foot. Ogden, by contrast, thought the lost put three men "at the mercy of the Canadians & Iroquois." This was a revealing statement, considering that in just a month's time Ogden will be saying that the freemen deserting the expedition "stole" horses that were the property of Hudson's Bay. At this time, he was saying that the horses were their private property. The three men sustained the loss. They had to make the best deal they could with the other "Canadians & Iroquois" trappers to obtain mounts and to hire room on the back of pack animals to transport their traps, lodges, and other equipment. "[O]n that account," he concluded, "& the loss they will Sustain in their hunts I feel for them."[20]

In a letter to Hudson's Bay headquarters, Ogden confessed that he could not make the freemen guard their horses. "I had often from our starting represented to the Freemen the necessity of guarding their horses at night but in vain," he explained, "they [the Blackfoot] may as well steal them for if we tie them at night, they will die for want of food."[21]

One more illustration may be warranted to demonstrate the difficulty that even Peter Ogden had in regulating freemen as members of a trapping party. On the 8th of April several of the men came into camp after having spotted or escaped from a Blood war party. One man, Antoine Benoit, remained out. On the 10th "they found his body naked, Scalp taken[,] a Ball in the body one in the head & three Stabs with a Knife." The shock was enough, Ogden expected, to convince everyone that they were in dangerous territory. It did, but not in the way he hoped. "This caused me some trouble to induce the Freemen to continue in the direction I wished," he explained to headquarters. He wanted to continue toward the Bear River as he had been instructed. They wanted to go back, away from the Blackfoot River, which had been named by Donald McKenzie because he had encountered Blackfoot there.[22] Ogden talked them out of turning around. One reason he succeeded was that the stream was rich in beaver. And that created a new problem. The freemen, to set their traps in places they thought most likely to pay off, scattered far and wide, exposing themselves much as Benoit had done.

Three days after Benoit's body was found, Ogden promulgated specific rules, or what he termed "orders to the Freemen."

1st   No Man to Sleep out of the Camp
2nd   No one to set his Traps before Sun rise.
3rd   Not to Set their Traps before the Camp is encamped.
4th   If traps are in the rear of Camp to be raised ere it start

"[I]t has been well explained to all if they infringe on the above rules they shall forfeit their Beaver," Ogden wrote with surprising optimism, "as for quarrelling with them past experience has proved nothing is to be gained but trouble & vexation & I am in hopes this will serve as a greater check than any other punishment I could inflict on them."[23]

It was not much of a check. Within four days the freemen were not only ignoring Ogden's orders to stay close to camp, they were breaking all his rules. They ignored the Bloods, and trapped in small parties, hoping to move ahead and trap a dam site before being discovered by the remainder of the brigade. "The instructions given to the camp a few days ago by Mr. Ogden are not well attended to," Kittson lamented, "another party that left us yesterday have again divided into different small bands." Next day Ogden tried again to assert discipline. "Fresh orders were given to the camp to keep together." He did not impress everyone. On the following day, "Two men absent although against orders." And on the day after that there were even more. "Two of the men, that are behind came up to us, the remaining four are still following the Pienoir [Portneuf] river. Several of the men have again gone ahead, therefore let rules be made they will be soon broken through."[24]

CHAPTER EIGHT

We Must Endeavour to Annoy Them

The Snake country expedition of 1825 had a unique feature. Not one but two journals record its story. There were two Hudson's Bay Company officers on the expedition, Peter Skene Ogden and William Kittson, and each kept a separate journal. On all the other expeditions only one journal was kept.

Kittson's journal is important. We would know little of Ogden's troubles with the freemen if Kittson had not discussed them. Ogden did not mention many of the incidents. Perhaps he did not want to let his superiors in the company know that he was not in control of the freemen, but that is not certain. There is much that the journals do not tell us. They were not written for history. They were written so that company headquarters could evaluate needs and expenses, and written for future leaders of Snake country expeditions to study for routes, problems, and locations of beaver caught each year. When traveling the tributaries of the Bitteroot River, Ogden noted that "Three small Rivers were Crossed Some Years Since abounding in Beaver but now not a vestige left." Later, when the brigade was in a camp trapping beaver, Kittson rode out to investigate "the present state of the snows and grass in this defile, leading to the same route Mr. Finan McDonald took to come out of the Snake river." Both men knew about the beaver and about McDonald's route from speaking to leaders of earlier expeditions, or from listening to their men who had trapped the river and accompanied McDonald, or from reading reports and journals.[1]

There is a great deal that Ogden and Kittson do not tell us. Ogden does not mention many events that we would find interesting for what they reveal of the social and camp life of Snake country expeditions. Not many days out from Flathead Post, he began his daily journal by noting, "We [did] not raise Camp for various reasons," but explains none of the reasons. He did not say that they remained where they were because a woman on the expedition gave birth that day. That detail would not have been of any importance to people reading the journal at company headquarters, so Ogden passed it over.[2]

We owe everything we know about the Snake country expeditions to the fact that Hudson's Bay required that officers in charge of certain activities keep journals. But there is also much lost to history due to the purpose for which the journals were written. With no other matter do we have so much to regret than the fact the journal writers of 1824 and 1825 did not take the trouble to comment on the American trappers who traveled with them for three months. It was not until the expedition was nine days on the road that they were first mentioned. "Seven Americans who followed Mr. Ross to the Flat Heads joined us this evening and intend to keep with us untill out of danger," was all Kittson said. Scholars of British Columbia claimed that the Americans were with the expedition "much to Ogden's disgust." How they know this, they do not say. Except for noting, at various times, where the Americans were, Ogden made no comment about them at all.[3]

As Kittson said, the seven Americans had gone to Flathead Post with Alexander Ross, when he returned from the Snake country expedition in November. A series of events, some of which we can only guess at, led to the meeting between Ross and the American trappers. After the expedition had passed by the fringes of Piegan territory and arrived at the relative safety of the main branch of the Snake River, Ross had given in to demands of his Iroquois, and permitted them to leave the expedition to trap as a separate group. He recorded in his journal that it was a mistake to do so, and he was right. The Iroquois ran into trouble with Shoshonean-speaking natives, and were attacked by a group who took from them most of their possessions—nine hundred beaver, fifty-four traps, twenty-seven horses, five guns, and even some of their clothing. At least, that was what they told a suspicious Ross, that they had lost nine hundred beaver. All they had left, they reported, was 105 beaver conveniently hidden in a cache. They were in desperate circumstances when they chanced on a party of seven American trappers from St. Louis, perhaps in the vicinity of today's Blackfoot, Idaho. It is at this point that many details of the Iroquois story become ambiguous. The version that seems to be most generally accepted by historians is that the Iroquois offered the 105 beaver pelts they still possessed to the Americans, in exchange for being taken to the place where they were to rendezvous with Ross. The Iroquois, some of whom were quite familiar with the Snake River region, did not need to be guided by the Americans, all of whom must have been new to the country. If they did make an agreement of this sort, which is doubtful, they wanted American protection from Snakes and Piegans.

The appearance of the Americans at Ross's camp marks the dramatic turning point in Snake country history and of the fortunes of the Hudson's Bay Company in the Oregon country. Ross's shock on seeing Americans must have been immeasurable, There, standing before him was the one event above all else he had been ordered to avoid. Do not, Governor Simpson had instructed, make an "opening" for the Americans. To keep them from being on the Snake River was the reason why the company ordered Ogden to denude the land. There might be only seven Americans but behind them Hudson's Bay could see an endless line. They were men, Ross decided, "whom I rather take to be spies than trappers." He thought he knew the Iroquois too well to believe what they told him. When aspects of the Iroquois story differed a bit from that told by the Americans, Ross guessed that the Iroquois had not lost pelts to the Shoshone, but had sold everything to the Americans for the higher prices paid by St. Louis traders. Then, too, the Americans may have offered to go with the Iroquois to meet Ross in hopes of obtaining more beaver by dealing behind his back with the other freemen. "I suspect these Americans have been on the lookout to decoy" more of the freemen, Ross wrote. When he learned that the seven Americans had trapped more than nine hundred beaver, Ross was not above trying to get the pelts for Hudson's Bay. "I made them several propositions but they would not accept lower than $3 a pound. I did not consider myself authorized to arrange at such prices." The real damage, he knew, would

occur when American prices became common knowledge on the Columbia. "The report of these men on the price of beaver," he noted in his
journal, already "had a very great influence on our trap[p]ers." Then,
in a matter-of-fact manner, he recorded what headquarters must have
regarded as ominous—not as ominous as the prices—but ominous
nonetheless. The Americans, he wrote, "accompanied us to the Flatheads. . . . They intend following us to the fort."[4]

Ross carefully reported details of the prices and the numbers of
beaver he was told the Americans had purchased from the Iroquois,
because that was what headquarters had to know. He said nothing about
the Americans themselves, except that there were seven. He did not
even mention their names. Headquarters was not interested in who they
were, but of course history would like to know. It is regrettable that neither he, Ogden, nor Kittson, tell us anything about these men, especially
their leader, who was Jedediah Strong Smith. History would surely want
to know anything Ogden might have said about Smith. There can never
be any agreement, of course, but arguably, with the exception of Sir
Alexander McKenzie and David Thompson, Ogden was the greatest
explorer of the North American West among British fur traders. Smith
was the greatest explorer among American trappers. Surely we would
learn much about the priorities of discovery if we could know what they
talked about when traveling together toward the unknown Bear River
with the Snake country expedition. These two men were opposite personalities. Ogden could outswear everyone, but Smith was the most
devout and religious of fur traders. He neither smoked nor drank, and,
perhaps most rare among mountain men, was clean-shaven.[5]

Instead of learning what the British thought of the Americans, we
can only guess that none of them—not Ogden, Ross, McLoughlin, or
Kittson—thought that Smith had any charactersitics or ideas that would
interest the Hudson's Bay Company. "There is a leading person with
them," Ross wrote in his journal the day that the seven Americans
arrived at his camp.[6] That was the only comment he would make about
Smith. Even as he and the Americans rode out of the Snake country to
the Flatheads he never mentioned their presence. A reader of his journal could easily forget that they were with him.

Later, when the Americans stayed at Flathead Post waiting to go back
to the Snake country with Ogden, they were virtually unnoticed in the

post journal. They were there for several weeks and must have been closely watched, yet Ross mentioned them only once. It was not an idea or a comment that caught his attention. It was a sale of beaver. "In the course of this day we traded from the American hunters I met in the Snake Country 49 beaver at Freemen's prices," Ross noted. That was all he said, but it tells us a great deal. Hudson's Bay hospitality may have taken care of them while they were at Flathead Post, but the Americans needed supplies if they were to depart with Ogden's expedition. In fact, they must have needed them very badly. Ross bought their beaver at his lowest prices.[7]

From the entry of 29 December, when he mentioned the Americans were with the expedition, Kittson had nothing more to say about them until 18 March, when the brigade had recrossed the Continental Divide. "The seven Americans are preparing to leave us to morrow and try to make their way to snake river," was all he said.[8]

After leaving Flathead Post the expedition had spent more than five weeks traveling south, then up the Missoula to the Bitterroot River, up the Bitterroot to its East Fork, and then across the Divide to hunt buffalo and lay in a supply of meat. There was much beaver as well as buffalo, and the men did put out their traps, but it was not the place they had come to trap for two reasons. First, they were trespassing on American territory. Second, the Blackfoot nations claimed the buffalo and for years had been making war on the Kootenais, Nez Perces, and other tribes that came east to hunt. The presence of the Blackfeet may explain why the Americans remained so long with Ogden. Even after the expedition recrossed the Continental Divide, they stayed with him for over a month, probably because of "signs" that Blackfoot warriors had also crossed the mountains in large numbers.[9]

Not much can be made of the fact that, during the first three months out from Flathead Post, Kittson mentioned the Americans only twice—to note that they had joined the brigade and to say that they were leaving. It might indicate that they had kept themselves well separated from the main group, but that is unlikely when we consider that there were only seven of them and the Blackfeet were reported to be all around. Another explanation is that Kittson had no reason to mention them. They may have gotten along so well with their Hudson's Bay hosts that there was no friction. Company headquarters would have expected both

Ogden and Kittson to discuss trouble in their journals, but not cam-
araderie around the campfire.

"The American traded some ammunition and Tobacco from us for
Beaver at the same price as our freemen," Kittson noted on the next
day. "About noon they left us well satisfied I hope with the care and
Attention we paid them. For since we had them with us no one in our
party ever took any advantage of or ill treated them." Then Kittson
offered the only personal observation of Smith made by any Hudson's
Bay officer that year. "One Jedidah S. Smith is at the head of them, a sly
cunning Yankey."[10]

No one today can know what Kittson meant. Any guess would be pure
speculation. About all that is revealed by the record is that, sly as Smith
may have been, he was not cunning enough to avoid freemen prices.
At least twice he had to sell his beaver at the lowest rates Hudson's Bay
offered, except, perhaps, to Indians. The fact that he packed those pelts
for almost three months after leaving Flathead Post may indicate that
he had been negotiating for a better deal.

Smith may have been impatient to start trapping the Snake River. He
separated from the expedition only three days after "Black Feet tracks
were Seen Near the Camp," a time of so much apprehension that even
the freemen stood guard at night. We know that Ogden was impatient
to start. He had been forced to halt momentarily because of "the Weak
State of our Horses." Two of them had been unable to reach the camp
the day Smith prepared to depart, "& it was with difficulty many others
did." The next day, when Smith left, Ogden felt "So anxious to proceed
that I shall again Send a party to examine another Defile to *examine* if
it is possible for us to Cross over even at the sacrifice of Horses, if we
Cannot we may give up all hopes of a Spring Hunt."[11]

Ogden entrusted the mission to Kittson. "Mr. Ogden has just now
ordered me to prepare against tomorrow to head a party of five men on
discovery," Kittson wrote in his journal immediately after he had noted
that the Americans were gone. That was what Odgen had said he was
going to do, but Kittson tells us that there was a second purpose that
Ogden did not mention in his journal. Kittson explained that he was to
ascertain "the present state of the snows and grass in the defile, . . . and
also to notice the way the Americans went." With those orders, Ogden
began a five-week period when, in the words of one of his modern-day

editors, he and Jedediah Smith "played hide and seek with each other." It would be, another historian has said, a period of "stringent competition."[12]

Kittson spent an eventful two days inspecting the pass. He had a dangerous encounter with a party of thirty Gros Ventres when both he and they were afoot. He escaped and was able to complete the mission. "The American's tracks was to the Southward of our way," he reported. Ogden could not have been pleased. The news meant that Smith was going the same way he was, and Smith was ahead.[13]

Kittson had found the pass too deep in snow for the brigade to cross in safety. Besides, the Gros Ventres were somewhere in that direction. Ogden decided to take a different route to the Snake River, and it was then that Smith's plans became clearer. "We are now near the foot of the defile," Kittson wrote two days later, referring to the pass they were to cross. "The Americans have, it seems, taken it, fortunately for them, had they taken the one I visited they would have met with certain death, as they appeared when with us not to be over watchful."[14]

Kittson seemed more interested than Ogden in the Americans. Ogden did not mention them at all—not even that they were in the one place above all where he did not want them: ahead. Once the expedition was through the pass, Kittson did not pick up the trail until six more days. That occurred when the brigade made camp "near where the Americans had passed a night not long since." It would be a week before he saw more signs of them. Soon after crossing the Snake River, he "met two of the Americans who told us their camp was nigh, up the river. Made for it and reached it about noon, when we found it without any person in care, the beaver they had taken 80 in number were spread on the ground." From that point on, the contacts would become intense.[15]

The day after Kittson found Smith's camp, Ogden mentioned the Americans for the first time. Anyone at headquarters reading his entry for the day would have supposed that Smith had been with him ever since leaving Flathead Post. "[T]he seven Americans who joined Mr. Ross last Summer & accompanied him to the Flat Heads & have been since with us intend seperating tomorrow," he wrote. They "requested to trade & tho' they found the prices high say the Freemans Tariff but being in Want they were obliged to Comply & traded 100 Lar[ge] & Sm[all] Beaver." Ogden must have felt he had gotten some revenge for the pelts that Smith had purchased from the Iroquois, for he added, "this is Some recompense for the Beaver they traded with our party last Summer."[16]

Kittson also emphasized the prices paid. The expedition got "54 Beavers from the Traps," he noted in his journal, "and traded 43 Large and 54 Small Beavers and 1 Otter from the Americans at the same tariff of our Freemen."[17] It is well worth marking that neither Ogden nor Kittson took notice of the fact that the economics of supply and demand determined bargain and sale transactions out in the Snake country. Although dealing with foreigners in a wilderness where there was no law, they took it as a given that deals could be struck much as they would be at a market back home, even if the purchaser thought the price unconscionable.

Almost immediately after Smith and his party left the camp, the expedition was alarmed by Blackfeet. One trapper was killed and for two days no one had time to think of the Americans. The men still had to put out and visit their traps, and there was constant danger and concern. Then the Americans appeared again. "[T]hey this day gave us an alarm," Kittson wrote, "however they were soon discovered and all was again restored to quietness." For once, Ogden provided more details. The brigade had come to a river, the Blackfoot, which he planned to explore. It had never been trapped and was well stocked with beaver. The company "encamped on a fine Spot for defence   after encamping the Free men Started with 100 Traps but they had not been absent an hour when two Came back full Speed Calling out Black Feet." A rescue party was despatched to round up the trappers, "but in the evening they all returned it proving to be a false report, for it proved to be the American party who had left us in the Night & who from not finding a Suitable place for fording the River had changed their route." Kittson had said that they had not known where the Americans were—"we not knowing what route they had taken"—but again Ogden, by saying that the Americans "had left us in the night" gives the impression the two parties had been together.[18]

We can be confident that after that scare the two groups remained separated for almost a week. Ogden next heard of Smith's whereabouts six days later from his men. He was, he said, "informed by the Trappers who had gone a head with their Traps yesterday that they had Seen the Americans about ten miles ahead of us at their encampment." From what the men could see, the Americans had trapped fifty beaver that day, a very good catch for only seven men. The news upset Ogden. "[T]hese fellows by going a head will Secure the Beaver," he feared. He decided to take the competition directly to Smith. After all, he had many more men and it should be easy to make that advantage pay. "I assembled the Freemen," he explained, "& Selected 15 with orders to proceed to the Sources of this River & Secure all they Could   this may be means . . . of Sending them [the Americans] off Sooner than they probably intend   at all events we must endeavour to annoy them as much as we possibility Can."[19]

The next day the main part of the expedition, including Ogden, passed Smith's party. Smith tried to keep pace. "The Americans followed us this day & have encamped three Miles a head but this will avail them naught . . . we have traps 12 Miles a head."[20]

With so many more men, Ogden should have had the advantage. Moreover, the two parties had reached the headwaters of the Portneuf River, moving farther from Blackfoot war roads, and he could risk spreading the trappers more and more afield. However, what he ordered the men to do was often not determinative of events. The freemen generally were not obeying his instructions, except on those days when Blackfeet were actually seen.

The next day, the 18th of April, Ogden realized the Portneuf was not rich in beaver. "I must abandon for the present this route & retrace our steps," he explained. "The Americans have also been obliged to retrace back their Steps & will I presume follow us altho' they will nearly double their distance." Something was wrong with his calculations. By next evening, the 19th, the Americans were again ahead. "Trappers Started with their traps to overtake the Americans who are not far a head," he noted. It may be that Smith was making him angry. "[O]wing to the Americans being a head," he wrote on the 20th, "some of the trappers keep in Company with them so as to annoy them & with the hopes they will Steer another Course." The clear implication is that they were acting on his orders, that he sent them to "annoy" Smith. If so, the situation was becoming more than a game of hide and seek. Ogden may have been reverting to the rough tactics he had used when he and Samuel Black worked for the North West Company. We cannot be certain, however. In his journal that same day, Kittson implied that the trappers who had gone ahead were disobeying orders. "Several of the men have again gone ahead," he wrote, "therefore let rules be made they will soon be broken through." Perhaps they were so busy, Ogden could not keep Kittson informed about all his plans.[21]

Whether ordered or not, annoying Smith may have worked. Neither Ogden nor Kittson mentioned the Americans for another week. One reason may have been the presence of Piegans and Bloods. In the night they took about twenty horses belonging to the freemen, which, of course, were unguarded. Smith may have decided to get away from the expedition while raiders were in the area. On the 26th the brigade reached its objective, Bear River, a stream that Ogden was instructed to explore at least as far as where it emptied into the Colorado. "[T]he Americans have gone upwards and we are to follow it downwards in order to find where it runs to," Kittson wrote on arrival. Ogden thought the contrary directions made his prospects more promising than Smith's. "[T]he upper part," of Bear River "has been trapped twice," he pointed out, "but the lower part never has been."[22]

Ogden made slow progress going down the Bear. There were some beaver, but there also were Blackfoot warriors, causing the trappers to be more cautious and, at times, to remain close to camp. Then, on the 3d of May, he met a war party of seven Snakes, and the entire complexion of the expedition changed. The Snakes, Ogden reported, "inform us that a party of 25 Americans wintered near this & are gone in the same direction we had intended going   if this be true which I have no reason to doubt it will be a fatal blow to our expectations."[23]

A biographer has claimed that "Ogden's only concern about the Americans was apprehension that the beaver population would have been decimated by such a large number of trappers in the area for so long a time."[24] That cannot be correct. The news gave him much to be apprehensive about, and the amount of beaver on the lower reaches of Bear River would not have been very high on the list. He could not have received worse news than word that a party of Americans had wintered on the Bear. It was not just a matter of learning that there were many more Americans in the vicinity than anyone at Hudson's Bay had anticipated. They had been trapping a river that he had expected to find stocked with beaver because it had never been trapped before. How many other streams could he expect to find trapped? The Colorado, perhaps, or even the Buenaventura? Ogden did not know who the Americans were, where they came from, or how they were supplied. Surely he was puzzled about how they managed to spend an entire winter on the Bear. He certainly would have been very alarmed to learn that there were now American traders transporting supplies over the mountains from St. Louis, allowing these men to stay in the field all year. He also had to be worried about what would occur when the freemen met them. It was bad enough for Hudson's Bay Company's efforts to keep costs low in the Snake country to discover that these Americans had been trading with the Indians. The seven Snake warriors not only had four good guns, they had plenty of ammunition—"having procured it from the Americans." That information warned Ogden of two threats to Hudson's Bay prosperity. It could mean that some Americans were arriving west of the Rockies with either surplus goods or with goods to trade. More certainly, it meant that the Snakes had acquired ammunition at a lower price than the company charged Indians and the Snakes would expect to purchase as least as cheaply from then on.

We can only guess, but it is more than likely that Ogden would have retreated had he any idea how many Americans were in the area. It may be that his instructions to trap Bear River, and his own predilections for exploration, kept him going downstream. It certainly was not success that directed his course. "[B]ut few traps in the Water," he lamented on the 8th of May, "the Americans have taken nearly all the Beaver   they are a Selfish Set   they leave nothing for their Friends   we act differently."[25] The joke undoubtedly was meant for Simpson. After all, he had sent Ogden to strip the Bear so clean of beaver that nothing would be left for the Americans.

Bear River greatly disappointed Ogden. Hudson's Bay had had unusual expectations for the stream. Michel Bourdon, who may have seen it even before Donald McKenzie, had been very optimistic, reporting the river rich in beaver. On arriving, Ogden could see that the trappers who had wintered on the stream had done a respectable job picking it relatively clean of the tamer animals. "[T]he Americans must have taken a number of Beaver here," he wrote on that first day, "there are Still many left but no doubt very wild nearly all the Traps in the Camp were Set. 9 Beaver this day." On the third day he was thinking of moving elsewhere. "[T]he trappers inform me that they have Some hopes of finding a few

Beaver if not I shall Soon change my Course." The traps had produced seventy pelts by evening, and Ogden felt better. He became optimistic enough to hope that the Americans had worked the river too soon in the season and, although he had been later arriving on the Bear than had been planned, he might be the first to trap the upper reaches of the tributary streams. "[I]t would appear the Americans trapped only the lower part of these Forks," he wrote, hopefully. "[F]rom the quantity of Snow at the time it was impossible for them to proceed to their Sources & if we are so fortunate as to find Beaver it will be So much in our favour."[26]

The expedition had crossed the line that soon would divide the future state of Idaho from the future state of Utah. It had also reached the river that Ogden had been sent to explore and to strip clean of beaver before the Americans learned about it. We will never know, but it is possible that Governor Simpson had been unusually emphatic in insisting to Ogden that the Bear was surely rich in beaver and the Americans were to harvest none of it. As he progressed down the stream, Ogden seemed especially intent on impressing headquarters in his journal that he was making every effort possible to find the animals and trap everything available before the Americans had a chance. "[W]e did not move this day so as to give the Traps every chance & at the same time not waste Beaver," he wrote on 12 May, "indeed they are by far too Scarce, altho' from the different [accounts] we have received of the Snake Country I was as well as many others almost led to believe they were very numerous; but I am now of a Contrary opinion, indeed there is nothing like Seeing then a man Can *believe.*"[27]

In one respect the trappers were not doing as badly as Ogden indicated. They caught their "Second thousand" beaver on the 13th, and that put them ahead of the expedition of the year before. The trappers of 1824 "did not Complete their first thousand before the 16th from thus so far we ought not nor should we complain." Still, as they explored the smaller forks of the Bear and the Little Bear, it was evident that they had arrived a little too late. "[T]hey are small [streams] and have been well furnished in beaver," Kittson noted, "but the Americans got the best of them."[28]

There just was not enough beaver and, frustrated, many of the trappers began to drift over the mountains to see what they could find in the streams to the east. Ogden followed. Again the initial prospects were encouraging. "[T]his Country looks well & by all accounts promises equally So, it does not appear the Americans have Come this Way, so much in our favour." On the 17th of May they trapped 244 beaver.[29] And although the weather was "becoming very warm Still the Beaver are in their Prime." He even began to think that they might have the river to themselves. "[I]t is to be regretted that this Spot is not ten times as large I presume the Americans intended returning this way but they will be as we were on Bear River, *taken in* they ought to keep at home [and] not infringe on their neighbours territories."[30]

Ogden's remarks may have been casually entered into his journal without too much thought. But they should not be casually passed over. What he just said may help to explain the legal argument that he would adopt a few days later when challenged about the right of a British citizen to be on the waters running into Great Salt Lake. The Americans, he complained, "ought to keep at home [and] not infringe on their neighbours territories." He seems to have been claiming two things. First, that he was either in British territory or in an area that was contested between Great Britain and Mexico. Second, that the United States had no jurisdictional claim thereabouts, which made the American trappers trespassers on "their neighbours territories." Just what he meant about the United States is puzzling. Unless he was joking (as when complaining that, unlike the British, Americans left no beaver for their "friends"), he must have meant that he was not in the Oregon country, which the United States claimed jointly with Great Britain, and which claim was recognized by Great Britain. Or, he was saying he was somewhere that the United States did not claim. But that assertion could have been inconsistent with the claim that he was in British territory. The only British rights to lands south of the Columbia River were based on its claim to Oregon.

Before the week was over, Ogden would have to straighten out his thoughts and be more precise about the geography, but for the moment he did not have to worry about just where he was. It was enough to know that at last the expedition was in rich beaver country. Even Kittson was optimistic. "No signs of Americans having been here and the beaver are numerous," he wrote. "This place Mr. Ogden named new hole and the river bears the same name." "I have named [it] New River as no whites have ever been here before," Ogden explained. Today the river is called Ogden River and the valley is Ogden Hole. Just to the southwest is Ogden Peak. The members of the expedition never reached the site of present-day Ogden, Utah. They were, however, moving right along. Within a week, New River was "nearly exhausted of its riches & for So Small a Space it not being more than 6 miles in length & 3 in breadth has certainly well repaid us for the time we have spent. I only wish we could find a dozen *Spots* equal to it." Ogden would not find those spots any time soon. The exhaustion of New River would be his last period of sustained trapping in the streams southeast of the Snake River. On the next day the Americans were back.[31]

CHAPTER NINE

Do You Know in Whose Country You Are?

The expedition had been a challenge to Peter Skene Ogden. Looking back during his retreat out of the Snake country in July, he saw the first half of the trip as one series of disasters. First, one of the Iroquois trappers had been killed. Then the brigade was seriously delayed by ice and snow. Next, "a party of 6 Men were again attacked by a war-party but effected their escape." The attackers were Bloods who returned soon after and ran off eighteen horses. "[O]n the 1st April we reached the Great Snake River, and commenced trapping with tolerable Success but were not long allowed to remain quiet, for on the 5th a War-party of Blood Indians killed (Antoine Benoit a freeman) while in the act of raising his traps, took his Scalp[,] 16 Beavers and three horses and effected their escape." The killing increased Ogden's difficulty with the freemen. They wanted to change direction, away from the Blackfoot warpaths. Ogden talked them into continuing towards Bear River, "and all was then going on well, but again of short duration for on the 23d a party of Blood Indians & Piegans succeeded in again stealing 20 horses from the Freemen."[1] Once more Ogden nearly lost control. "[T]he Freemen then came forward and expressed their determination of abandoning the Country expressing themselves as follows 'to what end do we labour and toil, we are now at the commencement of the season and already one Man has been killed, and one half of our horses have been stolen.'

However threats and promises had the desired effect and the 5th May we reach'd Bear River."[2]

The Bear was another disappointment for Ogden. He had expected that it would be within the drainage system of the Colorado River, which would have led him to untrapped beaver fields and, perhaps, to the great Buenaventura, the river everyone believed flowed from the Rocky Mountains to the Pacific Ocean. Instead, he discovered that the Bear was an independent system, not overabundant in beaver. To find beaver, he was forced to leave the Bear and to cross a mountain range to the New or Ogden River, and then move on to another stream that he thought was an extension of the New but was a separate river, now called the Weber. There, at last, the expedition found an abundance of beaver. Prospects were clearly looking up when Ogden stopped at the site of today's Mountain Green, Utah. He waited for some of his trappers who were off in another direction. Here disaster struck again.

On 22 May the expedition was raising camp when two men rode in. They were freemen who had deserted from the Flathead Post in 1822. "One of them promised to keep with us," Kittson noted, "but the other, refused, yet said he would pay his debt."[3] That promise is a very important fact, and one that has too often been overlooked in studies of the Hudson's Bay Company. Most of the deserters whom Ogden would meet on his several Snake country expeditions, and whom he quoted, would tell him that they intended to pay their debts. Here, the first deserters ever encountered by a Snake country expedition indicated that, although they had left the Hudson's Bay jurisdiction owing money, they had not done so to avoid payment. They had deserted hoping to make money.

Ogden learned three very disturbing facts from the two deserters. First, they were trapping with a party of thirty men who, he noted, "were fitted out by the Spainards & Traders on the Missouri." The statement is vague and we cannot be certain what Ogden understood, except that he thought there were wide-ranging trappers in the area who got their supplies from both Mexicans and Americans. Second, he was told that his camp on the Weber was "now 15 days march from the Spanish Village." That village was Taos, which he knew was a center for the fur trade. It was startling to learn it was so much closer to the Bear River country than any Hudson's Bay posts. American trappers operating out of Taos had a much shorter supply route to the Snake country than did the British. And, third, the men told him "the whole Country [was] over-run with Americans." That was the worst news of all. The Americans were west of the Rockies in apparently large numbers. "Americans & Canadians all in pursuit of the Same object," he lamented, "of this we had Convincing proofs this Spring on Bears River."[4]

This was the second time Ogden had been told of sizable American parties trapping in the area. First, Snake warriors had reported American trappers who wintered on Bear River. Now it was evident that several other groups were in the general vicinity. No exact list has been compiled, partly because no journals have survived from the American side. William H. Ashley kept records and a diary, but he was not trapping. He was carrying supplies to the first rendezvous which would take place that summer west of the Rocky Mountains. He had several trapping parties out that year, at least two of which made contact with Ogden. One of these, of course, was the band of seven led by Jedediah Smith. A larger Ashley brigade was under the command of John H. Weber.

There was a third, important trapping party, which was not associated with Ashley. It was headed by Etienne Provost or Provot. He rode into Ogden's camp on the morning of 23 May. His brigade was remarkably international even by the standards of the fur trade. It consisted of two Hudson's Bay deserters, according to Kittson, plus "3 Canadians, a Russian, and an old Spaniard." Ogden said there were fifteen men in all, but that figure probably counts only those who came into his camp. Provost may have had a total of twenty to thirty men. Ogden also made contact that day with the group of trappers led by Weber. Weber had been trapping his way south from the Big Horn River. In his initial brigade he had a number of men who would leave their imprint on fur-trade history, Robert Campbell and Jim Bridger, for example, and, perhaps, David E. Jackson. Along the way he seems to have picked up smaller parties whom he met in the mountains. That was how Johnson Gardner came to be on the Weber River. He had traveled down from the Green with Weber.[5]

The gathering of so many trappers west of the Missouri River was unprecedented. A new era had dawned in the North American West. William H. Ashley was about to launch one of the most exciting and successful business enterprises in the history of the fur trade, the American rendezvous. By bringing supplies over the mountains, and buying fur as if at a medieval fair, Ashley did more than make it possible for trappers to remain in the West year after year, not having to bring their pelts in to St. Louis or to a trading post on the Missouri or Platte Rivers. He gave rise to what Washington Irving called a "new order of trappers." "In the old times of the great Northwest Company," Irving explained, "when the trade in furs was pursued chiefly about the lakes and rivers, the expeditions were carried on batteaux and canoes." Then the trade depended on *voyageurs* or boatmen, and remained close to the waterways in fixed permanent trading posts. "A totally different class has now sprung up, 'the Mountaineers,' the traders and trappers that scale the vast mountain chains and . . . move from place to place on horseback."[6]

It was this new phenomenon that the Snake country expedition encountered on Weber River. American trappers, either members of an independent party such as Provost's, or hired by fur companies to trap under leaders such as Smith and Weber, traveled vast distances, from the Yellowstone to the Bear, or the Arkansas to the Green. To arrive in the valleys of the Bear, the Ogden, and the Weber, they had, without hesitation, invaded the lands of proud and powerful peoples: the Arapahos, the Sioux, the Comanches, the Cheyennes, and even the Blackfeet. They were harvesting beaver pelts and other furs for sale to Ashley at his promised rendezvous, and then would ride out for a fall hunt, winter in some secluded valley, and near spring, when the ice started to melt, begin once more trapping beaver pelts and other furs.

Those American trappers would share one question during the months after meeting Ogden on the Weber River. They spent the fall, winter, and spring wondering if Ashley had made sufficient profits that summer to bring him back across the Rockies in 1826 for a second rendezvous. Events would prove that by every economic measure he had done very well and he returned in the summer of 1826 with more goods to buy more beaver. The rendezvous would become an annual gathering of mountain men. For Hudson's Bay it meant that the American presence in the Snake country would be permanent.

Before those events happened, however, Peter Skene Ogden had to deal with the American vanguard that met him at the Weber during the last week of May. On the 23rd of the month he was camped by the river, waiting for several of his freemen to rejoin the expedition. They had been absent for several days. It was a long enough time out of touch for Ogden to worry whether they had fallen in with one of the American parties and had sold their beaver for St. Louis prices. If so, they might not return at all. But if they did, he might have to deal with a serious matter of discipline as he believed that Hudson's Bay's claim on all furs trapped was superior to any right that the freemen had to sell them even in the Oregon country where the company's monopoly was not operative.

Ogden's apprehension must have increased in the afternoon following his meeting with Provost. Soon after Provost left, fourteen of the absent men "cast up," as Kittson expressed their arrival, "bringing with them a Strong party of Americans bearing Flags and under different heads." By being "under different heads," he meant that these men did not belong to one trapping party or company, but were a group collected from the various American camps nearby, men who wanted to support the returning freemen should they have trouble with Ogden, and, perhaps, harass the British brigade. There were twenty five of them, Ogden reported, and they came "with Colurs flying . . . headed by one Gardner they encamped within 100 yards of our encampment."[7]

The leader was Johnson Gardner, a little-known mountain man who, seven years later, in a contract with the American Fur Company, was described as a "Citizen of the United States and free hunter in the Indian Country." With his arrival there began what John S. Galbraith termed "one of the most famous incidents in the history of the fur trade."[8]

It has been suggested that the encounter between Ogden and Gardner was planned by the American trapping parties. That, for example, the two Hudson's Bay deserters who had appeared at Ogden's camp the day before had been sent to scout the situation. The Americans "were putting out feelers before approaching Ogden in force." The assertion is questionable. Most likely, Gardner was acting on his own. The subsequent behavior of other American leaders make it doubtful he had support. None of the American leaders, not even Smith or Weber, are mentioned by Ogden or Kittson. Besides, one of the two deserters rejoined Hudson's Bay employ and the other acknowledged his debts to the company. They do not seem to have been part of any plot. What is evident is that Gardner took it upon himself to confront Ogden. From what Kittson says, it appears that he believed Gardner had gathered a number of like-minded Americans who thought the British were intruding on American trapping grounds.[9]

William H. Ashley later claimed that American trappers became indignant when told that each night, on making camp, Ogden hoisted the British flag. In the years following the War of 1812, Americans were sensitive to any British insult, and carrying the Union Jack south of the Snake River basin was readily seen as an intentional insult to the United States. Ashley knew some of the men who confronted Ogden or who were camped in the immediate vicinity, but he himself was not present at the Weber and never met Ogden. What he said seems to be a politician's story told to justify what happened after the event. A better explanation is that the Americans invading Ogden's camp had become angry with the British after listening to the complaints of the Hudson's Bay freemen whom they encountered. They told tales of economic exploitation, of a company that kept them perpetually in debt by charging prices for goods which were exorbitant when compared to what it paid for beaver. It was a grievance that the fiercely independent mountain men could readily understand and, if given a chance, actively resent. That may explain why about twenty-five Americans followed Johnson Gardner into the British camp on Weber River. We will never know for certain. They may have been looking for trouble or they may have only wanted to persuade Ogden's remaining freemen to desert the expedition.[10]

Gardner seized the initiative. As soon as he arrived, Ogden said, he "lost no time in informing all hands in the Camp that they were in the United States Territories & were all free indebted or engaged." He was inviting them all to desert, not just the freemen, but the *engagés* as well. "Free or Engaged men were the same in this land of Liberty," Kittson quoted him as proclaiming, "whomsoever wished to go with him they were welcome. No man would dare opposed [*sic*] the measures they would take." Ogden and Kittson would not try to stop them. If they did, "he and his party were ready to stand by, any that wished to Desert Mr. Ogden."[11]

Gardner offered more than what he called freedom. He had brought economic incentive for desertion, for he was telling the Hudson's Bay people they could get much higher prices than what the company paid. He must have been claiming to speak for American traders in general, for he was a hired trapper, not a trader, and had no capital with which to purchase fur. "[T]hey would," he claimed, "pay Cash for their Beaver   3½ dollars p. lb., & their goods cheap in proportion." That was precisely what Ogden did not want his men to hear. The Americans, according to Gardner, offered eight times for beaver what Hudson's Bay was paying, and current mountain folklore held that American goods were cheaper than those Hudson's Bay sold. Ogden now guessed why some of his men had been absent. They had "been with the Americans no doubt plotting." Gardner had made his point. "[I]t was now night and nothing more transpired."[12]

By morning, Gardner probably knew that he had persuaded most of the freemen to desert the expedition. That day his arguments were mostly directed against Ogden, and he raised issues that gave the confrontation an entirely new aspect. Gardner was not merely angered at Hudson's Bay's because it was a monopoly that economically oppressed its employees. The British, he asserted—and seems to have believed— were trespassing in American territory, and he had the right to order them to leave.

Gardner started the day by going to Ogden's tent. It is regrettable that no American left a diary or other account of the quarrel. All we have are what Ogden and Kittson said in their journals and letters. As a consequence, we can understand the statements that Ogden made better than the arguments he attributed to Gardner. "[A]fter a few words of no import, he questioned me as follows   Do you know in whose Country you are? to which I made answer that I did not as it was not determined between Great Britain & America to whom it belonged." Ogden was referring to the treaty between the two nations providing for joint occupancy, and was also assuming that eventually the Oregon country would be divided between them. Only after the treaty was renegotiated would anyone know "to whom it belonged." According to Ogden, Gardner then attempted to bluff him. He answered "that it was known" to whom it belonged, "that it had been ceded to the latter," that is, Great Britain had ceded it to the United States. That meant, he went on, that "I had no licence to trap or trade" there, and should "return from whence I came." Odgen, of course, could not be certain whether Gardner was deceiving him, but he replied as though he did know. "I made answer [that] when we receive orders from the British Government we Shall obey, then he replied remain at your peril, he then departed."[13]

It will be recalled that five days earlier Ogden, finding the Americans had trapped Bear River before him, complained that they "ought to keep at home [and] not infringe on their neighbours territories."[14] The point was then made that his meaning is unclear. He was in today's state of Utah, and could have been saying that he was in that part of the Oregon country that the United States had ceded to Spain and that Great Britain still claimed. If so, he was correct about the United States, although he could not have known if he was still within territory that Britain claimed, partly because he was uncertain where he was and partly because the southern limits of British Oregon were imprecise. In the treaty of joint occupancy between the two nations, the southern border had not been given much attention because little was known of the geography south of the Columbia. Under the Adams-Onis Treaty of 1819, however, the United States and Spain had agreed on a boundary set by "Latitude, 42. North," running from where it struck the southern bank of the Arkansas River to the Pacific Ocean.[15] That boundary is now the northern state lines of Utah, Nevada, and California. When Ogden said the Americans should "not infringe on their neighbours territories," it is just possible he could have been referring to Mexican territory.[16] Because of Adams-Onis, American trappers on the Ogden, Weber, and much of the Bear rivers were trespassers in 1825. Ogden's rights were not affected by that treaty. Whether he also was trespassing depended on what Great Britain recognized as Mexican. If Hudson's Bay had not been told by the British government to keep north of the forty-second parallel, he was not, from the British perspective, trespassing. To be on the Weber was to be in an area that any practicing international lawyer could easily construe as within the jointly occupied Oregon country. The Mexican perspective, of course, was another matter, but was also irrelevant to Gardner's argument.

It is doubtful that Ogden ever heard of the Adams-Onis Treaty. He did not mention it when Johnson Gardner accused him of trespassing. He did not turn the argument back on Gardner and say that under American law it was Gardner who was trespassing. "Mr. Ogden," Kittson reported, "answered that as to the Country alluded to, he knew full well that it was still a disputed point between the two Governments."[17] He obviously was not thinking of Mexico, nor did he mention either that country or the Adams-Onis Treaty in his correspondence with his superiors at Hudson's Bay headquarters. In fact, Ogden probably gave no thought to Mexico, for he really did not know where he was. He understood that he had left the Bear River and guessed that he was near the headwaters of the Buenaventure or Sacramento. Otherwise the geography was quite vague. No one at that time understood it or could have told Ogden that he had entered the Great Basin of the North American West because the Great Basin was not yet known to exist.

Consider the confusion of John McLoughlin. He was in charge of the Columbia department and was the officer who authorized Snake country expeditions, telling them where to go and what rivers to trap. If anyone should have known the geography of the Snake country it was McLoughlin, yet he could be as uncertain as anyone else. He wanted the people at London headquarters to understand that Ogden, even though no longer "on the waters of the Columbia"—that is, even though he had passed beyond the drainage area of the Snake River— was not on the eastern, or American, side of the Continental Divide. "I think," McLoughlin explained. "he was Either on the head waters of a River that falls at St. Francisco or on those of a River said to fall into the Ocean a little South of the Um[p]qua." Like Ogden, McLoughlin thought the expedition had reached the headwaters of the Sacramento or Bue- naventure. Had the trappers made bullboats and floated down Bear River, they eventually would have drifted into San Francisco Bay.[18]

Even if we are surprised by the substance of the argument between Ogden and Gardner, we should not hesitate to recognize how much it turned on legal questions. There, in the isolation of the western moun- tains, beyond the reach of any coercive tribunal, in the area of the Great Salt Lake—a body of water not yet known in London, Washington, or Mexico City—men who made their living by trapping beaver argued aspects not only of territorial jurisdiction and private law but also of international and even transnational law. Seeking to take advantage of their extreme isolation from government, company, and all sources of information, Gardner tried to bluff Ogden in one, perhaps two, instances. The first was the claim that joint occupation of Oregon had ended and Great Britain had ceded the territory to the United States. The cession could easily have happened with neither Gardner's nor Ogden's hear- ing of it, but Ogden could not know whether Gardner had more recent information. Gardner was in touch with other American mountain men who wintered in the Rockies, as well as with the contractees of William H. Ashley who were in communication with St. Louis. Even if Gardner knew that no new agreements had been negotiated between Great Britain and the United States, it strengthened his argument to bluff the British and make Ogden uneasy.

It is not likely Gardner was saying that they were on the east side of the Continental Divide. Every Hudson's Bay officer in the Columbia department knew that that was United States territory, and Ogden had strict orders from London not to go over the mountains to the American side. He did go over, of course, as he had when he went from Flathead Post to hunt buffalo on the headwaters of the Missouri before crossing back to the Snake (or to the waters of the Columbia drainage basin), and as he would again after retreating from the Weber and returning north, when he trapped beaver near the Madison. There, when on the Weber River, dealing with Gardner, Ogden knew he was west of the Continental Divide, and, it must be assumed, Gardner did also. It was then common fur-trade knowledge that the Bear and the Green rivers were Pacific waters. The Great Salt Lake was just about to become known to westerners—Charles McKay, the Piegan interpreter, had told Kittson that from a mountain he had seen a large body of water to the south, and Washington would be told that some trapper, probably Jim Bridger, had floated a bullboat down to the mouth of Bear River where he had tasted salt water. When he got back to camp, some of Ashley's men guessed that he had been to the Pacific.

It would not be for a year or two more before the fur men learned that all rivers flowed into the lake, and none flowed out. There was as yet no notion of a Great Basin. That was why both Ogden and Jedediah Smith were searching for the headwaters of the one or two great rivers that they knew had to flow westward to empty into the Pacific. With that search so well known, it is very unlikely Gardner was bluffing about being on the east of the Continental Divide. He not only knew he was west of the mountains, he realized that Ogden and all his men knew that as well. Unless there had been a new treaty and cessation of territory, they were not on land indisputably belonging to the United States. He would not have tried a bluff on that point.

Ogden knew one fact about the Weber River that he did not share with Gardner. He may not have thought he was in Mexican jurisdiction, but as he was south of the Columbia River he knew that he was in country that Hudson's Bay expected would be ceded to the United States. After all, he was far south of territory the company was so certain would soon be American that he had been ordered to strip it clear of beaver. This is information he certainly did not want the Americans to learn. Knowledge that the British were laying waste to the region's resources well could have led to more trouble.

The argument has been made that Gardner probably knew that he had crossed into territory that the United States had ceded to Spain. Although there was little likelihood Ogden was familiar with the Adams-Onis Treaty, it was somewhat known in the American West that John Quincy Adams had used that treaty—in negotiating the purchase of Florida—to strengthen the United States claim to the Oregon country by adding to it whatever rights Spain possessed. That was why Adams had Spain cede to the United States all its rights to Oregon north of the forty-second parallel, in return for whatever claims to territory south of the parallel that the United States might have acquired when it purchased Louisiana from France. Gardner, it has been said, probably knew all of this.[19]

It is more likely irrelevant whether Gardner was aware of the Adams-Onis Treaty. Even if he knew of it, there is little chance he understood that he was in territory that it ceded to Spain, because there is little likelihood he had any idea where the forty-second parallel was located, let alone that there even was a parallel. Ogden, with the network of geographical information that Hudson's Bay furnished its officers, should have been better informed than Gardner. Yet we may doubt if he gave any thought to latitudes. His right to be where he was, trapping on the Weber River, was not affected by the treaty. Keep in mind that it was between the United States and Spain only, and, as said before, had left unresolved the boundary between British Oregon and the newly independent Republic of Mexico. Ogden had no reason to care where the forty-second latitude was. All he probably understood was that he was far south of any place that Hudson's Bay Company and, presumably Great Britain, intended to claim. When company headquarters in London decided not to ask the British government to seek compensation from the United States for Gardner's interference with Ogden's expedition, it noted "that Mr. Ogden must have been to the southward of the 49° latitude," indicating that even after the fact the company was not sure where he had been.[20]

The best conclusion is that neither Ogden nor Gardner knew where Mexican sovereignty began, and neither cared. We have to guess about Gardner, for he was an American and we have no idea what he thought about Mexican sovereignty. Most likely, he paid it no heed. Most American trappers were contemptuous of it, at least until they found themselves in Mexican jails. But Ogden was a Hudson's Bay officer, and he was expected to know and follow company policy. Most of Hudson's Bay contact with Mexico was in Ultra California, not in the area of the Great Salt Lake. For the most part, Hudson's Bay treated Mexican sovereignty as irrelevant.

United States authority was treated with far greater respect. The policy controlling Ogden's conduct when meeting Americans such as Gardner had been outlined by McLoughlin, who, in turn, got the law from the company's governing committee in London. That body had instructed its officers in North America, "That by the treaty of 1818 the Lands on the west side of the Rocky Mountains are free to ourselves and the subjects of the United states for ten years from the date of it which will expire in 1828." From this ruling McLoughlin drew the conclusion that "the Americans have no right to assume any authority or claim this Country as part of their Territory."[21] For McLoughin, this meant not only that Hudson's Bay could trap waters well south of the Snake River basin but that it could use force if push came to shove. When he learned of Ogden's confrontation with Gardner, and was told that Gardner had threatened "that the Americans would be at the Flat Head and Kootonais this fall and would drive us from their Territory," McLoughlin wrote to the chief factors and chief traders in his department, quoting the ruling he had received from the governing committee. "[B]y this you see we are justified in resisting to the Utmost of our power any attack on our persons and property or any assumption of authority over us by the Americans—Indeed so confident am I of our being justified in this that had we a party sufficiently strong to defend itself from the natives and that could be depended on, I would have no hesitation to make another attempt in that quarter if it was merely for one year to defy them to put their threats in Execution and to counter act the evil impression the vaunting assertions of Gardner . . . will have on the Indians and remaining freemen."[22]

These were fighting words that attributed far too much significance to Johnson Gardner. McLoughlin admitted that Gardner had put no threats "in Execution," and he surely understood that Gardner did not speak for the United States. Yet he was prepared to dispatch an expedition authorized to use force to maintain British rights to an area south of the Columbia River basin where Hudson's Bay people had long conceded that King George's writ would never run.

CHAPTER TEN

Go We Will Where We Shall Be Paid

John McLoughlin did not want trouble with the Americans. He would have sent a trapping expedition to enforce British rights against the American fur trappers only because he, like everyone else in the Hudson's Bay Company, at least for a while, believed that Johnson Gardner had threatened Peter Ogden with violence.

It is not possible to give a scale of value to the several aspects of the Ogden-Gardner confrontation that most angered Hudson's Bay officers. It seems a reasonable guess that the most disturbing fact of the affair was learning how many American trappers had suddenly appeared west of the Continental Divide. Next, they may have been most shocked by the freemen who not only deserted but took with them beaver pelts that all officers who are on record said belonged to the company. Perhaps, too, they were even more upset if, like some later scholars of the fur trade, they believed the pelts had been seized by violence. Ogden created the impression of violence by what he said in his journal and his letters. He never directly said that violence had occurred, he only implied that it had. He may not have intended to do so; it may have been only that he emphasized Gardner's boasts and threats, and did not dwell on or even notice the deserters' eagerness to break free of Hudson's Bay's monopoly and to sell their pelts at American prices.

Ogden did not hide the facts. He reported some of the freemen's criticisms. It is, rather, that he did not think them important. It was not until he was well away from the Weber that he began to appreciate that the freemen had genuine grievances. By the time he returned to the Columbia, he had become convinced that, to compete with the Americans, Hudson's Bay would have to treat the freemen differently. When still on the Weber, however, he did not yet realize how much the freemen felt exploited and how much they wanted to change their circumstances. While they thought they were freeing themselves economically by leaving the expedition, he thought them deserters stealing company property and did not credit their complaints.

Certainly the complaints were forcefully stated. After attempting to bluff Ogden without success, Gardner left his tent and went over to the lodge of John Grey, a leader of the Iroquois. Among Hudson's Bay officers, he was one of the most mistrusted and despised of the freemen. The year before, he had given Alexander Ross more trouble than any other member of that trouble-ridden Snake country expedition. He was, Ross claimed, "a turbulent blackguard, a damned rascal." The wonder is that Ross had allowed him to go on Ogden's expedition. Surely it was a tribute to his value as a trapper and Indian fighter that he was included. Even his severest critics granted his courage. Dale Morgan would describe him as "reputed among the bravest and most spirited of mountain men." Unreliable as he was, his worth to the brigade must have outweighed all defects.[1]

Most accounts of the Jackson Gardner incident cast Ogden in the role of the passive victim. In fact, he was aggressive, seizing horses and traps from deserters that they had intended to take with them and that, he claimed, were Hudson's Bay property. He even sent Charles McKay, the translator, over to Gardner's camp to reclaim a horse that had been taken there—a far more confrontational action than anything Gardner attempted. The horse was brought back to the Hudson's Bay camp. In perhaps the boldest move of the entire day, Ogden actually followed Gardner into Grey's lodge. It was a bit reckless, as he had no idea how Grey would react. That he took the risk indicates how alarmed he must have been on seeing Gardner going into the Iroquois' lodge. Surely he was worried they were intriguing together, but he could not have hoped to stop the plotting or persuade them they were wrong.

Once inside the lodge, Ogden had to be astonished by the fury with which Grey turned on him. Perhaps the argument verged near violence.

We have no evidence except what Ogden says, and it may not matter since no violence occurred. What did happen is that he learned of the freemen's discontent in no uncertain terms. Ogden was interpreting the argument for his fellow officers of Hudson's Bay, but even his account could not hide the anger against Hudson's Bay Company.

> [O]n entering this villain Gray [*sic*] said, I must now tell you, that all the Iroquois as well as myself have long wished for an opportunity to join the Americans, and if we did not the last three Years, it was owing to our bad luck in not meeting them, but now we go, and all you can say or do cannot prevent us. During this conversation Gardner was silent, but on going out he said you have had these Men too long in your Service and have most shamefully imposed on them, treating them as *Slaves* selling them Goods at high prices and giving them nothing for their Furs, Gray then said that is all true and alluding to the Gentlemen [*i.e.*, Hudson's Bay officers] he had been with in the Columbia, they are says he the greatest villains in the World, and if they were here I would shoot them, but as for you Sir you have dealt fair with us all. We have now been five years in your Service, the longer we remain the more indebted we become altho' we give 150 Beaver a year, we are now in a free Country and have friends to support us, and go we will, and if every Man in the Camp does not leave you they do not seek their own interest.[2]

The time would arrive when Hudson's Bay Company officers understood Grey's last argument. Many wondered how Ogden had kept any freemen with him. John McLoughlin, who at first missed the economic grievance and tried to argue that the Iroquois had no just complaints, eventually came around to thinking it was "more surprising that any remained than that any ran away."[3]

Ogden now realized that Gardner had been raising more than geography lessons when he had asked if he knew what country they were in. He had also been telling him that the Iroquois were in a country where Hudson's Bay's monopoly was unenforceable. "Gardner," Ogden wrote, "lost no time informing all *hands* that they were in the United States Territorys and that they were all free." He meant that they were free to make contracts and sales without concern for parliamentary restraints. Or, to use Gardner's own extremist language, they were no longer "slaves."[4]

Grey adopted Gardner's legal theory. His boast that he was "now in a free Country" has been interpreted as a claim that the expedition was in the United States.[5] As Grey was an American by birth and apparently thought of himself as an American,[6] that meaning is quite possible. In light of the general context of what he said and the specific arguments that Ogden was careful to quote him as making, it seems more likely that Grey was claiming economic rather than political freedom. He, of course, did not have the learning to express his argument in terms of law, but he was in fact making claim to a valid legal principle. He was asserting his right under American constitutional law not to be bound by any agreement or understanding he had made with Hudson's Bay as the provisions of the contract had been driven by the company's monopolistic powers granted by parliamentary legislation. If a lawyer had been there to put the contention into legal terms, he would have said that Grey was claiming that that monopoly was illegal in the country south of the Snake River, and contracts made with the monopoly were unenforceable as contrary to public policy.

Much more was being contended in the argument between Grey and Ogden than honoring agreements and respecting property rights. Cultures were in conflict—philosophical cultures and, perhaps, legal cultures. Two theories or economic philosophies clashed, one of monopoly and restrained, legislatively protected enterprise conducted as a quasi-governmental body supposedly in the public interest; the other of free trade, open markets, and unrestrained competition.

There had always been an antimonopoly streak in American politics and law. Dislike of economic privilege and uncontrolled private power was an established given in America constitutionalism, and was a prominent aspect of the then-dominant Jacksonian political persuasion. A related populist culture had worked itself into the mentality of the fur trade, as when a St. Louis merchant was warned that public opinion would not allow one company to dominate the business. Be careful, Ramsay Crooks told Pierre Chouteau in 1834, "your business so much resembles a monopoly that there will always be strong jealousies against you." Even Lewis and Clark had compared America's free-market economy to the trade restraints of Rupert's Land when they told Canadian traders that American rule in the Louisiana Territory would mean that "[e]very one shall be free to trade after his own manner."[7]

It would be wrong to push the dichotomy to nationalistic lengths. It was not a matter of British political culture against American, or English legal theory against American. There was as much opposition to monopoly in Great Britain as in the United States. It had been forbidden in England for two hundred years.[8] The monopoly had been conferred on the Hudson's Bay Company to be an instrument of imperial policy, not domestic policy. In fact, monopoly was so contrary to British political theory that attacks upon Hudson's Bay privileges "won easy applause in Parliament."[9] The monopoly was even criticized by officers of the company, and those supporting it often were hard pressed to defend it.[10] The strongest arguments for monopoly were nationalistic and humane: nationalistic because the monopoly preserved for Great Britain a vital area of commerce that otherwise might be dominated by Russians and Americans;[11] humane because monopoly preserved the Indians from the debauchery that always resulted from competition in the fur trade, especially when rivals competed with liquor. There is evidence that last argument, together with the contention that a monopoly was more likely to practice conservation and protect the environment than was a company in free trade, persuaded Parliament to create the monopoly in 1821.[12]

Grey exploited this antimonopoly sentiment. It might be thought he knew nothing about it, but, in fact, he was not only literate (as were others among the Iroquois), he had in his youth received what has been called "a white man's education." To be sure, none of the Hudson's Bay officers in the Columbia would give him credit for principled thought. For them, all the Iroquois were unmanageable, and John Grey was the worst of all. They may have misunderstood him, but more likely they never took the trouble to get to know him. Of course, he may have been unusually stubborn and contentious, and they resented that behavior from a freeman. More likely, however, what they found offensive was his intelligence and the fact that he was educated enough to question how the monopoly computed debts.[13]

Having lectured Ogden about his rights, Grey asserted his economic independence. "[H]e then gave orders to his Partners to raise Camp," Ogden wrote in his journal, "& immediately all the Iroquois were in motion, & made ready to Start   this example was Soon followed by others at this time   the Americans headed by Gardner & accompanied by two of our Iroquois who had been with them the last two years advanced to Support & assist all who were inclined to desert."[14]

Except for the journal kept by his clerk, William Kittson, Ogden is our only eyewitness to what happened. The words were his, but it is worth reminding ourselves that he was writing to his superiors in the Hudson's Bay Company, explaining how he had lost over seven hundred beaver pelts. He was not addressing historians who would want to know such things as whether he told the freemen they had no right to take the pelts, what the freemen answered, and in what context people on either side spoke of "ownership," "possession," "theft," and "right."

What Ogden chose to write and how he wrote it has shaped all subsequent accounts of what occurred on the Weber River that day in 1825. The last sentence in the passage just quoted is an example of his choice of words controlling later interpretations. He said that Gardner and two Iroquois "advanced" to support anyone wanting to desert. Whether intended or not, the implication is that they were threatening to use force should Hudson's Bay people attempt to prevent the desertions. When Ogden emphasized the word "desertion," it is possible he meant only to suggest that the freemen were committing a delict against the company or British law, or that they were breaking an implied contract that they had made when they joined the expedition. Yet, the suggestion that force was threatened should he attempt to restrain them from leaving or from taking the furs they had trapped, and also the way he used the word "desert," put Gardner and the two Iroquois in the wrong, not only with Ogden's fellow Hudson's Bay officers but with subsequent scholars of the fur trade.

It is never asked on what grounds Ogden could legally have held the men in the company's service, had he been physically able to do so. They had agreed to go on the expedition, and surely understood that both its safety and success depended on their continued presence. That knowledge could be said to create an implied obligation or at least a promise to remain until the brigade was out of danger. If so, it was a contract for which Hudson's Bay Company furnished no consideration except organizing and commanding the expedition, or, by accepting the freemen as members of the party, putting itself in a position where it depended on them. If Ogden had claimed that the men were obliged to remain with the brigade, he would have been asserting an obligation for which the company owed no counter obligation. It furnished the freemen no food, shelter, or clothing. Practice and humanity dictated that if a man was injured or sick the expedition did not abandon him. The members of the expedition carried him until he recovered, until he died, or until they got back to the Columbia. That protection was reassuring to the sick trapper, but was hardly sufficient consideration to create a binding contract on the freemen not to abandon the brigade. After all, Ogden would have done as much for Johnson Gardner had he been found alone and wounded on the trail.

Hudson's Bay people tended to think of the obligations of the freemen not in terms of service but of debt. This perspective had been demonstrated the year before by Alexander Ross when he forced John Grey to remain with the expedition of 1824. Grey announced he was so unhappy with the progress Ross was making that he was leaving, taking his property, including his horses and traps. An armed Ross confronted him. If he paid his debts, Grey was told, he could take the horses and traps. He could not leave with the horses and traps while owing money. Ross prevailed. Knowing he could not survive without horses, Grey remained with the expedition.[15] If we were to convert Ross's actions into legal theory, it would be that the company had an implied lien on Grey's horses and traps.

The same theory apparently determined what Ogden did that day on Weber River. He tried to obtain possession of the horses that the freemen had been riding by a claim of right that may have depended as much on debt as it did on ownership or contract. When an Iroquois named Lazard began to take some horses (we may assume the ones sold him on credit back at Flathead Post), Ogden resisted. "I was determined not to allow him or others to pillage us of our Horses as they had already taken two say [of] Old Pierres which has been lent him, they desisted & we secured the ten Horses but not without enduring the most opprob[r]ious terms they could think of from both Americans and Iroquois."[16]

Old Pierre, it will be recalled, was the Iroquois who had lost all his horses when he did not guard then on a night Blood raiders were in the vicinity. The Bloods ran them off, and from what Ogden said, Old Pierre had borrowed the horses he was riding when the expedition reached the Weber. Ogden's diary entry just after the taking of the horses made it clear that Old Pierre would have to borrow from other freemen. If so, Hudson's Bay might not have had any interest in the animals unless the lender had acquired them at Flathead Post on credit and had not yet paid for them. If they were borrowed from an *engagé* they may have been his property, but, more likely, they were horses on which Hudson's Bay had a property claim.[17]

Ogden did not secure every horse or every trap that he believed he had the right to possess. Some had been taken into the American camp before he had realized Grey and other freemen were deserting. What he did do, when he asserted either his claim of ownership or his claim to a creditor's lien, was keep possession of ten that otherwise would have been taken. His most articulated grievance against Gardner, however, was not the horses or traps but the desertions, and the fact that Gardner—or some other American for whom Gardner spoke—had already taken custody of many furs and was asking the Hudson's Bay freemen to bring more. He continued to promise that they could receive eight times the price Hudson's Bay paid for beaver. It was the freemen's response to this offer that led Ogden to report that he had been subdued by superior force: "Thus we were overpowered by numbers and with the exception of a part they succeeded in carrying off their Furs to the amount of 700 Beavers—in fact many of them had conveyed them in the night to the American camp. Situated and circumstanced as I then was, not knowing friend from foe, I cannot but consider it was a fortunate circumstance I did not fire; had I, I have not the least doubt all was gone. Furs and property, indeed that was their Plan [that] I should fire and assuredly they did all they could to make me, and I was fully aware of their Plan and so saved what remained, before this affair we had nearly Three Thousand Beaver and were doing well."[18] In truth, Ogden had been "overpowered" not by force but by higher prices, and considering the odds, decided it was not worthwhile to fire his gun.

Again, it must be emphasized that Ogden was writing for his Hudson's Bay superiors. His way of describing this event has become more important than the facts he chose to relate. He indicated that he felt threatened and students of the fur trade in the transboundary North American West have generally adopted his perspective of American armed aggression.

The Gardner-Ogden confrontation has acquired importance in fur-trade history. It is the best-known recorded incident occurring in the western mountains proving the lawlessness of American mountain men when encountering the law-abiding agents of Hudson's Bay Company. It has been called "the famous British-American clash of 1825—when the 'cold fur war' nearly exploded into a hot shooting war."[19] It is seldom noted, however, that it apparently came closest to degenerating "into a hot shooting war" when Ogden drew his gun (remember, he said "it was a fortunate circumstance I did not fire"). There was no claim by either Ogden or Kittson that they were threatened by American weapons (the only armed threat mentioned by either officer came from an Iroquois, a Hudson's Bay deserter). Yet the incident fits the stereotype of the American mountain men, and with them violence can always be implied even from nonviolence. For example, "Johnson Gardner," it has been written, "at the head of twenty-five flag-waving Americans, rode boldly into the British camp with obvious hostile intentions. Ogden's cool action prevented the fracas from developing into a shooting war."[20]

The stereotype easily becomes the evidence. "By distributing liquor among Ogden's men a general desertion was brought about," F. T. Elliott wrote, referring to Gardner's tactics.[21] There is no evidence that Gardner had liquor. Neither Ogden nor Kittson say anything about alcohol.[22] If Gardner had whiskey with him, even if it had not been given the freemen, Ogden would have mentioned the fact, knowing it would make him appear harassed at headquarters and make Gardner seem even more threatening. Elliott, however, did not need evidence from Ogden. He had the stereotype. Gardner was an American fur trapper in Indian country. Of course he had liquor.

A far more serious, and also more defensible charge made in the historical literature is that the furs taken from Ogden's to Gardner's camp were stolen.[23] "[T]he transaction," Gardner's biographer asserted, "was but thinly-veiled robbery, accomplished by inducing Ogden's Iroquois trappers to desert." "This was," Frederick Merk agreed, "no friendly call for the exchange of trappers amenities. A lawless spirit of trade rivalry and national resentment at the activities of the Hudson's Bay Company in the Oregon country brought Johnson Gardner."[24]

Important as events at Peter Ogden's camp on Weber River may have been for students of the far-western fur trade, they would be even more important if scholars took an interest in transboundary legal history. This was the only serious fracas to occur between Hudson's Bay officers and American mountain men, and there may be no better known incident for examining the degree of transboundary criminal behavior in the Pacific Northwest during the years when Great Britain and the United States jointly occupied the Oregon country. Three elements of that behavior should be considered: the charge of violence, the claim that Hudson's Bay horses and fur were stolen, and the lawfulness of the act of desertion.

The violence was partly in the confrontation and largely in the words. Johnson Gardner rode into the Hudson's Bay camp in a belligerent mood, accusing the British of illegally trapping in the United States, and announcing to the freemen that they were now "free" and that the Americans would pay high prices for their pelts. It was easy for McLoughlin, Simpson, and other company officers to consider that this appearance, if not itself an act of violence, threatened violence. Yet Ogden's only mention of violence occurred when he wrote that "the Americans with Gardner at their head accompanied by two of our Iroquois who deserted from our party in 1821 advanced to support and assist all who would join them. Lajaux an Iroquois now called out we are in numbers far greater, let us pillage, on saying this he cock'd his gun and took his aim, another then seized two of the Companys horses, but Mr. Kit[t]son Mr. McKay and two of the engaged men coming to our assistance we saved them."[25]

Ogden meant this account to convey the impression of American violence or threat of violence. But consider that he came closest to describing violence when he said a gun was cocked and aimed. We may reasonably assume that everyone possessed a weapon. Yet only two men with guns are specifically said to have prepared their weapons to fire. They were the Iroquois, Lajaux, and Peter Ogden, both of Hudson's Bay Company.

"Even in the heat of passion," one of Ogden's biographers claimed, "Ogden could see that his opponents were trying to goad him into firing, which would then give them an excuse to fire back." Well, maybe. Admittedly, Ogden made the same charge, once in his journal and at least twice in letters. "I did not fire," he wrote, "indeed their plan was that I should fire first." But why? Why would the Americans have wanted him to fire first? Did they need an excuse to fire back? If so, to whom would they want to justify themselves except to Smith, Weber, Ashley, and the other American trappers in the area? In that case, they must have reasoned that violence started by them would be condemned on the American side. That would, however, not explain why the deserting freemen would have wanted an excuse.[26]

These men, both Canadian freemen and the American trappers, were angry at Hudson's Bay. The freemen were angry about how the company kept them in debt year after year and expedition after expedition. No matter how they struggled, or what dangers or hardships they endured, they generally ended every year or every expedition with as much debt, or even greater, than when they had started. Americans prices had been much more to them than the promise of money. They had been a revelation. If they had not suspected before, they were convinced now that they had been exploited by Hudson's Bay.

The American trappers may have been more angry. The year before, some of the freemen had left the Snake country expedition for a few days to raid a Snake camp for horses. Snakes had been killed and the Snakes needed to obtain revenge. The first mountain men the Snakes reached were Americans led by Etienne Provost. On the Jordan River, a leading Snake chief persuaded Provost to lay aside his weapons and smoke the pipe. While the trappers were smoking, the Snakes turned on them. Provost and one or more of his men escaped, but at least seven Americans and one deserter from Hudson's Bay were killed. Americans blamed Hudson's Bay and, not too surprisingly, Ogden agreed. The expedition of 1824 had raided the Snakes and, predictably, they took revenge. But, Ogden insisted, Alexander Ross should not be blamed. "[T]he murder of 7 Americans & Patrick O'Connor [the Hudson's Bay deserter] was owing to that unfortunate thieving expedition, but I am confident Mr. Ross did all in his power to prevent their going, but with villains in this cursed & ill fated Country no man Can inforce obedience to his Commands." Actually, Ogden was wrong and probably knew that he was. Ross should have prevented the raid. Ogden was right, however, when he said that the Americans were "greatly irritated . . . against us, and they would most willingly shoot us if they dared."[27]

Perhaps Ogden was making excuses, but he had to be wrong. Ross may have been a relatively weak, ineffective leader, but he should have prevented the raid. It was simply too risky. If anything went wrong, the

Snakes were certain to hold Hudson's Bay employees liable, and, if they found none, by extension would hold any mountain men, of any nationality, liable. That was just what happened and the Americans were right if they said Ross was to blame.[28]

When we consider the remarkable degree of anger that was directed against Hudson's Bay Company—the anger of the freemen and the anger of the American trappers—what occurred on Weber River to Ogden and his men, does not live up to the reputation for violence of the "Wild West."

Twenty-three freemen deserted to Gardner. Besides these men, Gardner had the support of the American trappers whom he had led into Odgen's camp. By Ogden's own account only four men stood with him against the Americans, yet he and these four men prevented the Iroquois from taking horses which they, the Iroquois, thought of as their property, but on which, they knew, Hudson's Bay also had a claim. Some of this behavior must be attributed to shared values concerning rights of ownership, but just what rights is not obvious because of the way that Ogden reported events.

John McLoughlin would express anger at the *engagés* who did not help Ogden keep possession of the horses that the deserting freemen claimed. At least nine servants gave no support.[29] Because of "their behaviour . . . the Iroquois walked off with their Furs, Horses and traps, all of which were certainly our property," he wrote. "[T]he Engagees," he concluded, "evinced the most disgracefull, I might say, criminal, neglect of their Duty."[30] Just what McLoughlin expected the engaged servants to have done aside from assisting Ogden to retain property he had under his actual, physical possession, he did not say. By asserting that the furs, horses, and traps "were certainly our property," he implied that the men would have been justified going to Gardner's camp to recover what items had already been taken there. But since Ogden made no move to take back anything except a horse (which he sent McKay to retrieve), it is unlikely that McLoughlin was criticizing the men on that score.

Ogden, like McLoughlin, said that the horses and traps that the freemen had taken from his camp to Gardner's camp were company property. It was an easy assumption to make. Many of those who have written about the Ogden-Gardner incident have stated or implied that when Gardner admitted the horses and traps to his camp he received stolen goods. We will never be certain just what the freemen believed, but it is quite unlikely they thought they were embezzling Hudson's Bay property. They had good grounds for thinking of the horses as *theirs*, if not actually their property. It was not a significant factor that they had purchased the animals on credit and still owed the company for their purchase. They had been riding them since leaving Flathead Post, and they were responsible for them. Had a gun been fired inadvertently and killed a horse purchased by a freeman on credit from the company, we know that Ogden would have said that horse was the property of the freemen. Its death was his loss, not the company's. Every time a horse was lost, whether from drowning or being run off by Blackfeet, Ogden attributed the loss to the man possessing the animal. He did not on those occasions say that the horse was the company's property. It might be thought that Ogden adopted this attitude because ownership did not matter from his perspective. The freeman still owed Hudson's Bay for the dead horse and, except for the fact the company could no longer physically reclaim the animal, its financial position was little affected by conceding ownership. But when the members of the expedition were starving and freemen killed horses for food, Ogden credited the possessors of each slain horse with ownership of the meat because they had *owned* the horses killed. He did not say that he, as the partisan, had the right to make them share the food.[31]

If British legal principles were applied, it is evident that, against the freemen's sense that *they* owned the horses and traps they possessed, Ogden asserted a claim right, a sort of lien the company customarily exercised to secure its loans. It is reasonable, therefore, to conclude that both sides assumed they *owned* something, and, if so, that ownership justified the use of force, if necessary, to retain what was theirs.

It cannot be said just what McLoughlin or Ogden intended to claim, for it is unlikely that they gave the question any thought. McLoughlin said that the horses and traps (and also the furs) "were certainly our property," and that may be what he meant, that Hudson's Bay had exclusive property rights to the horses and traps (and even to the pelts). He would have been on firmer ground had he instead asserted that the company had a claim right to the goods stronger than the freeman's claim of ownership. It was stronger because the freemen were all in debt to the company for the horses and traps (and, it could be argued, that, by implication, the fur, as soon as trapped and brought to camp, was pledged to pay the debt). On the Weber River they attempted to take the furs, horses, and traps to Gardner, beyond the power of Hudson's Bay to secure its claims. That right to secure the debts did not transmute ownership from the freemen to the company, but it gave Hudson's Bay stronger grounds to assert its claim right and retain possession.

It is unlikely but still possible that when McLoughlin said the furs, horses, and traps "were certainly our property" he did not mean absolute ownership but a claim to a right because in the same paragraph he went on to insist that freemen debts had been voluntarily assumed. "[N]one of them were ever induced to Buy a single Article and . . . they are in Debt much against our will," he wrote, referring to himself and the other officers in the Columbia department, "and these advances had been made to oblige and accommodate them when at the time we ran the risk of loseing our property by their death, and in return if they did not murder Mr. Ogden and pillage him of the property in his possession it is not from want of a will."[32]

McLoughlin was wrong when he said the freemen insisted on borrowing against the company's will, and all the Hudson's Bay officers to whom he wrote knew he was wrong. The company was responsible for the financial predicament of the freemen, and soon even McLoughlin, by reforming the tariff of prices, would acknowledge that fact. He was right, however, that the freemen could have killed and pillaged Ogden. He says it was not from want of a will they held back, but in his surviving letters he never asked what restrained them.

McLoughlin may not have meant it, but he made a very relevant point when he said the freemen did not "pillage him of the property in his possession." It may be that the dominant concept that settled the issue of right that morning on Weber River was not debt, lien, contract, or ownership, but *possession*. Although he was overwhelmingly outnumbered, Odgen kept the horses that were in his camp, that is, the horses in his possession. The freemen kept the horses they had placed in Gardner's camp, that is, the horses that were in their possession. By Ogden's own account, neither group got more. They did not resort to force to get others, not even the ones they claimed were theirs. Instead they respected a rule of possession.

Accounts of the Ogden-Gardner confrontation generally do not consider concepts such as possession or even ask if there were any rules determining events. The assumption has been that, due to the threat of violence, Ogden had to allow the Americans to make off with everything that took their fancy. Yet, aside from the confrontation over the ten horses, the only mention of violence was when William Kittson reported that "we hear that the Americans and Iroquois are coming tomorrow to pillage us,"[33] and Ogden wrote of Lajoux's cocking and aiming his gun.[34] From this flimsy evidence, Frederick Merk concluded that the freemen "actually attempted in Gardner's heartening presence to pillage Ogden's camp." It might be possible to postulate different meanings to what Merk says, depending on what he intended by "attempted." No one, apparently, has asked. Instead, his assertion that the freemen, encouraged by the Americans, tried to pillage Hudson's Bay property, has set the tone for most interpretations of what occurred but not all. McLoughlin, hardly an impartial observer, reached a quite different conclusion about American actions. "[T]he Americans appear to me," he reported to London, "to have Given no assistance to our Deserters except countenancing and receiving them in their party.[35] Although Merk's thesis is somewhat defensible and has enjoyed the widest support, it is just as feasible to argue that the freemen did not attempt to pillage Ogden's camp and they were not encouraged by the Americans to do so.

Perhaps Merk concluded that the freemen attempted to pillage Ogden's camp because he believed they had already done so and what they had done once, they would attempt again. In other words, the horses, traps, and beaver skins that the freemen took with them to Gardner's camp were pillaged property. To conclude that actual possession was the criterion that settled how animals and traps were divided does not resolve the question of whether the freemen "stole" Hudson's Bay property. Rights of possession are not the same as rights of ownership. Both Merk and the company's governing committee in London use the same word, "spoliation," to describe what happened. In fact, many students of Snake country history and all the officers of Hudson's Bay have agreed that the delivery of seven hundred beaver skins to Gardner's camp by the freemen was an unlawful conversion of property. It is a conclusion too easily assumed.[36]

It is necessary to consider the question of ownership all over again. Hudson's Bay's claim to own the horses and traps the freemen transferred from Ogden's camp to Gardner's was not the same as its claim to own the beaver pelts. There is a difference in the facts that makes a difference in the applicable law. Hudson's Bay claim to the horses and traps arose from the fact that the freemen had purchased them on credit and still owed the purchase money to the company. Beaver pelts were different. They were trapped, not purchased. They were not obtained by credit.

From everything said in the letters that went back and forth from the Columbia to York Factory and company headquarters in London, it is evident that Hudson's Bay officers made no distinction between the horses and traps on one hand, and the pelts on the other. To them, taking beaver was the same as taking horses—both acts were stealing property belonging to Hudson's Bay, and Gardner was an accessory to the crime. All the factors and traders of the company understood what McLouglin meant when he wrote of "the Indignity of seeing people going off with our property." However, the matter of ownership may not have been as straightforward as McLoughlin and his colleagues assumed. McLoughlin inadvertently implied as much when he described items that "were certainly our property" as the property of the freemen ("their Furs, Horses and traps").[37] He was using a manner of expression common among Hudson's Bay officers, which may or may not indicate that they were not as certain as they claimed to be about who owned what. In one of his accounts of the affair on Weber River, Ogden referred to the beaver taken to Gardner's camp and which he never saw again as "our Furs," meaning the company's, and also as "their Furs," apparently meaning the freemen's, or, at least, fur in the freemen's possession.[38]

There is difficulty with the generally accepted view that Hudson's Bay was the owner of the horses and traps that the deserting freemen took with them. By the custom of the trade—established by frequent usage and freemen acquiescence—Hudson's Bay had a proprietary right of repossession that can best be described as a self-help version of a common-law creditor's lien. Ogden exercised that proprietary interest when he stopped the freemen from taking the horses that had not yet been removed from his camp. It is also possible that a custom of the trade restricted freemen from taking property in this category without Odgen's permission. If so, the company was stating valid legal doctrine when it said the freemen converted property belonging to it when they took horses and traps with them to Gardner's camp.

Against the likelihood such custom existed is the certainty that the company treated the freemen as the owners of the horses and traps purchased on credit for all purposes involving risks and loss. It is difficult to see why, except for trade custom, the freemen could not take the horses wherever they pleased as long as the debt was not due and as long as they intended to pay the debt. An obvious answer could be that the debt was due on demand. However, the evidence so far uncovered of Hudson's Bay practices indicate the debt was due when the expedition returned to its base on the Columbia. That, too, was a trade custom.

The best guess is that little thought was given to when debts were due. Debts were carried for so long by so many that, as far as the meager historical records indicate, payments were determined by opportunity. If any custom existed, it was probably that debts were due when the debtor returned to the base post with made beaver. After all, as the trapper could not lawfully sell to anyone but Hudson's Bay in most regions where the company operated, the company knew it would obtain whatever skins were trapped. The only other potential purchaser was a different freeman such as a hunter who sold surplus meat for beaver fur which he would resell to Hudson's Bay.[39] Indians did not buy beaver.

There is another consideration. Despite the way that Ogden interpreted events, it is not evident that the deserting freemen were repudiating their debts. A few twentieth-century observers have assumed that they were. "Most of them," a scholar has written of the freemen of the Columbia,

> were under obligation to the Company for equipment and supplies, but they were not a class to feel a strong moral tie and there was no tribunal in which a legal obligation could be enforced. The only obligation which they felt was to repay the advances, and they carried these obligations lightly. The fact that the advances by the Company had made possible the trip and the resultant catches, was a mere incident. Accordingly they felt no overpowering obligation to repay the debt by selling the furs taken on that expedition to the Company.[40]

That is a barely defensible assessment, yet there is reason to think that not all things on the Snake country were as obvious as they appear or as we would expect them to be. It is true that many of the freemen felt no obligation to sell to the company when they could obtain higher prices, but, except to the officers of Hudson's Bay, that was not the same as saying there was no moral or legal duty to repay, whether or not the debt was enforceable. In fact, evidence indicates that the freemen felt a duty to repay.

Two days before meeting Gardner, it will be recalled, Ogden's expedition had encountered two men who had deserted from Donald McKenzie's brigade of 1821. Kittson reported that one joined Ogden and the other said "he would pay his debt."[41] Both of these freemen were Iroquois, and on the morning before the mass desertions, when Ogden was having his first conversation with Gardner, the two met with Kittson to discuss what sums they owed to Hudson's Bay Company.[42] This conduct must have meant something, for had they intended to repudiate their debts, they could have told Kittson they were not paying, and there was little he or Ogden could have done. The same could be true for some or all of the men who later that day deserted the expedition and moved their lodges to Gardner's camp. It is sensible to assume they equated desertion with debt avoidance, but that conclusion could be mistaken. In fact, before leaving Ogden and joining the Americans, three of the twelve deserters paid their debts.[43]

Although McLoughlin and Governor Simpson both complained of the loss to the company of the seven hundred pelts taken to Gardner's camp and later sold to William H. Ashley, the loss was not as great as they claimed. Hudson's Bay did lose the substantial profits it would have made had it sold the furs on the London market, but that did not mean losing the debts those furs were supposed to secure. Over the next few years, various of the deserters repaid the company what they owed. The following year, for example, Ogden, on his second Snake country expedition, was near the American Falls when he was "surprised by the arrival of a Party of Americans and some of our deserters of last Year." He not only had the "satisfaction" of purchasing ninety-three beaver and seventy-two otter skins from the Americans at a favorable rate, but also settled accounts with at least three deserters. "[W]e received 81½ Beavers in part payment of their debts due to the Company also two notes of hand from Mr. Montour for his Balance [and from] Gabriel Prudhommes and Pierre Tevanitogans also we secured all the Skins they had."[44] There may have been extended pressure on these freemen to settle their accounts, propelled by their hope to return to the Columbia and work again for Hudson's Bay, or their desire to rejoin their families living near a Hudson's Bay trading post. But from the isolated, lonely location, the surrounding circumstances, and what Ogden says, the payments appear to have been voluntary.[45] That Ogden bothered to negotiate notes is evidence that he expected payment.

One of Ogden's freemen on that second expedition was the son of a trapper named Thiery Goddin who had deserted the year before. The son had also been a member of Ogden's first expedition and had refused to desert. Now he wanted to rejoin his father. Ogden "gave him his liberty . . . the Americans having advanced three Beaver Skins to make up the number." The father apparently paid nothing, but all was not lost. Over a year later, on his fourth Snake country expedition, Ogden met a large party of American mountain men, with whom he traded supplies for pelts. "I also received from Thiery Goddin thirty-five large beaver in payment of his debt with the Company. . . . [T]his is so much secured and more than I ever expected to have received from him."[46]

The company may not have lost everything even when deserters did not repay. On that fourth expedition, Ogden also ran into an American trapping party led by Robert Campbell, who told him that Old Pierre, one of the leaders of the Iroquois deserters, had been killed by Blackfeet, his body hacked to pieces. Old Pierre owed "a considerable debt to the concern," Ogden noted, "but as we have a mortgage on his property in Canada I am in hopes we shall recover it."[47]

The question still remains as to whether it is correct for scholars of the Snake country to say that the beaver the deserters took to Gardner's camp had been company property. The beaver, it must be emphasized, fell under a category of property different from the horses and traps. It had not been obtained on credit. Hudson's Bay Company could still claim the pelts, but it could not do so on the same debt theory that it claimed the horses and traps.

Hudson's Bay officers missed the distinction. They described the beaver taken to Gardner's camp as stolen property with the same terms used when they wrote of the horses and traps being stolen, as if the beaver was the property of the company in the same way the horses and traps were. Perhaps they were mistakenly drawing an analogy to Rupert's Land, where the company's legislative monopoly gave it the exclusive right to purchase beaver. That legislation did not give the company a property interest in the pelts that were trapped within its jurisdiction, for there was no legal obligation that trappers sell their fur to anyone. Moreover, the monopoly was limited to Rupert's Land and, perhaps, New Caledonia. If it applied at all in the Oregon country, it specifically did not prohibit freemen to buy from or sell to Americans, and did not restrict freemen who were American citizens—for example, some of the Iroquois—from doing business with whomever they wished.

Hudson's Bay officers, such as McLoughlin, who claimed that the company was the primary owner of the pelts that the freemen "stole" from Ogden and took to Gardner's camp, never stated the legal theory on which they based Hudson's Bay's claim. It would not have been a creditor's lien. The goods that had been furnished the freemen on credit were to be paid for by the beaver each freeman collected, but the company did not claim title from the moment the animals were caught in the freeman's traps. The theory could have been debt, however, as the freemen owed heavy debts to Hudson's Bay. But, if so, the same objection arose, for the company did not assert ownership at the moment the beaver was caught. Suppose a freeman had trapped three beavers downstream from the expedition's camp, and, as he was carrying them back to his tent to be skinned, was attacked by Piegans and the pelts taken from him. Ogden would not have said that the skins, when taken, had belonged to Hudson's Bay and reduced the trapper's debt by three beavers. It was not property belonging to the company that the company had lost. The trapper sustained the loss. The company considered the beaver his—to skin, to eat, or to lose.

Perhaps it is possible that, had the company thought about the matter and formulated an argument, it would have asserted that it had the same claim in the nature of a creditor's lien on the pelts that it had on the horses and traps. But, considering that the act of Parliament granting Hudson's Bay the privilege of operating on the western side of the Rocky Mountains south of New Caledonia had provided that American rights were not affected by the grant, it is possible that the company was not authorized to prohibit private trading with the mountain men for whom Gardner purported to speak. The company could have had an understanding with the freemen that if they joined a Snake country expedition they had to sell it the pelts they trapped, but if the pelts belonged to the freemen the legislation preserving American rights might preclude an implied contract not to sell to Americans, as such a contract would have interfered with the American right to purchase.

Any claim to a lien on the horses and traps that Hudson's Bay owned was proportionally stronger if the deserters were not only absconding, but did so intending never to pay their debts. That was even more true for Hudson's Bay's claim to the beaver trapped by freemen. If there was any lien at all on the trapped fur, it had to be based on the company's need to protect itself from debtors practicing debt avoidance. But then, the opposite extreme ought to establish an opposite right. If the deserting freemen intended to repay, then sale of their beaver skins at the prices Gardner quoted would put them in a much stronger financial position, making it more likely they could repay. Gardner, after all, had told the freemen that St. Louis traders would pay them more than eight times what Hudson's Bay would give.

The freemen of the Columbia had found in the promises of Johnson Gardner more than the competitive market for which they had been searching ever since they first began trapping the Snake country. Through him, they obtained even more than the freedom of trade that John Grey said the Iroquois had been after for at least five years. The prices promised were so much higher than they had been receiving, and costs of goods might possibly be so much lower than they had been paying, that it took no rationalizing to conclude that Hudson's Bay had been treating them so shamefully, they had every right to desert the expedition. The prices demonstrated what Gardner and Grey meant when they told Ogden that the company treated freemen as slaves, and what a later historian meant when he said they had been in "a virtual state of servitude."[48] As Ogden was told by one of the deserters, "go we will where we shall be paid for our Furs & not be imposed & cheated as we are in the Columbia."[49] The grievance alone created the right to desert.

CHAPTER ELEVEN

They Are Now to Be Found in All Parts of the Snake Country

Ogden had to retreat. There were two reasons why he had to return up the Bear River to the Snake, backtracking over the route he had just traveled. The first was because, as he put it, the expedition was "Surrounded on all Sides by enemies." Even if he thought there was a chance to recover any of the property that the freemen had taken with them, and which he believed was property of the company, it would have been foolhardy to have stayed even half a day. Again, it would be best to ask what it was that Ogden feared. It was not American violence that drove him away, it was American money. "[T]o remain in this quarter any longer it would merely be to trap beaver for the Americans," he explained the day after he had confronted Gardner in John Grey's lodge. "I Seriously apprehend there are Still more of the Trappers who would Willing join them indeed the tempting offers made them independant the low price they Sell their goods are too great for them to resist & altho' I represented to them all these offers were held out to them as so many baits   Still it is without effect."[1]

Ogden had a second and even more persuasive reason to retreat—he could not go forward. His plan, once he had traveled the length of the Bear, had been "to take a West course with the hopes both of finding Beaver and discovering the Umpqua River."[2] Ever since realizing that the Bear was an independent water system and did not empty into the Colorado, he had known the expedition would not be trapping on the Colorado and, perhaps, would not locate the headwaters of the Sacramento, but he still expected to explore and open a new road to the Columbia by finding a route via the Umpqua. No such way existed, of course, for the Umpqua was far to the west, beyond a coastal mountain range, and had Ogden tried to find it he would have encountered great hardship and might have covered distances he did not wish to travel. But that was one reason he had come to the Bear: to map the geography of the region and let headquarters know in what directions rivers flowed to and from beaver. Although that was a prime purpose of the expedition, and he preferred exploring to every other task connected with the fur trade, it was too dangerous for him to head west. Disappointed as he may have been, Ogden simply did not have enough men to explore the unknown. "I have now no other alternative left," he explained, "but direct my Course towards of Salmon River without loss of time, to follow up my Second intentions in proceeding by the Walla Walla *route* is now in a manner rendered impracticable as our numbers are by far too few."[3]

Ogden's meaning is not clear. He seems to be saying that just as he was unable to return to the Columbia at Fort Vancouver, because he had too few men to go in search of the headwaters of the Umpqua or the Willamette, he also could not go in by way of Fort Nez Perces. That left only Spokane House and Flathead Post. As he was heading for the Lemhi drainage, which he referred to as the Salmon, it seems evident he meant to end the trip at Flathead Post, the last place that he wanted to go.

It may be that Ogden had no choice but to head for Flathead Post. He had lost twenty-three men and had less than that number left. So few remained that he was dependent on each of them. In fact, his need of them may have given the freemen as much voice in decisions as he had. At least they had a veto. Unable to proceed without them, Ogden had to bow to the demands of his men as he never would again on any of his remaining trips to the Snake country. He did not dare let the party divide and, if the freemen would not follow him, he had to go where they wanted. "[N]early half the Trappers are determined to return to Fort des Prairies," he noted, meaning that they wanted to go to Edmonton House on the North Saskatchewan River. "[I]f we divide again neither party would ever Stand a chance of reaching the Columbia." What could he do? "[T]here is now No alternative," he concluded,

"I must bend & Submit to the will of the party." That is why he headed for the Flatheads rather than the Walla Walla.[4]

The freemen surely believed that it would be easier to go to Edmonton House from Flathead Post than from either Fort Nez Perces or Spokane House. From the Flatheads they could head directly north to the Columbia via the Kootenay River, cross by Howse Pass to Rocky Mountain House, and go down the Saskatchewan to Edmonton House. Whether these men would have dared separate from Ogden so close to Blackfoot country and strike out on their own to Flathead Post is unlikely. Yet what can we assume but that Ogden felt he could take no chances? He had to go to Flathead Post.

For some reason Ogden believed he had to justify disobeying orders. At least he told Simpson that, had he opened new routes to the Columbia, the Americans would have followed. Even if he had had enough men for a trek west to search out the Umpaqua, he pleaded, "I am not of opinion it would have been good policy in me to have open'd a short cut for the Americans to Fort George, we have done enough and suffered also without increasing the load."[5] It was a lame excuse in a situation that needed no excuses. Had the freemen not deserted, we can be certain Ogden would have headed west into unknown regions, looking for the Buenaventura and the Umpqua. If he had enough trappers to strip the streams clean of beaver, he would not have given a second thought to opening paths for Americans. He knew they could find the way on their own. He was more convincing when saying the Americans were the reason he fled the Weber immediately, not waiting to see if any of the deserters changed their minds.

The day started when five more freemen, none of whom were Iroquois, told Kittson they were deserting. One, Nicholas Montour, had been a clerk with the North West Company, and was treated with the respect due an officer, called "Mister" by Kittson, Ogden, and McLoughlin. He asked to see his account. "I showed him the ammount of Debt due by him to the Company," Kittson reported, "he then said to Mr. Ogden, I have about £289 in the Companys hands for which they seem not to give me Interest, let them now keep it altogether for my Debt and that of Prudhomme's." Gabriel Prudhomme was one of the four men deserting that morning with Montour. "I endeavoured to reason with Mr. Montour but all in vain," Ogden wrote. Montour repeated that "the

Company turned me out of doors and have £260 of my money in their hands, which they intend to defraud me of, as they have refused to give me Interest for, but they may keep it now for my debt and Prudhommes which we have contracted in the Columbia."[6]

Montour was expressing a grievance when saying "the Company turned me out." He probably meant that when the two companies merged in 1821 he had not been retained as an officer. He had been relegated to the status of freeman. Again, however, the probative fact for us is that a deserting freeman voluntarily undertook to pay at least two debts. Montour did not desert in order to avoid his obligations to Hudson's Bay, nor, apparently, did Prudhomme. In fact, unless he had been accumulating enormous debts during the past four years, Montour seems to have been giving up more money than he could possibly owe. It is almost certain he had not recently acquired new debts. McLoughlin agreed with him that when the North West Company merged with Hudson's Bay, and Montour "went free," the new company had continued to hold in his name a large sum, and during the four years since, he had deposited even more money into his account.[7] We can not be certain, however. Within a year, Montour and Ogden met on the Snake River, and Montour gave Hudson's Bay a note covering his remaining debts. The implication is that the money on deposit had not been sufficient to pay what both men owed when they deserted. Of course, it could have been enough to pay Montour's debts, but not pay both men's. The note could have been to cover the difference.[8]

That a freeman was willing to lose so much is striking evidence of how much better he expected his situation to be trapping for American prices. Montour surely thought both he and Prudhomme would do so well that he could afford to lose the money he was leaving behind. Then, again, he may have been so upset at how Hudson's Bay had treated him that he just wanted to get away. In any event, the gamble paid off handsomely. In less than a year Montour wrote an officer of the Hudson's Bay "that since he has been with the Americans that he has made 2000 Dollars by his hunts," adding that after one more hunt or season "he will be able to retire from the Indian Territories."[9]

Ogden noticed none of Montour's personal grievances and economic complaints. Again, what he saw were American menaces and suggestions of violence. All he reported was that Montour and Prudhomme "were immediately surrounded by the Americans who assisted them in loading, and like all villains appeared to exult in their villainy." Kittson better understood why the two men were deserting. "It was of no use in us to argue or point out their foolishness," he explained, "go they must."[10]

It was at this time, when Ogden was leaving, that Gardner made the threat which would anger McLoughlin so much that he would consider sending a retaliatory expedition to the vicinity of the Bear and Weber Rivers. "[O]n my mounting my Horse," Ogden wrote that day, "Gardner Came forward & Said you will See us shortly not only in the Columbia but at the Flat Heads & Cootanies as we are determined you Shall no longer remain in our Territory." Ogden answered that Hudson's Bay would abandon the Oregon country only when ordered by the British government. "[I]n answer to this he said our Troops will reach the Columbia this Fall and make you, we then separated." The last boast should have told McLoughlin that Gardner was a vainglorious braggart who spoke for no one but himself. In 1825, American troops would have had a difficult time getting by the great bend of the Missouri River, let alone to the Columbia.[11]

"We are now ready to start though our party is now small still I have a hope of its reaching the Point of Destination without danger, although we were again to loose men," Kittson wrote with evident apprehension. "I kept behind all day through Mr. Ogdens orders, fearing that more would leave us on the road." The brigade was too small as it was, but there were five or six trappers still absent, and Ogden could not take chances. Although he did not say so, it is possible Kittson was told to use force to stop more desertions even if the men did not try to take property with them.[12]

Late that night two of the missing men arrived and told Ogden he would not be getting their beaver.

> By their accounts as they were on their return to the Camp yesterday they fell in with an American party from 30 to 40 men as they Say Troops, who on Seeing them Called to them to advance which they did, their traps 15 in number   16 Beaver & their two Horses were taken from them they were then told if they would remain with them & not return & Join me their property would be restored to them otherwise not,   they were Strictly guarded

during the day & while in the act of changing Watches about mid-
night last night they effected their escape leaving all behind them.

Ogden did not believe the story. He suspected the men had sold their
beaver to the Americans and had returned to the expedition because
both had wives and horses in the camp. "[P]erhaps they will now Watch
an opportunity to return   if they do which they Can easily effect without their Furs both day & night   we shall however watch them." Kittson had no doubts. "All well told," he observed, "but I thought it lies."
He rode "all day behind watching the movements of several suspicious
fellows who lurked in the rear of the party." Next day both he and
Thomas McKay, the interpreter, kept "watch behind." That night Ogden
was depressed. "Our Camp is now dull & gloomy," he told his journal.[13]

"We Strongly suspect this morning that a party is forming to desert,"
Ogden noted in his next entry, "this they Can easily effect at any time
but with their Furs not conveniently." He was right. Kittson kept a sharp
eye in the rear. "On our way three more villains were looking out for
an opportunity to desert with their furs but were too well watched," he
wrote. By next morning two of the three decided that by the time they
could escape with the beaver, horses, and traps that they wanted to
take, it would be too late to get back to the Americans. "Two of the
Canadian Freemen gave up their furs, Traps and a couple of horses
and said to Mr. Ogden they would go back to join the rest of the villains that left us, and as it was in vain for us to stop them, they seperated." Again, it should be marked that one of the men "paid up his debt."
The other man had "still a balance against him." Later an Iroquois
slipped by Kittson. "He took nothing with him but his riding horse. Left
wife and furs behind."[14]

Ogden was beginning to appreciate why the trappers were deserting
Hudson's Bay. "Three men deserted," he noted that evening, "leaving
all behind them Women, Children, Horses, Traps & Furs so greatly are
they prepossessed in favor of the Americans that they sacrificed all to
join them." He could not afford to lose more. Although still several days
away from reaching the Snake River, he was in an area where Blackfoot
war parties had been seen earlier in the month. "I cannot make too
great progress," he complained, "otherwise I apprehend many more
will leave us,   our Numbers are now So few that if any war party

Comes across us we shall Stand a poor chance of escaping." He meant "any war party," not just Piegan or other Blackfoot, but also Nez Perce and Snake, any except Flathead and Kootenai. No more men would desert, however, and almost every day, despite the danger, the little brigade set traps and skinned beaver.[15]

After reaching Snake River, Ogden was irritated when two Flatheads told him "many wonderful accounts" of the Americans "which they have received from the Peagans." They also reported an encampment of their nation on Henry's Fork, where there were letters for him. As he had just had a Blackfoot scare, he decided to go there immediately. "I was glad to learn the Flat Heads were at Henry's Forks," he observed, "as that quarter is I believe still rich in beaver but being the general rendezvouz of all the War Tribes & our party being weak I did not dare attempt going in that direction, but Shall now loose no time in reaching it as we Shall have the Flat Heads to protect us, & if no American trappers have been there since our party was last there in 1823 I am in hopes we Shall find Beaver." He was referring to the Snake country expedition that had been led by Finan McDonald, and his notes told him that the brigade had found Henry's Fork rich in beaver, but had taken only three hundred skins before it had been attacked by Blackfeet. That was when Michel Bourdon, who had been the leader of the 1822 expedition the year before, and five trappers had been killed. McDonald had fled the area and, as far as Ogden knew, no one had trapped the river since. "[W]e have Still Some hopes the Season will not be entirely lost," he wrote, expressing his first optimism in two weeks, "but what will we have compared to the Hunt we Should have made if those Villains had not deserted us."[16]

Next morning, "as we were on the eve of Starting" for Henry's Fork, Ogden was alarmed to discover that "5 of the Half Breeds were on the eve of Starting to go in quest of the lower Snakes to Steal Horses." A similar raid for horses had occurred the year before. Freemen from the expedition led by Alexander Ross had raided a Snake camp for horses, some Snakes had been killed, and eight members of the American trapping party led by Etienne Provost had paid the blood price when Snakes killed them in retaliation. It took Ogden or Kittson some time, "but after considerable pe[r]suasion [the five men] were at length diverted from their object."[17]

That horse raid of the year before and the abortive raid that Ogden prevented in 1825 provide a measure of how rapidly international contact between the British and Americans was altered from commercial competition into common risk and shared liability as American parties began to move with more frequency into the Oregon country. No other events so dramatically illustrate how interdependent the British and Americans were in the Snake country. The safety of one nationality was linked to the conduct of the other. The raid by Ross's men of the year before cost American lives. Had Ogden not stopped this raid other Americans—or British or Canadians—might have had to pay a blood price.[18]

Henry's Fork was not so rich in beaver as Ogden had hoped. "[O]ur time was not entirely lost," however, "and the Flatheads were also following our example." He meant that the Flatheads were catching beaver and the reason his time on Henry's Fork was not entirely lost was that he knew any animals they trapped he would be able to purchase. "[B]ut scarcely ten days elapsed when 5 Tents of Americans containing from 30 to 40 Men were discovered, they were coming down the same River we were trapping." Not too surprisingly, the area was also infested with Piegans. They were, however, not war parties but horse raiders, and not too well armed at that. One band of thirty that Ogden met had only four guns, and, as a result, the expedition encountered no trouble from them. In fact, they were so amiable that Ogden traded with them. Selling tobacco and beads, he obtained one hundred twelve beaver and three horses. But no matter how much beaver they had to sell, there were some prices he would not pay. "[T]hey made many & repeated demands for ammunition but all in Vain"; he would not let them have any. "[W]e have already too many enemies in this quarter," he explained, "too well provided in arms & ammunition without adding to the quantity." In fact, he claimed he should not have traded with them even for tobacco, "but I apprehend their Furs would Soon find their way to the American Camp, so eager were they to obtain tobacco." Competition against the Americans was beginning to determine more and more decisions in the Snake country.[19]

Ogden then abandoned Henry's Fork. It was a revealing turn of events, showing how rapidly circumstances could change in the Snake country. It was not the numerous Piegan bands and the threat of attack that drove Ogden to abandon the rich beaver hunts on Henry's Fork as they had forced Finan McDonald to flee just two years before. It was the Americans and the threat of economic competition. "[K]nowing too well from dear bought experience the loss I should sustain if the Freemen were once more to meet with them and the tempting offers they would make the Flatheads I resolved on leaving" Henry's Fork.[20] He then turned east, looking for the pass through the Rocky Mountains that would take him to the drainage of the Missouri.

By now Ogden had had much time for reflection and realized that the economics of the Hudson's Bay Company's operations west of the Rockies were changed forever by the laws of competition. Back in American territory, on the headwaters of the Missouri, and on his way to Flathead Post, he had a chance to send a letter to Governor Simpson and the other officers of the honorable company. "You need not anticipate another expedition [in the] ensuing Year to this Country," he warned, "for not a freeman will return, and should they, it would be to join the Americans,   there is Gentlemen a wide difference with their prices and ours, they have opened a communication with waggons over land from St. Louis to the first Spanish Settlement call'd Taa's where they fit out their Trappers and receive their Furs in return and they say they intend reaching the Columbia also with Waggons, not impossible so far as I have seen."[21]

Ogden had been talking with Jedediah Smith, Etienne Provost, John H. Weber, and probably other American trappers. He realized what beaver trails they were following, he had been told the plans of William H. Ashley, and he could see the future. He even foresaw the Oregon Trail and envisioned that wagons could roll all the way from the lower Missouri to the Columbia. He could not yet realize that those wagons would spell the end of British rule south of New Caledonia. He thought the real threat to Hudson's Bay was from American prices. He also may not have understood how rapidly events were moving, which was very fast indeed. The monopoly that Parliament granted the company would last in the Oregon country but half a decade.

The Oregon Trail meant the end of British control of the Columbia River country, but in 1825 it lay in the future. The event that was to spell the end for Hudson's Bay's monopoly in the Snake country was just starting to occur at the time Ogden had crossed Monida Pass in the Continental Divide and had entered United States territory. It was the great American fur rendezvous inaugurated that summer by William H. Ashley. Ashley had transported trade goods by river boat from St. Louis to the Platte, and then by pack horse and wagons across the plains and over the mountains. On the day when Ogden encountered a band of Piegans who made Snake country history by saying they wanted to trade rather than fight, Ashley was traveling near Echo Canyon in today's Utah. When he learned "that Johnson Guardner—& party of whom we are now in se[a]rch had ascended the small river," he changed directions and went after them. Ashley had heard of what had happened on Weber River and, knowing the deserters were with Gardner, wanted to buy the seven hundred pelts the deserters were said to have.[22] He made contact and the freemen had at last found the market they had so long sought.[23]

The first rendezvous was conducted on Camas Prairie in present-day Summit County, Utah. "On the 1st day of July," Ashley explained, "all the men in my employ or with whom I had any concern in the Country, together with twenty nine who had recently withdrawn from the Hudson Bay Company, making in all 120 men, were assembled in two camps near each other."[24] The Canadian freemen sold the pelts that they had trapped with Ogden's Snake country expedition and William H. Ashley earned the scorn of Governor Simpson and other officers of Hudson's Bay.[25] They exaggerated his profits, saying he had carried back to St. Louis up to six thousand beaver skins worth from $75,000 to $200,000. They actually were worth $45,000 to $50,000 in St. Louis, more than enough to ensure Ashley's fortune. What Hudson's Bay found galling was that several thousand of those dollars were earned from pelts that the company's officers in the Columbia department thought they should be shipping to London.[26]

Ogden, of course, agreed with Simpson that Ashley had knowingly purchased stolen property. Still, he could not help but admire Ashley for his remarkable enterprise, the annual gathering of fur trappers west of the Rockies known as the rendezvous. By creating the rendezvous, Ogden believed, Ashley had brought an unprecedented level of prosperity to American mountain men. It was true that the goods purchased there were not as cheap as Hudson's Bay officials had feared. They were sold "at least 150 per cent dearer than we do, but again they have the advantage of receiving them on the waters of the Snake Country, and an American trapper, from the short distance he has to travel, not obliged to transport provisions, requires only half the number of horses we do, and are also very moderate in their advances."[27] The rendezvous threatened to do more than reduce most of the costs of American fur trappers. It possibly meant Hudson's Bay would never match American prices.

> In all the different expeditions to the Snake Country two thirds of the time is lost in travelling to and from headquarters, far different is the mode the Americans conduct their trapping expeditions,   their trappers remain five and six years in their hunting grounds and their equippers meet them annually secure their furs and give them their supplies and although great the expence and danger they have to conduct their business in this way, and surely there is a wide difference in the prices they pay for their Furs and sell their Goods compared to us a difference of 200 PC.[28]

By 1828, Ogden's comparisons would become personal, after he learned that Ashley had sold the rendezvous business to three men whom he knew: Jedediah Smith, whose prosperity apparently surprised Ogden, William Sublette, who had been a member of Smith's trapping party that had traveled with Ogden from Flathead Post to the Snake River; and David E. Jackson, whom Ogden would soon meet in the Snake country. As he thought about their good fortune the comparison between him and the three young Americans became painful.

> For three years . . . General Ashl[e]y transported supplies to this country and in that period has cleared eighty thousand dollars and retired, selling the remainder of his goods on hand at an advance of 150 per cent payable in five years in beaver at five dollars per lb or in cash optional with the purchasers. Three young men, Smith, Jackson and Soblitz [Sublette] purchased them, and who have the first year made a gain of twenty thousand dollars. It is to be observed, finding themselves alone [*i.e.,* without competition at the rendezvous], they sold their goods one third dearer than Ashley did, but have held out a promise of a reduction in their prices this year.

The unrestrained free movements of the American competition were the envy of many Hudson's Bay officers. Probably on no other did the comparison hang more heavily than on Peter Skene Ogden. "What a contrast between these young men and myself," he complained. "They have been only six years in the country, and without doubt in as many more will be independent men."[29]

Ogden's party was already too small to travel with safety in the Snake country, yet in the middle of July he divided it another time. He had recrossed the Continental Divide from east to west through Gibbon Pass. The brigade was not out of danger but at least was on the other side of the mountains, moving away from Blackfoot country. He had somehow overcome the freemen's opposition and planned to return to the Columbia at Fort Nez Perces. But in the meanwhile, the company had set in motion plans to receive the pelts at Flathead Post, from whence they were to be transported to Fort Vancouver via Spokane House. He had no choice but to send his packs of furs to the Flatheads. That was why Ogden separated from Kittson, who would take the beaver to Flathead Post and eventually to the Spokanes. As there was a party of Flatheads returning home from hunting buffalo, Kittson had their escort and needed to take with him only two men to handle the packs. Still, three men were a serious loss for Ogden because he had to return to the Snake River and faced a three-and-a-half months' trip before arriving on the Walla Walla. Kittson was worried. "Early this morning I seperated with a sorrowful heart from Mr. Ogden," he wrote that day in his journal, "knowing him to be placed in a dangerous Country and most of his freemen ready to leave him at the first opportunity, however as I had to proceed I left him and began my journey homewards . . . , having with me the charge of 18 horses loaded with Furs."[30]

It took Kittson two weeks to reach the Flatheads and a month to deliver his cargo at Spokane House. "[N]ow that the furs are safely stored at this place," he wrote, "I make an end of my journal with an idea of having filled many sheets of paper with the troubles, vexations, and loss of an unfortunate Expedition, but bearing in mind that had we had good and honest men with us, this self same Snake Expedition would have turned out double the thousands of Beaver, to that of any other Expedition hitherto made in the Country. I think if the party had consisted of Canadians and no Iroquois we would have succeeded in the enterprise."[31] Kittson's last thoughts deserve scrutiny. Like Ogden and most other Hudson's Bay officers, he just did not understand why the freemen had deserted.

The expedition had actually done well. Ogden had not gotten the six thousand skins he had expected, but Kittson had brought to Spokane House 2,485 large and 1,210 small beaver, which McLoughlin estimated would bring a profit of £2000. He called the returns "very handsome," and they were, in fact, handsome enough to persuade both him and Simpson to continue sending expeditions to the Snake country.[32]

Peter Skene Ogden was less optimistic. There was beaver to be trapped in the Snake country, true enough, and there was plenty of it. But so were there plenty of Americans. Most depressing to him, he had just left the richest beaver country he had ever seen, and he knew the Americans would soon be there.

> [I]t was in the vicinity of Maria[s] River a fork of the Missouri . . . and it is on the said River that the Americans have it in contemplation to make an establishment and if strong enough to cope with [the] War Tribes of the Sascatchewan is the most suitable spot they could have selected   and if carried into effect we shall soon loose our Flathead & Cootany trade if we loose nothing more we may deem ourselfes lucky,   but from the high opinion they entertain of our success in the Columbia, we may apprehend a visit from them ere long, they are now by parties to be found in all parts of the Snake country,   from what I could learn there are three different Fur Companys . . . who offer and give as high as three to three and a half dollar p. lb. for the most indifferent Beaver and goods at a trifling value   independent of their wishes our freemen could not resist such tempting terms compared to ours.[33]

Ogden surely felt he was facing a relentless tide. Perhaps it could not be stopped, but he was ready to return to the Snake country and try.

CHAPTER TWELVE

The Cheapest Shop Will Carry the Day

At first, Governor George Simpson and Chief Factor John McLoughlin misinterpreted the importance of the deserters on Weber River. Their mistake was that they evaluated the Ogden-Gardner confrontation as they did every event, in terms of the costs to the company. John McLoughlin thought only of loss and villainy. "I certainly was very much disappointed when I learned the disasters we suffered in the Snakes," he told Hudson's Bay's chief North American officers. "[I]t was impossible to take more pains in every way to insure their [the freemen] getting their Supplies in due time, to enable them to hunt, and all these precautions and care are blasted by the Villany of these rascals. . . . [B]y the desertion of these Men we will loose Furs to the amount of about Three thousand pounds and their future Services." Governor Simpson estimated that Hudson's Bay had lost £600 by not collecting the freemen's debts. McLoughlin thought of loss more in terms of the beaver pelts that Ogden had been unable to bring back and that he would not trap in the future.

> By the desertion of these men the Concern has lost between two and three thousand Skins in furs and their future services, add to this the loss they caused by disabling the Remainder from going to where they intended and finally if the Saskatchewan freemen have determined on abandoning this side of the Mountains we

may say the desertion of these men will prevent our getting four thousand Skins annually from that part of the Country.[1]

By "Saskatchewan freemen" McLoughlin was referring to the trappers who had wanted Ogden to return via Flathead Post so that they could more easily cross to the east side of the mountains at Rocky Mountain House and go down the Saskatchewan to Edmonton House. He seems to be saying that if they had gone east, he might have had to abandon the Snake country expeditions. Earlier than most of his colleagues, he had come to realize the freemen were not just a nuisance to the company, they were needed if Hudson's Bay was to denude the Snake country.

At first, McLoughlin thought any difficulties could be solved by tossing a small sop to the men. Expecting that Snake country expeditions would be starting from Fort Nez Perces, he proposed that freemen purchase their supplies there at the lower prices charged at Fort Vancouver. Those prices, he hoped, might keep them from returning to the Saskatchewan or deserting to the Americans. Or, as he explained the plan, he would "offer them their Supplies at Walla Walla at the same price as if they took them here [Fort Vancouver] to induce them to remain on this side of the Mountains to hunt on the South side of the Columbia."[2]

The benefits for the freemen could not have amounted to much. The reason for the differences in prices was that supplies sold at Fort Vancouver came directly off the ships transporting manufactured goods from London. What was sold at Fort Nez Perces had to be carried by canoe from the lower Columbia to the Walla Walla River. Transportation added something to the costs, but whether a substantial amount is not revealed by available evidence. Of course, Columbia freemen had so little money, any reduction in costs had to help them.

McLoughlin simply had not understood the problem. He admitted as much two years after he discovered "that the High price charged for the Supplies was the cause of the difficulties." He even had an explanation. Although "we heard that they were complaining," he said of the freemen, "still we never had information before us to Enable us to Judge of the Costs of the Snake furs till I made out the Accounts." That statement sounds farfetched, but McLoughlin had an excuse. "It may be asked but why was not this looked into when Governor Simpson was in the Columbia," he wrote. "To this I beg to observe that the Snake Expedition account was so blended with that of Spokan[e], that unless a person had been on the Spot, it was impossible to make the two accounts out and it was only in the Spring of 1825 after we had received by the Brigade the necessary documents that we were able to make an approximation to the cost of a made Beaver from the Snakes, and M^r. Ogdens returns [of] fall 1825 are the first on which we could ascertain the costs of a made Beaver."[3]

When McLoughlin finally studied the accounts, they proved both surprising to him and, he implied, disturbing. "I send you the Tariffe the Freemen hitherto paid for their Supplies and the price allowed them for their furs," he wrote London headquarters. "[S]everal have killed a hundred and fifty made Beaver and this was not sufficient to pay [for] their Hunting supplies and their Losses in Horses and traps stolen by the Natives."[4] To say that a freeman trapping 150 beaver on an expedition could not pay his debts for the year, was the same as admitting that no freeman would ever work himself free of debt. Ogden came to that conclusion while out in the field on his second Snake country expedition. He had been thinking about the desertions on the Weber and, like McLoughlin, had finally realized that the company was as much to blame as the Iroquois.

> [F]rom the exorbitant price the Trappers paid for their Goods and horses is solely to be attributed their desertion and former misconduct, indeed from the enormous prices they have been charged with, the difficulties they had to encounter and subject to so many losses, it was almost impossible however industrious a Man might be to clear his annual expences, in fact his four horses and traps alone cost him One hundred fifty Large Beaver, nor could he depend on the latter for the year as they [the traps] have been of late years of an inferior quality, and seldom could a Trapper return to the depot without being obliged to renew both and the former at an advanced price.[5]

It was a remarkable reversal of attitudes. From placing all the blame for the desertions on the dishonesty and treachery of the freemen, Ogden told his fellow Hudson's Bay officers that the desertions were "solely to be attributed" to exorbitant prices. Moreover, he now understood that no trapper could repay his debts. No one could trap enough beaver to repay the costs of four horses and six traps.

After studying the figures for Ogden's expedition, McLoughlin found that the cost of a made beaver had been ten shillings and twopence halfpenny. More revealing, only two shillings of that amount represented the value of the goods received by the freemen. The balance of the cost, he concluded, had been "caused by losses incurred by desertion and by expences in sending clerks and servants to watch over" the freemen, referring to William Kittson, Thomas McKay, and the *engagés*.[6] There were two conclusions: the freemen had very good financial reasons for being discontented with Hudson's Bay and their discontent was costly to the company. As long as they remained dissatisfied and hostile, it would be unreasonably expensive to denude the Snake country and compete against the Americans. "[T]o charge such High prices was certainly most mistaken policy," he summed up in a letter to London, "as we had only a precarious tenure of the Country and we ought therefore to have allowed the trappers [to] have their supplies at as low a price as possible so as to get while in our power all the furs we could out of it." Over four months earlier, using some of the same words, he had made the same argument to Simpson. "[T]o have put so high a price on the supplies to these Freemen when this expedition was set a going was certainly bad policy as we always have held a precarious tenure of that part of the Country and the Natives will not hunt Beaver, and it is well known all the difficulties, disappointments and losses this Expedition has suffered have been caused by the high price the Trappers paid for their Supplies."[7]

McLoughlin's understanding had turned full circle. When Simpson had visited the Columbia in 1826, he had asked the cause of the freemen's "misconduct." McLoughlin had told him that "it proceeded from their bad disposition." Now, after a year and a half of looking at accounts, he had a new perspective. It had been enormous debts that drove the freemen to desert and, he realized, the debts were the result of company policy, not the fault of the freemen.[8]

McLoughlin thought the difficulty easily solved. Of course the company had to raise a bit the price paid for beaver but, more importantly, it should lower the cost of goods sold the men. The Americans could continue to pay more for beaver pelts than could Hudson's Bay, but that advantage was somewhat offset by higher American charges for supplies. It did not take Fort Vancouver long to discover that the company could generally undersell the Americans. That was because of the costs of transporting merchandise to the rendezvous. Hudson's Bay's products came to the Columbia by sea—relatively cheap freight compared with horse caravans out of St. Louis that had to pass through Pawnee country to get to the gathering of the American trappers on either side of the mountains.

The solution seemed so sensible and so urgent that McLoughlin acted on his own authority, telling his superiors that the reforms would be implemented before they had time to receive and reply to his report. "As it is certain if the Americans fall in with our party," he wrote, "Unless we give more for Beaver than we have hitherto our people will desert us. We therefore have agreed to give them 10/- for Every full Grown Beaver—half this amount for a cub and to allow them [to] purchase personal necessaries according to their abilities and means of from ten to fifteen pounds at European servants prices and hunting Implements at Inventory prices."[9]

"[T]he measure adopted," McLoughlin assured London headquarters, "will be beneficial to the Concern, as the High prices charged the Freemen and trappers for their supplies . . . drove our people to desert from us and to work for others whom they are now Guiding to Countries Rich in Beaver and in opposition to us." As he told Simpson, it was "certainly much better [and] much more effectual to allow the expences we are obliged to incurr at once to the Hunter, it secures their fidelity[,] equips them more completely and stimulates them to exert themselves."[10]

> In anticipation of your approval I have promised the Freemen 10s. for every large Beaver and half that sum for a cub and I beg to observe as I said in my letter to the Honble. Committee that I consider the measure will be advantageous to the concern, and if we wished to retain these Men we had no alternative left.

So the point would not be missed, he reminded Simpson of the Americans. "If we have to compete for the trade the cheapest Shop will ultimately carry the day."[11]

Simpson agreed. "We now when too late perceive that our former system of trade with those people was bad," he wrote of the freemen.[12] Happily the problem could be corrected without much cost. In fact, he hoped, it would be no more expensive than the previous system. "The Expence will be a mere triffle as the Men are on the spot, they will have no Wages or if any merely nominal, . . . and their pay will be the price we shall give for their Skins which must be liberal or nominally high in order to sound as well as that offered by the Americans, but their supplies will of course be charged at prices to be regulated by the prices given for their Skins."[13] "We therefore entreat," he instructed McLoughlin, "that no exertions be spared to explore and Trap every part of the country and as the service is both dangerous and laborious we wish our people to be treated with kindness and liberality, and such prices given for hunts as will afford them a fair remuneration for their services and their supplies sold on such terms as would convince them that by desertion they would seriously injure their own interests."[14]

London headquarters endorsed both policies. It was even more willing than Simpson to pay whatever price necessary to denude the Snake country and drive the Americans back across the Rockies. "We can afford to pay as good a price as the Americans," the London governor and committee assured Simpson, "and where there is risk of meeting their parties it is necessary to pay as much or something more to avoid the risk of a result similar to that of Mr. Ogden. By attempting to make such expeditions too profitable the whole may be lost and it is extremely desirable to hunt as bare as possible all the Country South of the Columbia and West of the Mountains."[15]

Claiming that he was writing of the spring of 1826—a time when Ogden had been out on his second Snake country expedition and before the reformed system of prices had had a chance to be tested in the field—McLoughlin announced that it was a success.

> Mr. Ogden saw most of these Deserters and on their hearing the terms our Servants had for their furs and the prices they paid for their supplies—they Expressed themselves as sorry (at least in conversation with our men) that they had left us and declared that had they Anticipated any Reduction on the price of Goods they would have remained, I am of Opinion it is the Dread of many had that if they came here they would be taken from their families and sent out of the country prevented them from coming to this place with Mr. Ogden.[16]

McLoughlin was referring to a meeting that Ogden had with a party of trappers employed by William H. Ashley. He met them somewhere along the Snake River on the 10th of April, and he did report that the deserters told him they regretted leaving the expedition and wished they were back on the Columbia. Even so, McLoughlin interpreted his words more optimistically than he would have done. Nine months before McLoughlin wrote, but after his encounter with the deserters—when he was working his way back from his second Snake expedition—Ogden had not been as certain as McLoughlin thought he was that the reforms were effective. Reflecting on the current status of the Snake country expedition, he regretted "that the present Plan had not been adopted many years since." Moreover, he feared, the reforms had not gone far enough. They did not match American prices and American competition.

> [A]s we now have every reason to suppose not only from the infor-
> mation I have obtained from the different American traders and
> other sources, that the Americans will soon establish themselves
> in the Columbia, it was full time *if we are allowed to remain* on the
> North side of the River to reduce the Freemans tariff, otherwise
> how can we expect to retain one of them in our Service, and
> under their present terms it is doubtful we shall; although some
> articles are sold by the Americans higher than we now sell, still
> there is a wide difference in the price they pay for Beaver say three
> dollars p lb delivered in the Snake country and three and a half
> to four at St Louis.[17]

Even while out in the field on his fourth Snake country expedition, Ogden felt that higher prices gave the Americans too great an advantage. "Although our trappers have their goods on moderate terms, the price of their beaver is certainly low, compared to the Americans," he complained in his journal. "With them beaver large and small are averaged at five dollars each, with us two dollars for a large and one dollar for a small beaver. Here then there is certainly a wide difference." He also advised that when calculating prices, the company should take into account the fact that, although American trappers had "free liberty to trade with natives," Hudson's Bay freemen were forbidden to buy beaver or other furs from Indians. "[A]lso it is optional with them [American trappers] to take their furs to St Louis where they obtain five and [one] half dollars per lb.; one third of the American trappers follow this plan."[18]

In truth, Hudson's Bay's prospects were much more favorable than Ogden realized. The prices of goods that Ashley sold at rendezvous were rising just at the time when expenses for Hudson's Bay freemen were falling. Under the reformed system introduced by McLoughlin, and approved by Simpson and London headquarters, the freemen paid only £2 apiece for horses. American trappers had to pay from $150 to $300 for a horse, and some cost as much as $500. During 1826 or 1827 an American lost a horse on the Yellowstone and two in today's central Utah. He calculated that his loss could not be less than $450. Under the new Hudson's Bay system, moreover, when the freemen returned from an expedition the company would take back the traps and horses that had been issued at the start of the trip, charging the purchasers only for those that had been lost and for the cost of repairing traps, saddles, and other products that had been damaged. Supplies that had to be paid for or which a freeman wished to retain as personal property, were now sold at the same rates that *engagés* paid, which was 50 percent above prime cost of importation. Only two or three months after Ogden complained that the Americans still had the advantage, Hudson's Bay got convincing evidence that its new prices were competitive. Some of the freemen who had deserted from his brigade on the Weber River went to Flathead Post to sell their hunts at Hudson's Bay terms.[19]

No matter how successfully Hudson's Bay Company reduced the discrepancy between American and British prices, the primary task of the Snake country expedition did not change. It was still to denude the land. The expedition, London headquarters ordered in 1827, was "to hunt as bare as possible all the Country South of the Columbia and West of the Mountains." The emphasis was on the word *west.* Snake country brigades were ordered to remain west of the Rocky Mountains. Specifically, they were told not to cross the Continental Divide south of the forty-ninth latitude. They were to remain in the Oregon country.[20] Nothing was said of Mexican territory. The implication was that if the expedition crossed a border it should be into Alta California, never into the United States.

London's command was not new. Officially, the Snake country expedition had always been ordered to avoid American jurisdiction. There was a new insistence, however, and the reason was that London

misunderstood where the confrontation between Ogden and Gardner occurred. Headquarters believed it had taken place east of the
Rocky Mountains, in the United States. That was why the company
did not ask the British government to demand compensation from
Washington. "[I]t was never our wish that trapping parties should
hunt beyond the Neutral ground, which by the Convention of 1818
is to be free to the subjects of Great Britain and the United States for
a period of Ten years," the governor and committee in London wrote
McLoughlin.

> Had the spoilation taken place on the West side of the Mountains
> on the neutral ground which from the statement of Mr. Ogden
> appears not to have been the fact, we might have submitted such
> a case to [the] Ministers, as might have induced them to seek
> redress or a restitution of the property from the United States Gov-
> ernment, but as the transaction took place on the United States
> territory, we fear we must be compelled to bear the loss unless you
> are able to prove distinctly that it occurred on the West side of the
> Rocky Mountains.[21]

London headquarters was mistaken. Headquarters believed "that Mr.
Ogden must have been to the southward of the 49° of latitude and to
the Eastward of the Rocky Mountains,"[22] because it learned of the confrontation between Ogden and Gardner when it was forwarded a copy
of the letter that Ogden had written to Hudson's Bay traders and factors in North America. In that letter he had first described what had
occurred on the Weber. He had sent it from the field, after the incident
but while still on the expedition, before he returned to Fort Nez Perces.
He had composed it at the headwaters of the Beaverhead River, a stream
that is formed by the junction of the Red Rock River and Horse Prairie
Creek. Since, however, it was dated from "East Fork, Missouri," and
reported his confrontation with Gardner, the designation "East Fork,
Missouri" caused London headquarters to believe that the confrontation had occurred on the Missouri. It is not surprising that Hudson's
Bay's London officers were confused about the jurisdiction. After all,
neither Ogden nor Gardner had known what country they were in. In
fact, Ogden was not right about being on the "East Fork, Missouri" at
the time he wrote the letter. He was actually on an east branch of the

west fork. The west fork of the Missouri is the Jefferson, and the Beaver-head is one of the main branches of the Jefferson.[23]

As a result of the misunderstanding, London headquarters not only refrained from protesting to Washington, it sent McLoughlin new instructions to keep the Snake country expedition out of American territory. "We have most particularly to desire," he was told, "that all our officers will in future confine themselves and the Parties entrusted to their charge within the limits of the Companys Territories or the Neutral Ground till the Boundaries of the two Powers are defined, and any inattention to this instruction, on the matter being made known to us will be attended with our serious displeasure." Or, as Governor Simpson was warned, "the parties must have positive instructions not to cross to the East of the Mountains south of 49 degrees north latitude."[24]

McLoughlin went immediately to Ogden's defense, first telling London that he thought Ogden had been on the headwaters of the Sacramento when he met Gardner, and, if not there, certainly in the drainage system of some river emptying into the Pacific.[25] It was some months before McLoughlin realized that he, like everyone else, did not know where the expedition had been. When he did, he changed his defense of Ogden. True, the brigade had crossed to the east side of the Continental Divide, he admitted, but that had been the usual route from the Flatheads to the Snake country. Alexander Ross had gone that way and Ogden had been given no orders to take a different route. McLoughlin was apparently stung by the reproaches, not just from London but also from Simpson, and he replied in no uncertain terms that Ogden had not disobeyed orders. He more than implied that Simpson had known where Ross had gone and where Ogden had been told to go. Simpson had not acted when he had his chance to keep the expedition west of the Continental Divide and should not now blame Ogden after the fact.

> I can only say I find no document here to show that any directions were given not to cross the Eastside of the Mountains by the Gentlemen who outfitted the Snake expedition prior to Mr. Ogden, and he conceived he was right in following the route of the preceding expeditions, since it had been sanctioned by his predecessors, who outfitted it from the Flatheads, indeed as long as the Snake expedition was outfitted from that place in consequence of

a very high range of Mountains that runs east and west between
the Snake country and the Flatheads people leaving the latter
place in the Fall to go to the former must cross to the East side of
the Rocky Mountains, proceed South and recross them to get to
the Snake Country.[26]

Simpson was aware of these facts. McLoughlin was not telling him anything he did not know. McLoughlin was being circumspect when saying
Ogden followed the precedent of his predecessors. What he meant was
that Ogden had been following the route laid out, at least by acquiescence, by Simpson. The implication was that the governor could have
kept the expedition west of the Continental Divide, and had no business
blaming Ogden for following a route he had been authorized to take.

In fact, Simpson would know that the Snake country expedition continued to cross to the east side of the mountains even after Ogden had
been ordered not to go there. There were solid reasons for crossing.
Far more buffalo roamed on the east side. Even when Ogden wintered
on the Snake River, he had to have meat and the surest place to get it
was across the Divide. Second, some of the best beaver grounds were
over there. After he wrote the letter from the "East Fork, Missouri,"
Ogden's small party had trapped about 1500 beaver before crossing
back to the Snake River. "These Furs," McLoughlin had clearly stated,
"were killed on the East side of the Mountains on the Head Waters of
the Missisourie."[27]

Those beaver had been so plentiful that Ogden had wanted to proceed at least to the vicinity of the Marias River, "but my cowardly freemen did not dare advance" so far into Blackfoot country. He knew that
Donald McKenzie, when he wintered on Bow River, had been instructed
by Hudson's Bay's North American headquarters to explore the Marias
"and the environs of the Missouri" for beaver. McKenzie had sensed discontent among the Blackfeet who asserted "that his intended Journey
was not to view the Country but to assist their enemies and the Americans." He had called a meeting of representatives of the Blackfoot tribes
to explain his intentions. His explorations, he told them, were "to ascertain the reports they [*i.e.*, Blackfeet] have given of the Country and the
richness of Beaver in the environs of the Missouri, which their enemies
the Crow Indians reaped the benefit of." The Crows were then well south

of the Missouri and, if actually hunting beaver, had to be working deep inside American jurisdiction. McKenzie's expedition occurred in 1822, and if it was then official company policy to explore that far into the United States, Ogden could reasonably have contended that he should not be faulted for going to the same general area in 1825.[28]

Both Simpson and McLoughlin had not only sanctioned Ogden's trespass over the mountains, they had ordered it. They had even laid out the route, telling him where to cross the Continental Divide and, perhaps, had authorized him to trap beaver on the Missouri waters.[29] But once London had understood where the Snake country expedition had been traveling, crossings over to the Missouri River side of the Rocky Mountains were ordered to be stopped, and they were, at least officially. Simpson made an effort to persuade headquarters that he was obeying its commands. In December 1828, for example, a leading American fur trapper, Joshua Pilcher, was in desperate financial straits. He had been president of the Missouri Fur Company but now was down on his luck. The trapping expedition he then was leading had not been successful, and he was in winter quarters, near Flathead Lake, short of men, trade goods, and equipment. Seeking an escape from his debts, he wrote Simpson proposing what most likely was a partnership. In exchange for supplies he would lead an Anglo-American expedition trapping the upper Missouri, using his citizenship as a cover and giving Hudson's Bay Company "legal" entry into the United States. Simpson knew the proposal would have violated the spirit if not the substance of American law, and probably took pleasure writing Pilcher a lesson in integrity and good citizenship. It was also an irresistible opportunity to persuade superiors in London that he was keeping his people west of the Rockies.

> I am aware that the Country watered by the sources of the Missouri, usually known by the name of the "Black feet Country" is a rich preserve of Beaver, and that a well organized Trading and Trapping Party would in all probability make valuable returns therein (altho' perhaps the most dangerous Service connected with the Indian Trade) would therefore readily entertain your proposition with the attention which its importance merits as regards capital, if a difficulty of a formidable character did not present itself, which is the Territorial rights of the United States Government to

that Country. These rights, we as British Subjects cannot infringe openly, and although the protecting Laws of your Government might be successfully evaded by the plan you suggest still I do not think it would be reputable to the Honble Hudsons Bay Co[mpan]y to make use of indirect means to acquire possession of a Trade to which it has no just claim. Under these circumstances I cannot fall in with your views and as regards Mr Ogden he cannot without acting in direct opposition to his instructions cross the height of Land.[30]

Two years later, in 1831, John Work succeeded Ogden as the leader of the Snake country expedition. McLoughlin was at a loss where to send "the Snake party" that fall, as so many areas had been trapped clean of beaver. Work proposed going east of the Flathead nation, but McLoughlin had serious reservations. "[T]he lands laying north of the Flatheads which Mr. Work mentioned I believe are on the East side of the Mountains," he wrote Simpson, "and if south of 49 we can not go there, and if north of 49 I think we ought not to go." They could not go south because it was American territory, and they ought not go north because that was Blackfoot country.[31]

CHAPTER THIRTEEN

It Is a Lottery with All Expeditions

Peter Skene Ogden had arrived at Fort Nez Perces from his first Snake country expedition about the 8th of November 1825. He had been instructed by John McLoughlin to go to the Walla Walla and not try to come into the Columbia at Fort Vancouver "if it prevents your returning in due time to your hunting ground." What "due time" meant in the Snake country was dramatically demonstrated when Ogden left on his second expedition on 20 November, just twelve days after coming in. He had been ordered to join forces with Finan McDonald, who had been sent to the Klamath Lake region to start trapping bare the area south of the lower Columbia River. Because of the threats of Johnson Gardner, McLoughlin said, the two expeditions should be joined, "to give protection against American attack."[1]

Ogden met McDonald on 9 December and was distressed to discover he had no guide who knew the country. Unwilling to penetrate unknown regions without a native to show the way, Ogden left McDonald and headed east across the valley of John Day River, then over the Blue Mountains, to Burnt River. This, too, was part of the Oregon country never trapped by the company, and, as he proceeded, Ogden carried out Governor Simpson's orders to strip it clean of beaver.[2] On the 2d of February, at Burnt River, Ogden paused to assess his progress. Although the hunt had been encouraging, the men had suffered almost beyond endurance.

We have now taken independent of what Mr. McDonalds party had before my giving him 485 Beavers and otters—one consolation however the number is small but Beaver is good, but for want of wrappers suffer greatly in the Snow, but the Men suffer still more so for want of shoes in this cold weather, and, in the Snow and Water   Men worse provided for in leather for such a long voyage I presume never were sent off from any Establishment before and none but ignorant Canadians would have consented. Altho' Ten horses have been killed by the Freemen and Servants for food still they could not make use of their skins as a substitute as our worn out horses required all to enable them to crawl.[3]

By "ignorant Canadians" Ogden meant the *engagés*. Apprehensive that the expedition might meet Americans in the region south of the lower Columbia, McLoughlin had been afraid to send many freemen on the expedition. He had, instead, greatly increased the percentage of company servants or what he termed "engaged Trappers."[4]

Traveling down Burnt River to its mouth, Ogden reached the first objective of his trip on the 11th of February: the Snake. It had been an extremely difficult month and a half. Both horses and men had gone as many as four days without food. He had had at least two desertions and he knew the trappers were desperate. Strikingly, however, he was more concerned about meeting Americans than about the suffering of his men. Even when he came near "the place where the Blackfeet Killed one of my Party last spring," he was more on the lookout for Americans than for Blackfeet. "[I]f the Americans have not visited that place since I left," he observed, "we surely shall find Beaver and Buffalo there." Just eight days later he met a party of Snakes who gave him bad news. The Snake nation was abandoning the area of the Malade and Raft Rivers "to avoid the Blackfeet Indians." That news did not seem to alarm him. He expressed no apprehension of the Blackfeet. More troubling was something else the Snakes told him.

[T]hey report that a party of Americans & Iroquois are not more than three days march from us . . . if this be the case which I have no cause to doubt our hunts are damn'd   we may now make provision and return empty handed and in lieu of our returns being equal to last year they will be far less indeed . . . with my discontented party I dread meeting the Americans, that some will attempt desertion I have not the least doubt after the sufferings they have endured can it be otherwise.[5]

Well before Ogden met any, signs of Americans had been everywhere. He wanted to trade with the Snakes but "they appear to be very independant of our Goods being nearly well armed and well Stocked in Ammunition Knives & Iron works—part of these supplies obtained last Summer from the Fort Nez Perces Indians and the remainder from the Americans." Just four days after writing these words he took a measure of the quantity of trade goods that were getting into the Snake country, British as well as American. He had encountered

another Snake Camp [of] about 200 Tents   it appears these fellows have spent their winter with the Americans and from their accounts have made peace with them   this I am inclin'd to beli[e]ve is the case as they have received an American Flag and appear pleased and contented with the reception they have received from them,   they have a number of American Knives and trinkets amongst them but all their Fire Arms except one Rifle have come from our quarter   altho not more than 100 men came to our Camp they had sixty Guns and ammunition appears not to be scarce amongst them and they appear eager to obtain more.[6]

On a Sunday morning just over two weeks later he met Americans. The expedition was camped on the Snake River, with Blackfeet all around. "About 10 oclock we were surprised by the arrival of a Party of Americans and some of our deserters of last Year   28 in all." Ogden did not take the trouble to identify them, but it is known that these trappers were a wintering party under contract with William H. Ashley. Their ranks included two more of the most famous legends of American fur-trade history, Jim Bridger and Thomas "Broken Hand" Fitzpatrick.

What Ogden had to tell his journal about the trappers gives us a very good indication why he had been so apprehensive of running into Americans—why he said "I dread meeting the Americans." He had anticipated that, like Johnson Gardner, they would challenge him and ask what right he had to be in the Snake country. His very first comments about the encounter show that he believed all American trappers would be repeats of Gardner. "[I]f we were surprised at seeing them," he wrote, "they were more so at seeing us from an Idea that their threats of last year would have prevented me from again returning to this quarter, but they find themselves mistaken They encamped at a short distance from our Camp   all quiet." Unquestionably, he believed Gardner had spoken for Ashley and that all Americans were instructed to harass him.[7]

Next day the reeducation of Peter Ogden began. Now that he had met the Americans whom he had been "dreading," he had to wonder what he had feared. He did not say so, but his comments indicate he found them the opposite of what he had expected. "The Strangers paid me a visit and I had a busy day in settling with them," he reported, "and more to my satisfaction and the Companys than last Year." By the end of the day when he wrote his journal entry, he was almost celebrating. Deserters of the year before had come forward to settle their accounts or, at least, to pay something of what they owed. Except for his meetings with Jedediah Smith and John H. Weber (and, perhaps, Etienne Provost), it was his first dealings with trappers who worked for Ashley. Johnson Gardner had not been one of Ashley's trappers; yet Ogden, equating Ashley's men with Gardner, had expected them to act as Gardner acted, and when they did not he was not only surprised, he was puzzled.[8]

All the deserters of the year before, who were with the Ashley party, paid Ogden something, either what they owed or what they could then afford. This also was the day when he accepted a note from Nicholas Montour, indicating that Montour's money deposited with Hudson's Bay, which he forfeited when deserting Ogden on Weber River the year before, had not been enough to satisfy his (or Prudhomme's) debts with the company. Ogden also received just under eighty-two beaver pelts from the deserters and he purchased ninety-three that belonged to Ashley.[9] The Americans did not have much to sell, for they had left winter quarters only recently and for approximately two weeks had the bad luck of working streams that Ogden had been trapping just ahead of them. As a result, "the few Beaver they had" Ogden "obtained from them." Some of the pelts he received "from our deserters in part payment of their debts." All the remainder he took "in trade with the Americans."[10]

Affairs between the two parties were so amiable that the British and Americans even exchanged men. Ogden gained two and lost one. "Goddin's Son having requested permission to join his father and being a worthless useless scamp I gave him his liberty he having paid his Debt in full   the Americans having advanced three Beaver Skins to make up the number."[11]

That Snake River meeting with Ashley's trappers was, for Ogden, a most puzzling turn of events. He had expected more desertions and instead rode away with an extra man. "[N]ot one of our Party appeared the least inclined to leave us," he noted in wonder, "not even a hint was given, so much to their Credit   if our last years Party had comported themselves equally well we should not have been under the necessity of returning to the Columbia with such miserable returns."[12]

Ogden just did not understand what had happened. He could think of only one important difference between this expedition and the one of the year before. This time he had a much higher percentage of *engagés*. No engaged servants had deserted in 1825. All the deserters on the Weber had been freemen. Now, in 1826, not one freeman had, in Ogden's words, as much as given "a hint" that he was thinking of leaving. The one man who left to join his father had asked permission and paid his debts. Ogden was sure that prices could not explain why his freemen did not desert this time. American rates continued to astonish him. "I cannot conceive," he wondered, "how the Americans can afford to sell their Beaver so as to reap profit when they pay $3 per lib. for coarse or fine but such is the case and Goods proportionably cheap."[13]

Ogden did not at first speculate why the freemen had remained with the expedition. He made a suggestion in his journal that he believed the freemen had talked to the deserters of the year before and had been advised not to desert. At least, he purported to understand that those who deserted on the Weber had become unhappy with their lot among the Americans and were now sorry that they had ever left him. "From what I could observe," he reported, "our deserters are already tired of their New Masters and from their manner I am of opinion will soon return to their old employers   they promise to reach the Flat Heads this Fall."[14]

After Ogden had a chance to mull over the question for a few months, he came up with no better explanation than the one he probably first thought of. The difference between his first and second expeditions, he wrote Governor Simpson and the chief factors and chief traders of Hudson's Bay, was the percentage of *engagés* he had the second time.

"[A]ltho' great were the Offers and temptations held out to desert, not one expressed the slightest inclination," he told his fellow North American officers, "this I presume however must be attributed to $^2/_3$ of the party being engaged Men which gave me a decided advantage over the remainder on all occasions."[15]

By saying not one "expressed the slightest inclination" to desert, Ogden was just repeating what he had said in his journal, that there was not a "hint" of desertion. But when he said "great were the Offers and temptations held out to desert," he again was exaggerating the threat, either because he still believed every American was another Gardner or because he wanted to impress his fellow officers with the difficulties he had overcome. In his journal, written at the time, there is not a suggestion of any great offers and temptations "held out to desert." In fact, it reads the exact opposite, for Ogden made no mention of conversations with the Americans. Instead, the entry makes it appear that he spent the entire time with them conducting the business of settling debts and buying furs.

Ogden did not even explain what he meant when he said that having two-thirds *engagés* gave him "a decided advantage" over the one-third who were freemen. The best that can be made of what he wrote is that he seemed to be claiming that he could have counted on his engaged servants to support him if the freemen defied him, and that was why the freemen did not desert. Could he have meant that the *engagés* would have used force to keep the freemen in camp? It is not likely if he remembered that only two of them physically backed him the year before when he, Kittson, and McKay faced down the deserters and kept them from taking ten horses over to Johnson Gardner's camp. If he expected them to support him in 1826 he must have had an entirely different group of engaged servants than he had had on his first Snake country expedition. More likely, however, he was guessing. He had expected the freemen to desert and he did not understand why they did not. The two-to-one advantage of the servants over the freemen was as good a reason as he could come up with.

If we heed only what Odgen said, the conclusion is thrust on us that he did not give as much thought to what had happened as he should have. The idea did not occur to him that the difference between what had happened on the Weber River in 1825 and the conduct of Ashley's men along the Snake in 1826 was that Johnson Gardner had been on the Weber. There were quite different men determining behavior on both occasions. The trappers of 1826 worked for Ashley. The two whom we know, Bridger and Fitzpatrick, were responsible, respected fur men who not only one day would lead their own trapping brigades but eventually would be partners owning a share of their trading companies. Gardner was a free-lance trapper who never raised capital and probably could not have raised any had he attempted to do so. He had never been a leader of men and, for all we know, could not have attracted followers had he tried. He is remembered more for his violence than his judgment. Ogden seldom took note of the distinction. The Americans he would meet on his remaining expeditions were of the stamp of Bridger and Fitzpatrick, yet it would be some time before he stopped expecting they would all be carbon copies of Gardner.

About three weeks before arriving at the Columbia to end his second Snake country expedition, Ogden was already planning his third trip. He wrote Simpson from Burnt River that the next expedition should "proceed at the opening of the Season to the Country beyond the Claminitts," by which he meant the Klamath nation. Beyond the Klamaths was California, with all its potential riches. Undoubtedly, one reason for going that way was to explore. He wanted to locate the sources of the Umpqua, and settle the question whether the Buenaventura emptied into the Pacific or into the Sacramento. But his strongest motivation was to trap the area before the Americans. He had been told that some Americans had already tried to get there but had failed because they had not taken sufficient provisions. "I have every reason to believe," he wrote Simpson, "that a party of Americans who started from the [Great Salt] Lake in May last for the purpose of penetrating to three large Rivers, which are said to be in the Vicinity of the Claminitt Country and rich in Beaver were obliged from starvation to retreat."[16]

Ogden must have heard the story from Ashley's men, from Bridger perhaps, or Fitzpatrick. Supposedly, Jedediah Smith had hoped to head west from the lake but had not had sufficient supplies. Had he succeeded, he would have come upon the Humboldt and trapped that stream. He would not have crossed the Sierra Nevada. Ogden was still quite confused about the geography of the area below the Willamette River, and was mistaken to think that the route west of Salt Lake went to the Klamaths. No Americans had attempted to penetrate the mountains south of the lower Columbia. The first to get anywhere west of the Great Salt Lake would be Smith when, three years later, he came up from California to the Columbia River.[17]

It really did not matter what immediate plans the Americans had. Even if Ogden had known there were no Americans planning to cross the Cascades, he was certain that soon there would be. The Klamath country, he explained, "still remains unexplored, but will not long remain so, as I am of opinion now that the Snake Country is fast on the decline, from this I conclude the Americans will soon make another attempt better provided now that they know as well as us do from experience that provisions are required to reach it."[18]

By saying the Snake country was "on the decline," Ogden was not referring to the decrease of beaver. It was, rather on decline in the minds American trappers. It was losing much of its attraction for them because of the severe losses they had recently suffered.

> [A]ltho many American Trappers are scattered over the Snake Country it is still [for Hudson's Bay] an object worthy of attention   the Headwaters or Sources of the South branch of the Columbia [*i.e.*, in the area of Henry's Fork] and its environs are still rich in Beaver, but a party less than Fifty could not trap with safety, it being in the vicinity of the great War road   in fact of all the War tribes; an American party attempted to reach the Crow Village by that route in Fall 1824   but all with the exception of one and he was wounded were *killed*   and since that period no attempt has been made, the severe loss the American trappers have sustained within the last three years, has caused them to act more prudently than formerly,   no less than 32 Men have been killed with the loss of all their Traps, horses and Beaver,   the greater part of this number have been killed by the Snakes who appear determined to destroy and annoy them whenever an opportunity offers.[19]

Ogden knew the Americans soon would be going to the Klamaths and beyond. What he wanted was to get there first and denude the beaver grounds. "I now beg leave to propose and in lieu of a better volunteer to lead a party to that quarter provided you should consider it worthy of a trial," he wrote Simpson. He even thought the timing urgent.

I shall now only add that if you feel inclined to send an expedition to that quarter no time should be lost as you may rely on it the Americans will not loose sight of it, and altho' they were not successful in their first attempt, they will not abandon it without giving it a few more trials, altho' they have the same obstacles to encounter in reaching it that we have,   the only difference between us   they take their departure from a Buffaloe country, whereas unfortunately if we go we must take a Supply of Provisions from the Establishment we start from.[20]

Ogden left Fort Vancouver on 11 September 1826. It was less than two months after he had completed his second expedition. His plan was to cross the Cascades before the weather became too severe, to find some sheltered valley in which to winter, and, with the first signs of spring, to push on to the Klamath country and beyond into today's California. He did not find the Buenaventura but that could not have been a serious disappointment, considering how much geography he was able to learn. He mapped the Umpqua and now knew that the Buenaventura flowed much farther south. He was not even discouraged that he found much of the country destitute of beaver. The Pit River was barren and so were the streams in the area where today's California meets today's Oregon. "At 2 P.M. we reached a large Fork nearly opposite our last nights encampment and our Guides informed us there was Beaver in it," he wrote in the expedition's journal when returning north somewhere in the area of Goose Lake, now dried up. "We encamped and the Trappers started with their [traps] but ret[urne]d with them in the evening the gre[a]ter part enraged and vexed at finding nothing   indeed it is enough to vex any man to see so many fine Streams and all destitute of Beaver." There was, however, a positive side to finding no animals. "We have certainly examined a large extent of Country and found nothing," he added, "still it is a satisfaction to know that this quarter is destitute of Beaver and unnecessary to send again, it is true is [sic] has not been explored without expence but this could not be avoided   it is a Lottery with all expeditions."[21]

Best of all, from Ogden's perspective, no beaver meant there would be no Americans. He met none on this expedition. He had beaten them to the Klamaths. But that did not mean Hudson's Bay had won the land south of the lower Columbia. What Ogden could not know was that at the very time he was riding north from Goose Lake, Jedediah Smith was crossing the Sierra Nevada out of California to the rendezvous of 1827. There he would report that the Bear River system and the Great Salt Lake lay in a geographical basin. Rivers did not drain out of it. There was no Buenaventura. Then he would ride back across the Mohave Desert to California, gather up his men, and lead them north, to see if he could reach the Columbia from the south.

CHAPTER FOURTEEN

Our Own People Are Now Perfectly Satisfied

At a time when Peter Skene Ogden was on his third Snake country expedition, trapping waters in today's Josephine County, Oregon, the governor and governing committee of Hudson's Bay Company in London issued new instructions for their North American governor, George Simpson. It may be that headquarters had just read the journal of Ogden's first expedition. Simpson was told his brigade leaders should behave differently from the way Ogden had behaved toward Jedediah Smith on the Snake River in 1825. They should employ less direct confrontation than sending men to beat the Americans downstream and trap the river banks ahead of them clear of beaver. London even wondered whether rules of conduct could be negotiated. "In the event of our trapping party falling in with any Americans in the Country common to both," Simpson was urged, "the leader ought to have instructions to endeavor to make an amicable arrangement as to the parts of the Country which each will take, to avoid interference, and to be careful to avoid giving just cause for accusing our people of any aggression against the Americans or violence except in a clear case of self defence."[1]

We might guess that this was foolish thinking. With the Snake country expeditions laying waste to the beaver population not for profit but to keep the Americans out of the country, and with the rates of prices set to destroy them as competition, one would expect that Hudson's Bay was asking for trouble, that there was bound to be conflict when British and American trapping parties met in the wilderness. We would be wrong. There was trouble—serious trouble—when one or the other met Black-foot, Piegan, or Blood war parties, but not when they met one another.

Ogden's fourth expedition did not go to western Oregon or to California. It returned instead to the Snake River. It was, however, different from his first and second trips in one important respect. Ogden implemented a schedule that had been proposed some years ago by Alexander Ross and other Hudson's Bay officers. He departed from Fort Nez Perces on the 7th of September 1827. He planned to remain in the field for ten or eleven months, until July 1828, making both a fall and a spring hunt, spending winter in quarters somewhere on Snake River. "[A]ltho it is now some years since trapping expeditions were first sent to the Snake country," Ogden explained to his fellow officers, "it is a fact the trappers have not yet made a fall hunt, and only the last two years were Spring hunts made, prior to this the Beaver taken in this Country were trapped in June, July and August and consequently were of a much inferior quality, and it was generally the opinion of all that no other could be procured, but by trapping at the proper Season it is as good as any Beaver procured in the Columbia, of this in my last returns I have given a most convincing proof."[2]

Although acknowledging that "many American Trappers are scattered over the Snake Country," Ogden insisted that trapping the area was still worth Hudson's Bay's time and effort. Governor Simpson agreed. "The Snake Expedition we look to as a very prominent branch of our business and we wish by all means that it be kept constantly employed," he told John McLoughlin, and to remind him that the main purpose was not trapping, he added, "it moreover does much good in over-running and destroying that extended country south of the Columbia which is the greatest temptation to our opponents."[3]

Ogden encountered Americans much sooner than he had expected. Only nine days after leaving the Columbia he shared his camp with four Cayuse who told him that three days earlier they had separated from a party of American trappers who were going to Fort Nez Perces to trade. "It may be so," Ogden wrote of this disturbing news, "but until I see them I shall not be convinced." Eleven days later he learned that the story was true. The first morning the brigade was on the main branch of the Weiser River, his men reported that "all along the river traps have

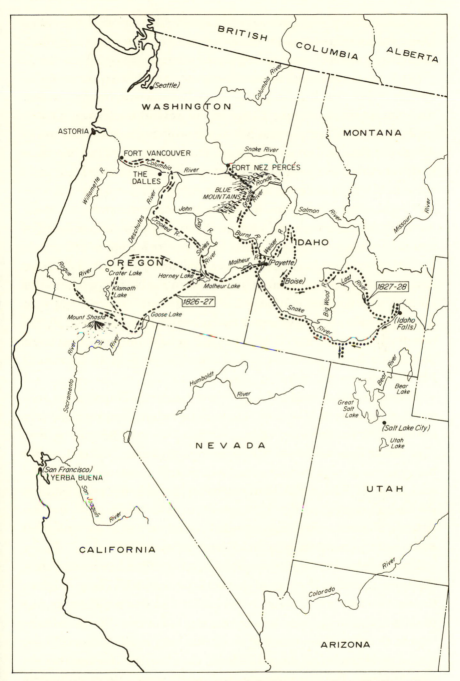

Snake Country Expeditions, 1826–27, 1827–28. From Gloria Griffen Cline, *Peter Skene Ogden and the Hudson's Bay Company* (Norman: University of Oklahoma Press, 1974).

been set and that most recently. Some are of opinion it is Americans, others Indians who have been trapping in this quarter." He soon discovered that the traps belonged to Americans. A man named John Johnson, who soon would be killed by Blackfeet, "made his appearance and informed us he and five others were on this stream a short distance from this." They were a party of forty men, six of whom "have gone with goods accompanied by a band of Nez Percy, to trade on the Columbia, and the remainder are dispersed in this quarter, so my hopes of returns in beaver which was yesterday rather sanguine are now blasted, and I am certainly at a loss how to act."[4]

Next day "two Americans and two of my deserters paid me a visit." They told him that they had left Bear River eleven weeks before and in that time had trapped only 130 beaver. They "complain of the scarcity of beaver in all directions and are equally at a loss with myself where to find any, and purpose following me and return with me to the Columbia, but so far I have given them no encouragement." His own men took only eight beaver that day and next. The only trappers having any success were a group of Nez Perces. "The Americans inform me they would not part with one [*i.e.,* beaver], I hope this may be true," Ogden noted. He hoped it true for it meant they were waiting to sell to him or to a Hudson's Bay post on the Columbia. Again, the Americans "informed me it was their intentions to follow me and accompany me to the Columbia. I informed them that if so I could not hold out better terms to them than my own men had. With this they are satisfied, and replied had they not seen me, it was their intention when their hunts were made to have gone to [Fort] Nez Percy and delivered their furs there, consequently they take their chance."[5]

Ogden's meeting with these Americans on Weiser River was one of those otherwise unimportant events that serve to sum up both change and predictable behavior in the Snake country. It was no longer news that there had been no desertions from Hudson's Bay to the Americans as there had been three years earlier. What did deserve attention was the success of McLoughlin's lower prices on supplies. The Americans wanted to buy at Hudson's Bay prices even if that cost them much lost time and distant travel. Hudson's Bay rates must have also been better than American rates for Indian purchasers if the Nez Perces would not sell their beaver to the Americans but were planning to carry it back to the Columbia for sale there. These events may not have surprised Ogden. Once he learned how much American goods cost at the rendezvous, he realized that Hudson's Bay had the advantage. What must have startled him, however, was to have Americans ask to stay with the expedition. They did not want to become members but they did intend traveling with him. He would have Americans with him for the remainder of the winter. Having the Americans along gave Ogden some amusement. On stormy days they did not bother going to their traps. While the Hudson's Bay freemen and *engagés* were up and down the river tending to business, Ogden passed the time in camp with the idle Americans. He even found comedy in the careless way they watched their horses. On the main branch of Big Wood River some of the trappers spotted Blackfeet. "It is evident they have discovered us, and will not allow us to remain quiet, for horses they must have," he observed. There were reported to be fifteen Blackfoot and, if all they wanted was one horse apiece, he wrote, "they can soon obtain them, as the last party of Americans we lately joined never keep watch, not long since they had them stolen. Still no guard and appear quite indifferent about them, *happy men.*"[6]

As the brigade moved from the Weiser to the Payette and then to the Boise, it found few beaver. On one day "Our traps did not give a beaver," and on the next "from sixty traps only three beaver." Ogden had an explanation. "[T]he Americans," he pointed out, "have almost resided on these rivers for the last eighteen months." He paused at the Boise only to wait "the return of the six trappers who started yesterday to examine the lower part of this river." He did not stop because he thought he might find beaver. "I have no hopes from it as the Americans have also cleared it." Four days later he decided to abandon that quarter of the Snake country. He had hoped to have three thousand beaver by that date. "It was from Wazers [Weiser], Payettes and this river we expected our returns, and we have now visited them and have produced only 140 beaver." He may have wondered if the Americans were beating Hudson's Bay at its own policy and denuding the land themselves.[7]

Wherever the brigade went during October, Ogden saw signs of Americans and sometimes even met them. On Willow Creek, near the east end of the Camas Prairie, he "found two tents of American freemen, five men. This party separated from the party that joined us on Wazers River, and although they have had the advantage of being ahead of us their success has been but indifferent." There simply were too few animals left. Two days later the expedition got fifteen beaver. "This is less certainly than I expected," he lamented, "but this part of the country was trapped only last spring by an American party and consequently we cannot expect many. Indeed the once famed Snake Country for beaver is a ruined one now, and granting it were allowed repose, which few on either side concerned are willing to give it, it would at least require four years to recruit."[8]

The five Americans encountered on Willow Creek also decided to go along with the expedition, making about eleven guest trappers traveling under Ogden's general command. With the brigade much strengthened, he could risk detaching small parties of six or more hunters who wanted to go off on their own for a day or two to find beaver. Even better, whenever the visitors needed something, they had to purchase from him. "The Americans being in want of supplies applied to trade," he explained the last week of the month. "We were some time ere we could agree as to terms, however finding me determined not to give way, they consented to trade paying 1/4 less than Indian tariff, and I obtained from them thirteen large beaver nineteen small and twenty-five musquash." On the same day he also settled with another of his deserters, taking "thirty-five large beaver in payment of his debt with the Company." Again Ogden noted that this was "more than I ever expected to have received from him."[9]

By the 1st of November, when on Big Lost River, Ogden had completely reversed himself. Until then he had been on his guard to avoid meeting Americans and getting away from them as quickly as possible. His new policy was "to prevail on the American party to remain with us," so that his detached trappers under Thomas McKay "may have time to trap the beaver they may find on the tracks they propose going." He was being devious and took delight in it. As the Americans "are not aware of this," he wrote with satisfaction, "it is so much the more in our favour," making it "my interest to amuse the American party" and "not hasten our progress." The scheme worked to the extent that the Americans remained with him the remainder of the month. His tricks did not get him as many furs as he hoped, however. When he detached McKay, sending him looking for new beaver streams, Ogden "had no idea that the Americans had already trapped all the rivers."[10]

On the morning of the 30th "the American party who have been in company with us since 18th October started for Salt Lake." He boasted that it had been a profitable time for him and a disastrous five weeks for them. "With them I traded thirty beaver," he counted, "and with the beaver the freemen have obtained from them in barter and formerly traded with me exceed one hundred, and during the time they have been with us, their success in trapping amounts only to twenty-six, so they have lost more by meeting with us than we have, and their hunt is miserable considering the advantage they had of being so long in advance." Burt Brown Barker summed up what Ogden was saying when he concluded, "Ogden got a good look at their tactics and energy, and accordingly lost all fear of them as competitors."[11]

By the 20th of December, Ogden was worrying about McKay's detached party. He had lost all contact with it. He had wanted to hire Snake guides to search for it but could get no Snake to go because of the severe weather. The cold also forced his main brigade into winter quarters near today's Pocatello, Idaho. He had been there for about three weeks when he was visited by two American trappers who came to tell him that they had been with McKay ten days before and report where he had been going and what condition his party was in. Ogden was grateful for the information. Although the men said that McKay had gone looking for him on the Lehmi River and hence had to be wintering a considerable distance away, he at least knew that he was alive and had some idea where he was. Some of the other things the men told him of their own incompetence and bad luck lowered even further his estimate of American trappers as commercial rivals.

> This is the Nez Percy part[y] of Americans that went to that country to trade horses, and are now on their return, and have little hopes from the quantity of snow of reaching their destination. From their accounts they traded forty-nine horses at an extravagant rate, averaging each according to their valuation of goods fifty dollars. Of the above they have lost nineteen, in crossing the plain that divides this from Days Defile; when in company with Mr McKay they were obliged to eat six. Mr McKay's party were also under the necessity of eating one, but had not one stolen, the

Americans [had] ten [taken] by the Snakes. . . . Their success in beaver and obtained by trade and trapping amounts to 200 skins, which they say is a miserable hunt. It was so far fortunate I sent a party in that direction, otherwise the beaver our side have was best.[12]

The Americans said that there had been seven men in their party, but they were "now reduced to six, one having remained with Mr McKay." When noting this news in his journal, Ogden made an interesting, even an important comment. "I was glad to learn from the Americans," he wrote, "that Mr McKay held out no encouragement for him to leave his employers." It is unlikely the two American trappers thought to tell him this without being asked. He must have enquired about how McKay had behaved and learned that he had done nothing underhanded. Interestingly, the subject came up again four days later when the other four men belonging to the party came in to camp and joined his winter quarters. They were led by Samuel Tulloch, who probably surprised him by saying he worked for Jedediah Smith. That also was news—that Smith now had his own company, Smith, Jackson, and Sublette.[13]

"This is a decent kind of fellow," Ogden wrote of Tulloch, making his first personal comment about any American mountain man except for Johnson Gardner. Even more to Ogden's satisfaction, Tulloch disassociated himself from Gardner's conduct on Weber River. He "informed me that the Company he belongs to would willingly enter into an agreement in regard to deserters, on both sides." Ogden's journal gives no indication he took up Tulloch's offer. Hudson's Bay's London headquarters had suggested agreement with the Americans about separated trapping areas so rival expeditions would not come too near each other, not a very practical idea. London had said nothing about making rules about deserters, a step that would have been more practical. Ogden did not even indicate he realized how it could have benefitted him. Instead, he missed the possibilities of what Tulloch said, and thought only that it demonstrated American weakness. "They appear alarmed, and may be not without cause," he wrote, apparently referring to all American trappers, although only Tulloch made the suggestion. He seems to have believed that not only was Hudson's Bay gaining the upper hand, the Americans knew that they had lost the advantage. Tulloch also told him "that the conduct of Gardner at our meeting four years since has not been approved of." Again, Ogden did not appreciate what Tulloch meant. He took the words in a less than friendly spirit. "I certainly should wonder," he observed, "if any man of principle did approve of such conduct." He was pleased with Tulloch's attitude but not won over. "So far very fair," he observed, "and I only wish in case of a general meeting they may conduct themselves decently." Still, he was impressed by the evident international good feelings that he was beginning to realize existed on the other side. "Tulloch I am happy to observe speaks highly of the treatment he received from Mr McKay."[14]

Tulloch joined the camp on the 24th of December and remained with Ogden for three months, until the 26th of March. Cooped up in winter quarters with idle hours on their hands, the two men had extensive conversations during those weeks, some of which Tulloch reported when he returned to St. Louis. One claim that Ogden was said to have made— that Hudson's Bay would exploit its advantage of charging prices one third less than those of the American rendezvous—William H. Ashley thought important enough to pass on to United States Senator Thomas Hart Benton of Missouri.

> Tulloch, one of the American partizans, a young man of excellent Character, fell in with & remained some days near the Encampment of a party of sixty men of the H. B. Comp[an]y under the command of a Mr. Ogden—Mr. T states that he had repeated conversations with Mr. O. concerning the operations of the British & American traders in that country, and expressed his opinion that the former would have to with draw from the country In Oct[obe]r 1828, when the privilege granting them intercourse & trade there should expire—but Mr. Ogden seemed to have no such idea, said the Hudson Bay Company had good friends at Washington City, as well as at home. That he felt Easy as it regarded any steps our government might take to remove them—and as to individual enterprise, he was Equally unconcerned, believing the company rich Enough to sacrifice more money by the sale of goods to Indians at reduced prices than any american compy would employ in the Fur trade in that quarter, and in that way they would soon exclude the American traders.[15]

No matter what measure of good will had been developing in the western mountains between British and American trappers, it certainly was not shared by Ashley sitting in his St. Louis office. He wanted the United States to station troops where they could protect the trappers, especially from the Blackfeet, and, to persuade Washington that the need was imperative, he was not above implying Hudson's Bay might be stirring up the Indians. Apparently he had planned to make even more extreme charges but toned down his remarks. In what appears to be an earlier draft of the letter to Benton he had said: "I mention this conversation between Mr. Tulloch & Mr. Ogden, merely to show you the ideas of the HBC in relation to those matters. They have already put into practice their p[l]an, as expressed by Mr. Ogden to monopolize that trade."[16] He gave the senator what he thought was evidence that the plan "had been previously concerted."

> Mr. [William] Sublette informs me that goods have been recently sold by the H B Compy to some of the Indian tribes who had previously confined their trade to our traders, for less than the probable cost of the articles, and not more than one tenth part of the sum they had before been in the habit of selling them for—with means like these, those traders may Effect there [*sic*] object, and our people there may anticipate much more serious times than they have heretofore experienced.[17]

By warning of "much more serious times," Ashley was not referring to commercial competition or diminished American profits. In that apparent early draft of the same letter he implied that Hudson's Bay Company had a much more serious policy in operation. "By such means as these," he had written, "they may effect their desired object & in proportion to their success we may reasonably anticipate the increase of Indian outrages."[18]

Tulloch told Ashley only that Hudson's Bay sold goods cheaper than he could. The Americans still had the advantage in the prices offered to buy beaver. Ogden referred to the higher rates just four days after he met Tulloch. A "Snake Chief, a stranger to me," came to camp to return traps that had been stolen and sell three beavers. Ogden showed his gratitude by giving him a scalper. "In fact had he gone to the American tent with his beaver," he explained, "he would have received three times the value of property he did from me; consequently I do not consider my scalper as lost." Had Ogden read Ashley's letter, he would have had a ready answer. It is likely that the conversation that Tulloch reported to Ashley took place on the 5th of January, because that evening Ogden was still thinking of the differences in prices when writing his daily journal entry. British costs might be lower, he admitted, but the price at which Americans purchased fur still gave them a decided advantage. "Although our trappers have their goods on moderate terms," he explained, referring to the cheaper rates his men paid for goods purchased from the company, the price they got for the beaver they sold was "certainly low, compared to the Americans." Beaver, large and small, sold to St. Louis traders averaged five dollars a skin, but "with us [it was] two dollars for a large and one dollar for a small beaver." He even doubted that the company's lower sales prices mattered much when he reckoned the much shorter distances American trappers traveled from the rendezvous to their trapping fields.[19]

By the middle of January, after Tulloch had been in camp about three weeks, Ogden adopted a rather surprising strategy. He decided to keep the Americans with him in winter quarters and not let them leave, even if he had to resort to devious tactics. The main American gathering was not far away, either in Bear River Valley or somewhere near Great Salt Lake. With a very large encampment of Snakes wintering near him for protection, Ogden did not want Tulloch going to the Bear and returning in a few weeks with trade goods. After Tulloch attempted to leave early in January and was forced back to camp by severe weather, Ogden decided to stop him for making a second attempt. "I principally dread their returning with liquor," he explained. "A small quantity they may succeed in bringing, if so it would be most advantageous to them but the reverse to me. I know not their intentions but had I the same opportunity or the same advantages they have, long since I would have had a good stock of liquor here, and every beaver in the camp would be mine." He also worried that they would return with more trappers, as many as twenty or thirty Americans. "This also would be most injurious to us, and this I dread, as all my hopes for a spring hunt are in this quarter, and in a word, as the party here have only ten traps, no good can result to us, if they succeed in reaching their Depot, and returning here."[20]

To keep Tulloch and his men from leaving, Ogden resorted to tactics that would have angered him, and would have raised hackles at York Factory, had they been used against a Hudson's Bay brigade. "The Americans are now more anxious to procure snow shoes, and I am equally so they should not," he explained on 16 January. "I have given orders to all not to make any for them. This day they offered twenty-five dollars for one pair and twenty for another." "The Americans constantly making offers to procure snow shoes but without success," he noted on the 18th, "and as far as my interest has any influence, I trust they will continue to meet with the same."[21]

Ogden did not say what "interest' and "influence" he used. It is not difficult to guess. Although many men in his camp probably could make snowshoes, the Americans most likely tried to buy them from the women of the expedition, at least those women who were independent of his control. They would have been the wives of freemen. He had less leverage over them than the wives of *engagés*. He paid them not to sell, or as he put it, he "bribed" them. That was the word he used when he said he could not stop the numerous Snakes wintering nearby from working for the Americans. "Tulloch, the American trader, started for the Indian camp, for the purpose of engaging an Indian to carry letters to the American Depot at Salt Lake," he noted on the 20th. "This I cannot prevent, it is impossible for me to bribe so many Indians. With my party I have succeeded in preventing them from procuring snow shoes; had I not, long since they would have reached that."[22]

Ogden was willing to do business with Tulloch, he just would not help him leave camp. "I traded two beaver with the American trader for tobacco," he wrote on the 23rd. "I have constantly supplied the Americans with meat, as they cannot procure any for want of snow shoes, and as I am the cause of this, it is my duty to assist." He may even have felt some slight sympathy for Tulloch's plight. "He is now very low spirited, as he cannot succeed in procuring a man to go to his cache, nor snow shoes, nor so far does he suspect that I prevent the men from making any for him," Ogden noted. "This day he again offered eight beaver or fifty dollars for a pair, and a prime horse to any one that would carry a letter to the American camp; in this also he has failed. It is reported in camp that he wishes to have fifty men, to assist us in trapping, but this we can well dispense with. I would rather prefer Mr McKay's party to assist us." Ogden was not troubled by what he was doing. In his mind, he could excuse it. After "consulting the interest of the Concern," he concluded that he was "fully justified in placing every impediment in their way, and shall continue so long as I have the means of preventing, even should I sacrifice property to obtain my ends."[23]

On the 24th, five Snakes arrived from Bear River and reported the American camps were breaking up. "The Americans are in three different places starving, no buffalo in that quarter this year, and [they] were reduced to eat their horses and dogs." The news greatly increased Tulloch's anxiety. "I suppose," Ogden commented, "we shall again hear of some new extravagant offer, and as I have already anticipated them, will I trust be of no avail to them." He must have meant that he had offered higher "bribes" to snowshoe makers. Next day the camp was alive with rumors.

> Reports arriving from all directions, relative to the distressed state of the Americans, horses dead and reduced to eat them, and their two principal caches destroyed. This I believe to be the case, as one of my men saw four yards [of] calico in the Snake camp. . . . The Americans here now appear determined to proceed and find their traders. They now discover it is to no purpose these extravagant offers, and are making snow shoes themselves. This they ought [to] have done two months since had they been clever, and would have had less snow, and long since would have been [t]here.[24]

Once the Americans started making snowshoes, Ogden knew there was no stopping them. Now he hoped the trip would take so long they would not return before the winter's ice began to melt and he had his traps in the water. He took in good grace the possibility they would succeed. When two of them finally started, he sent men along to see them to the Snake camp, where they planned to sleep the first night. He even did business with them. "Prior to their starting," he explained, "I traded two beaver from them and this with fourteen more the gamblers have secured is so many in our favour."[25]

Ogden called the American snowshoes "make-shifts" and he may have been right. Seven days after leaving, the men were back. They "made their appearance rather unexpectedly to all, but most agreeable to me, at the same time a most cruel disappointment to them, as those here expected they had reached their destination." The two men, he explained, had gotten only "as far as the sources of Portneufs River, when finding it a most fatiguing undertaking, they returned." He supposed that "if they do not make another attempt themselves they will not fail in making more extravagant offers and which I shall use my influence that they shall not be accepted."[26]

None of Tulloch's men got away before the winter weather broke, but to everyone's surprise on the 17th of February another American party arrived. It was led by a man destined to become one of the most successful St. Louis entrepreneurs, Irish-born Robert Campbell. Ogden no longer seemed irritated by these visitors. He may even have begun to welcome them, not only because they were white faces appearing in the wilderness but also because, as he said on this occasion, they usually brought him news. The only British news Campbell had was that the Duke of York had died, "and of course the old story from America, we shall soon be obliged to leave the Columbia; in regard to this however they appear to be more sanguine than hitherto." In other words, Campbell did not speak as Gardner had and certainly did not try to bluff him. "They have no doubt later news from America, than I have. Still nothing farther has transpired, at all events the treaty does not expire before ensuing November, and then we shall know what we have to expect, but I presume not before."[27]

Campbell also had a tale to tell about one of the trappers who had deserted the expedition of 1825. The man had done quite well trapping beaver with the Americans. The news was so surprising it started Ogden reflecting on the contrasting fortunes of the fur trade separating Hudson's Bay people from American fur men. "Old Goddin who left me in the fall under promise of returning [the] ensuing season," he reported,[28] "is now in a fair way of going to St Louis, having sold his eight horses and ten traps for fifteen hundred dollars. Independent of this he has his fall and spring hunt equal to six hundred more, which makes him an independent man." Once again, Ogden found the economic comparisons painful to consider. A man "[i]n the Hudson's Bay Company's service with the strictest economy almost depriving himself of common necessaries, barring accidents, in the course of ten years he might collect that sum." He then addressed Simpson and London headquarters directly.

Is it then surprising that men who consult their own interests, should give preference to the American service; and that they with the disadvantages they are subject to can afford to pay such an extravagant price for beaver, is also not surprising. If they paid all in goods the case would be different, but I know to the contrary. Considerable credit is due to my party for their behaviour, so far it is to be observed they are under a written contract, but if inclined to go, would lay little stress on it and still less in regard to their debts. We have however not yet reached home, and as we shall have some serious difficulty ere we do, I cannot venture to predict what may be the result.[29]

In a very real sense the legal ties in the Snake country expedition had been reversed since the trouble with Johnson Gardner in 1825. Then Ogden's hold on his men had been debt. Now it was contract. And it was Campbell, not Ogden, who complained about desertions and interference with contract. He accused Ogden of admitting into the brigade two Americans who deserted his employ when "heavily indebted" to the company of Smith, Jackson, and Sublette. These were two of the Americans who had joined in late September, telling Ogden they would "accompany me to the Columbia," and he replying that "I could not hold out better terms to them than my own men had."[30] Now he told Campbell he knew nothing about their debts. "I made reply that I had no knowledge of the same," Ogden recorded in his journal, "and as he was now here it was his duty to secure his debts and his men also, that so far they had deserved no encouragement from me, nor would they." It is not hard to imagine how outraged the officers of Hudson's Bay would have been if Ogden had reported that Gardner told him it was his job to secure his own debts. Yet, in lecturing Campbell and pointing out that his men were his responsibility, Ogden assumed a surprisingly high tone, claiming he was behaving much better than Gardner had. "I took the liberty," he wrote, "of observing, that my conduct towards their party was far different from what I had received four years since." Of course, Ogden was addressing Hudson's Bay officers and his words would not have been as hypocritical to them as they seem to us. Although Gardner had actively urged the Iroquois to desert, even harangued them, and Ogden may not have encouraged the two Americans to join him, the two situations might not have been as different as he expected his readers to believe. He gave no indication whether he took the trouble of asking the two Americans if they were deserting contractual obligations or were indebted to an American company. Certainly there is no evidence he was troubled as to whether or not they owed debts. Campbell could have asked him about this or even charged him with duplicity. Instead, like Tulloch before him, he apologized for Gardner. "He said it was far different [conduct], and regretted that at that time there was no regular Company in the country, otherwise I should have received far different treatment." Ogden accepted the apology with remarkably ill grace. "[S]ituated as they are dependent on me," he observed, "it is not their interest to say to the contrary. I have acted so far, honourable towards them, and shall continue so, and probably situated as we are, it is the best policy we can adopt."[31]

After a long conference, Campbell persuaded the two trappers to return to his employ. Ogden had hopes this would not work out. "[I]n my opinion one never will," he wrote. Whether the trapper returned did not much matter to Hudson's Bay. Ogden had made sure the company would not lose. He gave himself a creditor's priority over Campbell's claim to their beaver. "It was . . . well understood before they separated from me, that the debts they contracted in my camp should be discharged, to this all agreed. My share of debts are trifling and shall take good care to secure them."[32]

Due to extremely stormy weather, Campbell was unable to leave for three more days, plenty of time to do some business. He sold Ogden four beaver pelts for beads that he probably wanted for trading with the Snakes. He was on his way to open a trade for his company with the Flatheads, but he would not have needed the beads for them. They could get them more cheaply by trading at Flathead Post. Noticing that the expedition's horses were "very low," he offered to sell the men animals at sixteen large beaver a horse. The price was far too high, at least for the horses he was trying to sell. "It would certainly be a losing concern to purchase on these terms," Ogden reasoned, "for I am of opinion few of them will escape death, and if they do can render very little service this spring."[33] After Campbell left, Tulloch and his men remained.

Changes were occurring with remarkable rapidity in the Snake country. Ogden, who had complained so bitterly when Gardner enticed his freemen to desert, contracted with American freemen without asking them if they were indebted to their American contractees, and in a complete turnaround, freemen were now raising the issue. At least, American freemen were raising it. During the height of the winter, after several failed efforts, Ogden had sent one of his most trusted freemen, François Payette, alone, to find McKay. Payette succeed and returned with a trapper who "had left the Americans last fall" and joined McKay's detached party. He "came here to enquire if they [Smith, Jackson, and Sublette] had any claims against him, and as they said they had not, he has entered into an arrangement with me, on the same footing as our freemen."[34]

It could have been an impressive turn of events—a freeman coming forward to settle debts before changing employment. That this trapper did so may indicate that the word had gone out in the western mountains that neither Hudson's Bay nor the St. Louis companies would protect deserters from their financial obligations. But, also, the man may have come forward only because McKay, with more scruples than Ogden, told him he could not join a Hudson's Bay brigade unless he was free of debt. Ogden makes no mention of why the man inquired of his debts and may not have cared. He expressed no surprise at what, for him, should have been an totally unexpected turn of events. He had to be pleased, however, not only because Hudson's Bay was now taking recruits from the Americans but because he was getting a valuable trapper. "He is a Canadian by birth and a smart active young man, the American trader [Tulloch] has given him a good character, and from the offers he made him to return, I am of opinion he is entitled to it."[35]

The expedition abandoned winter quarters on the 15th of March and began again to trap Snake River. To Ogden's amusement the Americans came along but put out no traps. "It is true we take but very few beaver," he noted, "still it is surprising to me, the Americans, now five in number, who are more or less starving, do not make an attempt to take beaver, not one moves. Their only employment from morning till night is gambling. May they long continue so, in the interim my trappers are not idle, although their success is not great."[36]

It was not until the 26th that Tulloch and his men left the expedition. They had been traveling with it since December. "[W]e met and separated on good terms," Ogden observed. There is, however, no doubt he was relieved to see them go. "I am glad they are off, for while they were with us they caused more trouble than profit." The very next day two Americans "made their appearance from Salt Lake." They had been sent to escort Tulloch back to the company's base camp but had missed him.[37] It may have been quite unfortunate for Tulloch and his men that the newcomers had not arrived twenty-four hours earlier. At least it is possible that guides might have advised a different route. The one they took was disastrous. About three days after leaving the expedition, they were attacked by thirty or forty Blackfeet. Four men were killed and— or so Tulloch claimed—they lost "about four thousand dollars worth of furs, forty-four horses, & a considerable am[oun]t of merchandize."[38] If his furs were worth that much and he had so many horses, Tulloch had been much more successful than Ogden gave him credit for. One of the men killed was the younger brother of William Sublette, who had been a member of Jedediah Smith's party when it traveled with Ogden from Flathead Post to the Snake country in 1825. Ogden never mentioned either brother in his journals. He did not even say that he had met the brother of someone who had been with him three years earlier.[39]

William H. Ashley attempted to turn the tragedy into an international incident. A master at innuendoes, he first noted that "some time after separating from Mr. Ogden & party, but *while within fifteen miles of his Encampment*," Tulloch had been attacked. Next Ashley accused Ogden of buying plundered property. "Notwithstanding I cannot believe that Mr. Ogden himself, would dictate such conduct to Indians," he wrote Senator Benton, "yet there is no doubt in my mind but the furs thus plundered, were sold to him, or some one of his party, in the course, perhaps of twenty four hours after taken by the Indians, and the purchaser must of Known from whence they came."[40]

Ashley was dead wrong if he meant Ogden would ever encourage a native war party to attack American trappers. He would have defended Tulloch had he been able, especially against Blackfeet. There may, however, have been a bit more substance to the charge that Ogden would purchase plundered property. At least, he had implied so himself that past January when he discovered that a nearby band of Snakes had broken into two American caches and appropriated their contents. He then sent "two men with a trading assortment" to the Snakes on the chance they might have gotten some beaver. He never got Tulloch's furs, however, for the attackers had left them scattered about "the Plains." He did not even learn about the attack until he met a Snake war party over a month afterward. "Among the property they have, is the clothing, kettles, huts, shoes, also horses belonging to the American party, who spent the winter with me," he recorded. The Snakes told him that Tulloch had been attacked by Blackfeet and that they had later ambushed the Blackfeet.

> This to us all is a most convincing proof, they have been pillaged of all they had, and no doubt in my mind they are all murdered. Knowing what blood thirsty villains the Black Feet are and also how careless the Americans are, I am of opinion not one has escaped, more particularly so, if they attacked at dawn of day. The sight of this property and the mode by which it has been obtained caused a general gloom over the camp. Probably from the dangerous quarter we are going to, we may be doomed to the same fate. May God preserve us.[41]

Ashley was also wrong about Ogden purchasing Tulloch's property. He got none of it. "The Snake Indian party started at an early hour," he noted the day after meeting them. "They informed me they were on their way to Salt Lake in expectations of finding the Americans there, and intended to restore them their property and horses."[42] The trade goods they expected the Americans to give them as a reward would be worth more to the Snakes than Tulloch's property, even the horses.

The weeks with Tulloch was the last significant encounter Ogden had with Americans in his six Snake country expeditions.[43] He had reason to think that the tide of commercial affairs was turning in favor of Hudson's Bay. On this expedition he had given protection to Americans from September until November, and from late December until the end of March—for five out of six months. At first he had been despondent when he realized how much competition Hudson's Bay faced on the Snake. But as he came to know the Americans better, and began to buy their pelts at favorable prices, he had realized Hudson's Bay could compete. It had been particularly satisfying to have men leave the competition to join him, and, at the same time, none of his freemen deserted. Even the fact that Robert Campbell had been on his way to open a trade with the Flatheads, which must have appeared menacing in the winter, proved to be an insignificant event. The Flatheads had wanted American traders to come to their camps, but by the time Campbell got there, Governor Simpson boasted, it was too late for the Americans to get the Flathead business. Hudson's Bay's reformed tariff of prices had won back the market at Flathead Post. Even more striking, Simpson contended, the deserters were returning to Hudson's Bay.

> The Trade of the Flat Head Post Outfit 1827, was almost entirely lost to us, having fallen into the hands of the Americans, but fortunately made up by that of a party of freemen, who withdrew from our opponents, and delivered their Hunts to us last Spring at the Flat Head Post. These freemen are part of the band that deserted from Mr. Ogden in 1825, and who from the flattering prospects held out to them, conceived they would have made a fortune by changing sides; but the excellent footing on which the Trapping Expeditions were put, by Chief Factor McLoughlin after that disastrous affair, has proved highly advantageous in many points of view, as our own people are now perfectly satisfied with their situations, many of our late deserters find it advisable to return to their duty, and it has occasioned so much disaffection in the American camp, that several of their people have already joined us, and were we disposed to encourage desertion, very few would remain with them.[44]

Writing to London, Simpson was far too optimistic. He was using a few scattered triumphs to claim overall victory. Not even Flathead Post was secured until the next year, when the clerk in charge was authorized to buy furs below American prices. That step served to check the American advance from the south and east. In other areas of the Snake country in 1828 and 1829, the Americans were in retreat. They would not return with the numbers that had so alarmed Ogden in the fall of 1827. But other Americans were coming. The Snake country would not belong to Hudson's Bay.[45]

CHAPTER FIFTEEN

The Country Virtually Falls into Our Keeping

Peter Skene Ogden's fifth and sixth Snake country expeditions both steered west of the Bear River area, to the Humboldt River, which Ogden first reported and mapped, and even farther south into Mexican territory, quite far down the Colorado River, even across the Mohave Desert. He followed routes on which it was very unlikely the brigade would meet Americans except along the Snake River as it traveled from the Columbia to the Humboldt. That was the way the two expeditions turned out. Ogden met few Americans and had no more international encounters.

It was almost immaterial if the Americans retreated. The mere threat of their competition, even when they were not met, was what shaped the policy of Hudson's Bay Company in the Columbia department. In the relatively new hunting area around Fort Colvile, for example, Hudson's Bay suffered from a shortage of trappers. It did not want to bring new freemen across the mountains. It preferred to win back deserters. The extent to which they returned became a measure of the company's perceived triumph over the Americans. The clerk at Flathead Post, John Warren Dease, was instructed to undersell American prices, even if that meant taking short-term losses. When fourteen of the deserters came in to trade during the winter of 1827–28, John McLoughlin sensed victory. "I have reason to expect they will be followed by all the rest and perhaps by most it not all the Freemen trappers in the Snake Country," he wrote the company's governor and committee. Both he and Governor

George Simpson told their superiors that when Ogden returned from his third expedition in late July, 1828, he would bring back even more deserters. Those deserters would return, Simpson asserted, because "they find that our terms are more advantageous, and that they are more fairly dealt by with us, than with our opponents." McLoughlin instructed John Work at Fort Colvile to "assure them, that we will allow them their supplies as low as we can and pay them as high a price for their Beaver as possible." Simpson, McLoughlin, and the other Columbia officers told themselves that the new policy was successful because it was fair and made good business sense, but, in fact, it made sense to them because of American competition, not because of their new-found regard for the freemen's welfare.[1]

Although Ogden's fifth Snake country expedition of 1828–29 encountered no Americans, they were always on his mind. His reason for going southwest from the Snake River basin into today's state of Nevada was to get ahead of the Americans. During his second expedition he had heard from several Snakes that the rivers southwest of their nation were rich in beaver, and had thought of going there, but his horses were then jaded and he worried about supplies. "[T]here is certainly some fine Streams in that quarter that discharges into the Gulph of California," he had explained, still unaware of the geography, "but to reach them in a country similar to the one we are now in destitute of any Kind of resources   therefore without a Stock of provisions it is needless to make the attempt." He heard tales from the Snakes that Jedediah Smith had tried to go there and found the conditions too severe. Now over two years later, he decided to lead his fifth expedition southwest from the Snake River, if only to get there first.[2]

As he passed down the Snake River in October 1828 on his way to establishing winter quarters, Ogden encountered no Americans but he was prepared for them. After passing the mouth of Burnt River he detached a party of seven men under François Payette to trap the north side of the Snake while the main brigade traveled down the south side. "I gave Payette a small trading assortment in case of seeing Americans or Indians," he noted.[3] It would be easy to overlook these words. If they are read in haste with little attention, Ogden does not seem to be saying anything significant, but he was. He was saying he was no longer apprehensive of meeting Americans. Perhaps he even wanted to meet them—if they would exchange beaver for products of the "trading assortment" he was carrying. What we do not know, and what would be most revealing to find out, is whether any of his "trading assortment" was selected with the Americans alone in mind, items such as tobacco that American trappers would buy but the Snakes did not want.

Months later, when on the Humboldt River, he thought of the Americans again, mainly because he was so satisfied that he had beaten them across the mountains to an untrapped stream where every day his men were catching beaver.

> I will venture to say in no part of the country have I found beaver more abundant than in this river and I apprehend we will not soon find another to equal it. . . . I know of no other quarter excepting rivers that have been frequently almost yearly trapped and now almost destitute of beaver, but still small parties by gleaning, although dangerous to risk, may yet make tolerable hunts. This plan the Americans have latterly adopted but the advantage they have over us, their total numbers exceed eighty trappers and the fortunate make up for the loss of those who are defective, but this from the plan we follow would not answer. This year I have only twenty-eight trappers and fifteen are in two parties, and I shall be well pleased if one of the two escapes. I have now every reason to hope our returns will equal those of last year granting one of the two absent parties escape. The trappers now with me average 125 beaver per man and are truly well pleased with their success.[4]

The men would be even more pleased after the expedition returned to Fort Vancouver at the end of July. McLoughlin was very impressed with the condition of their beaver, which amounted "to four thousand" pelts. The fur was, McLoughlin reported, "remarkably well dressed and in the highest state of preservation, which, when it is considered some of these Furs have been Carried on Horses backs through the Country since last fall Winter & Summer, certainly does him [Ogden] great credit." He knew Ogden was responsible for the skins being in such splendid condition, but he also realized he had a chance to impress the freemen with the company's new pricing policy spreading the rewards among the freemen as well as the officers. "[T]hough we are not bound to allow them more than ten shillings per Made Beaver," he explained to London, "still we have deemed it adviseable to avail ourselves of the great care they have taken of their furs to allow them one Shilling more on each made Beaver."[5]

Ogden remained at Fort Vancouver but a brief time. He went to Fort Nez Perces where he waited for two months while buying horses from the natives for his sixth and final Snake country expedition. It is the one about which we know the least because on the return to the Columbia the expedition's only journal was lost when a canoe filled with men and furs disappeared in a whirlpool. He had led it to the Great Salt Lake, and then across the Mohave Desert to California. We know little else. We do not even know if there were any substantial contacts with American parties.

Just a few days before Ogden's fourth Snake country expedition had ended its journey at Fort Nez Perces, Jedediah Smith's party of American trappers had been nearly annilhilated on the Umpqua River by members of either the Kalawatset or Kuitshe nation.[6] Only Smith and two other men had escaped to Fort Vancouver where they were given shelter by Hudson's Bay.[7] Smith had come up to the Umpqua from California and there is some evidence that cannot be substantiated that Ogden's sixth expedition was guided to California by one of the survivors of Smith's party. And even if not, it is possible that Odgen had an account of the trail written by Smith.[8]

Governor Simpson may have been the only Hudson's Bay officer to find a connection between Ogden's last expedition and American competition. The expedition, he told the governor and committee in London, had "penetrated from the Interior as far South as some of the headwaters of a river running into the Bay of St Francisco, which we understood to be the Buona Ventura but is now ascertained to be the Sacramento." Now they better understood the geography and Hudson's Bay parties would never again be told to find the Buenaventura River. They would, however, be going back to central California. Ogden's "returns are less in value and in quantity that [*sic*] any we have had from that quarter but the Expedition still pays tolerably well, and it is our intention to keep it constantly employed while it clears its expenses." Ogden's invasion of Mexican territory did not upset Simpson. Only the Americans troubled him. "From Chief Trader Ogden's report," he explained, "I am concerned to find that the Country is much exhausted and still overrun by American Trappers." There was a positive side. Hudson's Bay's heartland was not threatened. The Americans were in the Snake country and California, but they were far from the Columbia. "[W]e were clear of opposition in the Columbia up to the date of last advices," he wrote in July 1831. The best advice was "that no apprehension of annoyance from the Americans was entertained."[9]

John Work succeeded Ogden as leader of the Snake country expedition. He was instructed to "endeavor to draw off any of the late deserters found attached to American camps—also if any respectable American trappers wish to join the Expedition there can be no objection if they deposit skins to cover the supplies they receive."[10] He had few meetings with Americans, however,[11] and only one is worth recounting for the light it sheds on the level of international rivalry in the Snake country. It puts a final cap on all the changes that had occurred since trapping expeditions of the two nations began running into one another. The American leader did more than refuse to allow an Iroquois to desert to him from Hudson's Bay. He actively supported Work and prevented the freeman from abandoning his debts.

The meeting occurred on the Snake River in April 1831. On the 8th of the month several of Work's trappers, whom he identified only as "half-breeds," attempted to leave the expedition. He stopped them from deserting. Four days later the brigade met an American party led by one of the foremost mountain entrepreneurs from St. Louis, Lucien B. Fontanelle. "Two of our men Bt Tyaquariche and A. Dumais wish to desert from us and accompany the Americans [to] whom they have applied to be received in their employ," Work noted. "Mr. Fontanelle came over and apprised me of the circumstances and stated that he had refused to have anything to do with them, or to receive some furs which they offered him until they had settled their accounts with me and paid up the debt which they owed the Honbl Hudson's Bay Company."[12]

In his party Fontanelle had some of Tyaquariche's relatives. They were Iroquois who had deserted from Ogden's expedition on the Weber in 1825. Tyaquariche apparently asserted that, no matter what Fontanelle said and no matter his debts, he was going to leave Work and join his relatives. He probably thought he had the upper hand, that Fontanelle would have to take him in, but the American showed how a strong-minded partisan could keep control of his brigade. "[T]his Mr.

Fontanelle said he could not prevent as they were freemen, but he could expect no supplies of any kind from him." One might think that Tyaquariche would have joined his relatives, and, through them, received whatever supplies he needed. We can only guess, but Fontanelle must have warned the relatives that if they took Tyaquariche in, he would cut them off. At least Work implied that some threat by Fontanelle forced Tyaquariche to come to terms. "Were people who have to deal with these scoundrels in this country to act mutually in a similar manner to Mr. Fontanelle," Work wrote, "there would be much less difficulty with roguish men and they would have less opportunity of putting their knavery in practice."[13] It is evident that Work had read Ogden's journals with the same lack of understanding with which they had been written. His standard, like Ogden's, for judging Americans in the Snake country was Johnson Gardner.

Next day Tyaquariche settled his account with Work. He "paid 15 beaver which is within 4 beaver of the amount of his debts, but he insisted on taking one of the Company's horses which was lent to him." Work refused to let him have it and there was a very dangerous confrontation that could have led to bloodshed, as weapons were pointed on both sides. Work stood his ground and prevailed, largely because he was physically supported not only by Fontanelle but by his own *métis* (but not by the Canadians in the brigade, either *engagés* or freemen). Tyaquariche had two horses of his own and Work thought of appropriating "one of them for the balance of the debt which he owes." Work did not seize the horse, and his reason tells us much about the permanency of Snake country family ties. He was, he wrote, "apprehensive had I done so he would have left his family consisting of a wife & three children on my hands, which would have greatly embarrassed me to take them back to their friends at Walla Walla." Work did not say that Tyaquariche threatened to leave his wife and children if the horse was taken from him. It was Work who was "apprehensive" of what might happen. Most of the Americans had moved across the river, but Fontanelle had "remained to the last," supporting Work against Tyaquariche. With all that, even though he was in a strong position, almost the opposite of Ogden's options on the Weber, Work was not in complete control. The wife and children kept him from executing judgment on the debt by appropriating Tyaquariche's second horse. The other man who wanted to desert,

A. Dumais, had less bargaining power. The unity of Work and Fontanelle left him no alternative but to back down. "Dumais," Work noted, "when he would not be allowed to go off without paying his debt and returning the Company's horses and traps said nothing more about the matter." In other words, he stayed with the expedition.[14]

Work had no other encounters with Americans that are worth recounting. There was, however, one incident that occurred on the penultimate day of 1831 which was indicative of how attitudes in the Snake country had changed since Peter Ogden's bitterness against Johnson Gardner six years earlier. "A party of twelve Americans passed in the morning on the way to [hunt] buffalo," he noted when on the Salmon River in today's Idaho. "They appeared to be very hungry but did not stop, or they would have received [been asked] to eat from [by] our people, indeed it was not known that they were so short of food till they were gone."[15] He did not think of them as commercial competition so much as fellow white men on the edge of the Blackfoot country who did not have to ask for assistance. He would have volunteered it.

It was not just a matter of better appreciation of the integrity and business ethics of the men on the other side. There was the belief among Hudson's Bay officers that the competition was over; they had won. "I broke up the American party in the Snake Country," McLoughlin had boasted that same year, 1831, "and I did this simply by underselling them and showing them we could afford to sell [to] the trappers at European servants' prices."[16] He meant the prices at which the company sold goods to the Orkneyan *engagés*. The effect was felt as far away as Fort Tecumseh, an American Fur Company trading post south of the Arikara villages beneath the great bend of the Missouri River. Again, we see the situation reversed from 1825. Now the Americans had difficulties controlling the freemen. "I think they will give us a great deal of trouble," Kenneth McKenzie wrote to Pierre Chouteau about the freemen in the area of today's Montana and the two Dakotas. "They put the devil in our engagés   moreover they traffic with indians & threaten to carry their furs to the British traders, who they say sell goods for nothing & I know myself they sell goods much cheaper than we can afford to do. It would be a good thing if those fellows could be stop[p]ed from carrying on such a commerce."[17] It might be good for the American Fur Company but there was only one way to stop the freemen from crossing the Rockies and selling their furs to Ogden or Work, or going to Flat-head Post or even to the Columbia. That was to buy at prices higher than Hudson's Bay was paying. Even after introducing steamboats to the Missouri, the American Fur Company could not undercut Hudson's Bay, which was always ready to go lower.

Governor Simpson was even more optimistic than McLoughlin. The Hudson's Bay policy of denuding the rivers of beaver, he pointed out, had done much more than drive American fur trappers from the Snake country. It also meant that American settlers could not push their way into the Oregon country. The Willamette River was "impassable even to hunters," he contended, and the Snake "route is unthinkable."

> I am of the opinion we have little to apprehend from settlers in this quarter [the Columbia] and from Indian traders nothing; as none except large capitalists could attempt it, and this attempt would cost a heavy sum of money, of which they could never recover much. This they are well aware of, therefore as regards formidable opposition I feel perfectly at ease unless the all-grasping policy of the American government should enduce it to embark some of its national wealth in furtherance of the object.[18]

Hudson's Bay became the aggressor. London's orders that Snake country expeditions remain west of the mountains were ignored. By 1830 the company even extended its "scorched-earth" policy toward the Missouri where John Work met and traded with American trappers.[19] He had hoped to push even farther and trap the upper Missouri before the Americans, but was stopped by too many battles fought with the Blackfeet. They had been obtaining more guns and ammunition now that the American Fur Company had opened Fort Union at the mouth of the Yellowstone and built Fort Piegan and Fort McKenzie at the mouth of the Marias. There was even one morning when Work was attacked by three hundred Blackfeet, or so he claimed. It was an incredible number, previously unknown in the western mountains. Work may have exaggerated, but he did not exaggerate the constant harassment as the Blackfeet hounded his trappers day after day. The war parties "were too numerous," he complained, "I was able to make no hunt." "[A]ll my perseverance and fortitude were scarcely sufficient to bear up against the danger, misery, and consequent anxiety to which I was exposed."[20]

It was not the Americans who drove Hudson's Bay back across the mountains. It was the Blackfeet. Work and the Snake country expedition did not go east again. His last important trapping excursion went south to California.[21]

A month after Work returned from California, London headquarters ordered an end to the Snake country brigades. "The operations of the Snake Expeditions had been very unprofitable for several years past, and attended with serious loss of life," McLoughlin was told. "[W]e therefore desire that if not abandoned this year it may be broke up next summer."[22]

Hudson's Bay was not ready to give up the struggle for the Snake country. It tried to establish a permanent presence on the river by purchasing Fort Hall from the Boston fur trader Nathaniel Wyeth. Located beyond the American Falls in today's southeast Idaho, Fort Hall's role in history was ironic, certainly not what Hudson's Bay Company intended. It became a way station on the Oregon Trail, a place of rest and sustentation for American emigrants, helping to ease the difficulties of the trip, speeding them on their way to the Willamette, the Columbia, and the Walla Walla.

There were some Hudson's Bay officers who continued to hope that Great Britain would do more than retain possession of the territory north of the Columbia; that it would keep part of the Snake country as well. As late as 1838 James Douglas was urging his colleagues to build another post even deeper into the Snake country than Fort Hall. He wanted it "established in the Youta [Utah] Country," south of Great Salt Lake, on the Mexican frontier. He urged the company to revive what he called "the Snake business," which, he reminded the governor and committee, had been instigated "to watch the movements and check the advance of opposition." There were still ways to do that, Douglas argued. To check the Americans in the Snake country, Hudson's Bay did not have to send out more trapping expeditions. The company had a resource it had not yet tapped. Indians were not as reliable trappers as a brigade of French Canadians led by Peter Skene Ogden but they were less costly and, if aroused, could be even more effective keeping Americans out of the country.

> I also feel most anxious to rouse the slumbering energies of the Natives and to place them, as hunters, in competition with the

American Trappers. The silent working of this system will teach the former to prize their natural rights of chace, which are not now appreciated, and excite a spirit of resistance, that may cause the expulsion of every intruder, and become the means of fortifying our tenure of the country. Such a spirit has been manifested by neighbouring Tribes, who have uniformly opposed the attempts made to trap their country and never fail to punish offenders, of that class, in a very summary manner.[23]

We cannot dismiss these suggestions merely because they are so extreme and made so late in Snake country history. Douglas is remembered as more than an important and respected officer of the Hudson's Bay Company. He was a future governor of British Columbia. No other member of the company would obtain greater political prominence in North America. It tells us a great deal about the thinking of Hudson's Bay officers that, as late as 1838, a man of his caliber was still formulating plans for keeping Americans out of the Snake country. Even more striking is the policy he wanted to adopt. By the "neighbouring Tribes" he meant the Blackfoot. What he wanted was to make the nations of the Snake country so dependent on trapping furs they would attack any American party entering their territories. A decade earlier William H. Ashley had claimed this already was Hudson's Bay policy. He had been wrong. But if Douglas's program had been adopted, Ashley might have been proven right.

Douglas did little to promote his plan. It may be that, like Simpson and McLoughlin, he began to think the Americans were routed. "Should the Americans traders actually withdraw," he hopefully wrote a year later, "the Country virtually falls into our keeping."[24] Like Simpson, McLoughlin, and even some Americans, Douglas believed the fur trappers were the vanguard of settlement. If the trappers moved permanently across the Rockies, the farmers and ranchers would follow. If the trappers retreated, the settlers would not come. What Simpson, McLoughlin, Ogden, and Douglas did not appreciate was that the American trappers were not in retreat geographically, only economically.

Drastic changes were occurring in the fur trade and the era of the mountain men would not long outlast the demise of the Snake country expedition. Europeans no longer were buying hats made from beaver.

In 1835, for the first time, buffalo robes sold better than beaver on the St. Louis market.[25] Five years later, hard times had come to the mountains, and many men could no longer make a living trapping streams that once had teemed with beaver. In February 1840 Francis Ermatinger, Hudson's Bay clerk in charge of Fort Hall, was visiting the company's posts on the Columbia River. "The Snake country is not as when you were here, a snug little party to conduct to their trapping ground," he lamented in a letter to his brother. "We have to deal with as lawless a rabble, the scum of all nations, as can possibly be gathered together. I left Fort Hall upon the 26th November and soon afterwards received an express informing me that a party of the scoundrels had been at the Fort and run off all the horses, at the same time left a note threatening my life and declaring that 'their fathers fought for the country and the Company shall not possess it.'"[26] The threat implied in that note would be the last echo of Johnson Gardner heard in the Snake country.

Some scholars of the fur trade, even historians employed by the United States government, have assumed there was violence whenever rival trapping parties met in the mountains. "[T]here was virtually no law west of the settlements," Merrill J. Mattes has written. "No claims or rights were recognized, except those which force alone could uphold."[27] Robert Newell would have been astonished had he read these words. He was an American mountain man in the Snake country during the difficult times of 1839 when some desperate "scoundrels" living at "Fort Misery" in Brown's Hole on the Yampo River had horses driven off by Sioux raiders. In revenge, they went over to Fort Hall and stole the Hudson's Bay horses, as Ermatinger would report to his brother, and also gathered up all the horses belonging to an old Snake Indian. Other mountain men were enraged. Newell joined with a party including Joe Meek, William Craig, and Kit Carson, under the leadership of Joseph R. Walker, to recover the horses. They were successful. The lesson to be marked is not just that the horses were restored. They were restored to the Hudson's Bay Company and to the old Snake Indian, two owners who were outside of and did not belong to the national or economic group to which these mountain men belonged. The men whom they attacked and from whom they recovered the horses did belong to their national and economic interest group. Taking the horses from their fellow American mountain men, they returned them to the British and the Snake because, as they understood either the law or the question of right, Hudson's Bay and the old Snake were the owners.[28]

"The horse-stealing episode was the low water mark of deterioration in the mountain men's relations with one another," observed Dorothy O. Johansen, who published Newell's account, and so it was. Francis Ermatinger, the Hudson's Bay officer most concerned with the event, had much the same perception when lamenting to his brother, "The Snake country is not as when you were here." Certainly Newell thought so when he both recalled the Snake country past and despaired of the future. "Shuch thing never has been Known till late," he wrote of mountain men stealing horses from other fur traders and from friendly Indians.[29]

In the mind of Robert Newell, either law or righteous behavior had departed from the western mountains and the time had come for the fur men to leave as well. That summer he attended the last American fur-trade rendezvous, and then, "convinced that the trapping era was over,"[30] on 27 September 1840, "with two waggons and my family I left fort hall for the Columbia and with some little Dif[f]iculty I arrived at Walla Walla thare I left one waggon and the other I had took down in a boat to vancouver and have it at this time on my farm about 25 miles from vancouver west."[31]

It has been said that Simpson's program of making barren the Snake country was a success, that it "resulted also in postponing for over twenty years the cession of the Oregon Country to the United States; and when this cession took place, it was largely caused by the influx of American settlers, and was in no way caused by American fur-traders."[32] Maybe— and then again, maybe not. Hudson's Bay program of denuding the beaver streams of the Snake country was successful in part. It created a shortage of fur-bearing animals and contributed to an economic depression in the valleys of the Bear, the Lemhi, the Boise, and the Snake Rivers. It accomplished what Simpson expected it would, driving American mountain men such as Newell from the trade. But Newell had not retreated to the beaver streams of the Missouri, the Yellowstone, the Green, or the Arkansas as Simpson anticipated. He went instead to the Columbia. The party he led amounted to much more than the sum of its numbers—three women and nine men, including the fur trappers Joe Meek, Caleb Wilkins, and, ironically, Francis Ermatinger, "the ranking trader of the Hudson's Bay in the Snake River Country."[33] They were the people who brought the first wagons to Oregon, proving correct Ogden's fearful prediction that one day wagons could travel from the lower Missouri to the Columbia River. Almost as important, Newell and Meek did the very thing that the Hudson's Bay Company most wanted to prevent. They settled in the Willamette Valley. Newell helped draft the organic law for Oregon, and served two terms as speaker of the house of representatives. Meek became the territory's sheriff, and, in one of the most memorable events in the state's history, rode horseback across the continent to help persuade Congress that it was time to enact the Oregon bill giving the country once ruled by Hudson's Bay an American government.[34]

Simpson had been both right and wrong. He was right that Hudson's Bay could strip the Snake country of beaver and hold the American fur trappers in check; wrong in thinking that the mountain men were the vanguard of settlement and that if they were stopped the settlers would have no one to follow. The mountain men, driven from their mountains, frequently became the original settlers; when they did not, they were often the ones who guided the settlers. The year after Newell's settling, the first wagon train from the Missouri frontier made it into Oregon, led part of the way by Thomas "Broken Hand" Fitzpatrick, one of those young men who two decades earlier came west, enlisted in the employ of William H. Ashley, and went on to become legends in the mountains. Behind them—behind those first wagons brought to the Oregon country by Newell and Fitzpatrick—stretched the thousands of overland emigrants, the men and women who would soon be passing through the trapped-over Snake country, and who would force proud, autonomous, aristocratic Hudson's Bay Company to retreat far beyond the Columbia River Valley, which it had so long coveted, into the relative isolation of New Caledonia.

Notes

CHAPTER 1: TO PREVENT DISPUTES AND DIFFERENCES

1. Karamanski, Book Review, p. 1706.

2. For discussion of a small but important aspect of Indian domestic and international law in the North American West, see *Patterns of Vengeance.*

3. Articles 1 and 2, Convention with Great Britain, 20 October 1818, 8 *United States Statutes at Large,* pp. 248–50.

4. Article 3, ibid., p. 249.

5. These and similar incidents are discussed in a chapter entitled "The Behaviorism of Property." *Law for the Elephant*, pp. 335–64. The cases are at pages 350, 351–52, 354–55.

6. Entry for 9 October 1849, Hoover, *Diary.*

7. Entry for 9 October 1849, Hoover, *Revised Journal.*

8. Entry for 23 August 1852, Conyers, "Diary."

9. Entry for 19 November 1849, Bruff, *Journals*, p. 645.

10. Entries for 13–14 December 1849, Bruff, *Journals*, pp. 660–61.

CHAPTER 2: THE WILD AND UNTRAMMELLED LIFE

1. For a social, institutional, and (to a much lesser extent) legal history of the Astorians, see Ronda, *Astoria.*

2. 1&2 Geo. 4, c. 66.

3. *West of Ashley*, p. 1.

4. See Ross, *Hunters.*

5. When Lord Selfkirk, the founder of Red River, and member of Hudson's Bay Company, was sent to Montreal for trial, Judge Isaac Ogden recused himself because his son, Peter Skene, was a "winterer" for the North West Company. Campbell, *North West Company*, p. 237.

6. Lorne Ste. Croix, "Charles Richard Ogden," *Dictionary of Canadian Biography* (1976) 9:610–11.

7. Glyndwr Williams, "Peter Skene Ogden," ibid. (1985) 8:660.

8. Cox, *Columbia River*, pp. 307–8.

9. Binns, *Ogden*, p. 19.

CHAPTER 3: ONE OF THE MOST UNPRINCIPLED MEN

1. Cline, *Ogden*, p. 13; Glyndwr Williams, "Peter Skene Ogden," in *Dictionary of Canadian Biography* (1985) 8:660.

2. [McGillivray], *On the Origin*, p. 6; entry for 16 October 1803, Harmon, *Journal*, p. 79.

3. Ross, *Hunters*, pp. 65–66.

4. Morton, "Jurisdiction Act," pp. 129–30.

5. Phillips, *Fur Trade*, 2: 295.

6. Robert S. Allen, "Peter Fidler," *Dictionary of Canadian Biography* (1987) 6:249–52 (quote on p. 250); Rich, *Fur Trade*, p. 214. For example, on 11 September 1805, Fidler wrote: "The French [*i.e.*, North Westers] have destroyed our garden, stolen our canoes, made a house to watch us, and put up two tents close to our house, not four yards from it, to keep every Indian away." Tyrrell, "Peter Fidler," p. 125. Fidler's post was Nottingham House. Black was a clerk at Fort Chipewyan.

7. Cline, *Ogden*, p. 14; Glyndwr Williams, "Peter Skene Ogden," in *Dictionary of Canadian Biography* (1985) 8:660.

8. Barker, Introduction to Ogden, pp. xvi–xvii; Binns, *Ogden*, pp. 33–34; Cline, *Ogden*, p. 14. Black must have been an officer, for Fidler always refers him as Mr., the Hudson's Bay address for an officer.

9. Cline, *Ogden*, p. 15. For a brief summary of what happened in 1811, see this book and Rich, *Fur Trade*, p. 213.

10. Entries for 21 January 1811 and 19 November 1810, in Patterson, Introduction to *Journal*, p. xxxii.

11. Robert S. Allen, "Peter Fidler," *Dictionary of Canadian Biography*, (1987) 6:249–52, at 251; Patterson, Introduction to *Journal*, p. xxxii.

12. Cline, *Ogden*, pp. 15–18; Rich, Robertson Appendix, p. 231.

13. Bird, *Edmonton Report;* entry for 31 December 1814, Bird, *Ninth Edmonton Journal.* The Paint River is now named Vermilion River.

14. Entry for 1 February 1815, Bird, *Ninth Edmonton Journal.* See entries for 1 April and 12 May 1815 for depositions by James Ross and James Spencer.

15. Letter from James Bird to Joseph Howse, and letter from James Bird to James Stewart McFarlane, 5 March 1815, Bird, *Ninth Edmonton Journal.*

16. Entry for 28 March 1815, Bird, *Ninth Edmonton Journal.*

17. Entry for 31 March 1815, ibid.

18. Glyndwr Williams, "Peter Skene Ogden," in *Dictionary of Canadian Biography*, (1985), 8:660.

19. Entry for 16 May 1816, Bird, *Tenth Edmonton Journal.* For a different version of the killing, see Cline, *Ogden*, p. 22.

20. Cline, *Ogden*, pp. 21, 22.

21. *Patterns of Vengeance*, pp. 75–84.

22. Entries for 4, 5 March 1817, Bird, *Fourth Carlton Journal.*

23. Entry for 26 April 1817, ibid.

24. Keep in mind how Bird's superiors at company headquarters might have reacted, especially those at York Factory. They understood the potential consequences of employing Indians in such a situation far more than would those in London. They held the belief that the Canadians and Americans of the North West Company were much more skilled dealing with Indians than were the Scottish–born officers of Hudson's Bay.

25. Cline, *Ogden*, p. 23.

26. Entry for 13 April 1817, Bird, *Fourth Carlton Journal;* information of John McLeod, 17 May 1817, *Documents of 1817;* McGregor, "Old Whitehead," p. 169; Barker, Introduction to Ogden, pp. xvii–xviii.

27. Wallace, "Explorer of Finlay River," p. 29.

28. Cline, *Ogden*, p. 22.

29. Cox, *Columbia River*, p. 308.

30. Ibid., p. 309.

31. Ibid., p. 308.

32. Binns, *Ogden*, p. 49; Morton, *Canadian West*, p. 711; Rich, *Fur Trade*, p. 232; Cline, *Ogden*, p. 25: Glyndwr Williams, "Peter Skene Ogden," in *Dictionary of Canadian Biography* (1985) 8:660.

33. Ross, *Hunters*, pp. 129–30; Karamanski, "Iroquois and Fur Trade," p. 9; Binns, *Ogden*, pp. 51, 62.

34. Rich, *Fur Trade*, p. 241; George Woodcock, "Cuthbert Grant," *Dictionary of Canadian Biography* (1985) 8:341–44; Patterson, Introduction to *Journal*, p. xlvi; Binns, *Ogden*, pp. 64–65.

35. Letter from Andrew Colvile to George Simpson, 10 March 1823, in Cline, *Ogden*, pp. 39–40.

36. Council of 5 July 1823, *Minutes of Northern Department*, pp. 52–53; Cline, *Ogden*, p. 42; Lamb, Introduction to McLoughlin *Letters*, pp. xxii; Glyndwr Williams, "Peter Skene Ogden," in *Dictionary of Canadian Biography* (1985) 8:660.

37. Letter from George Simpson to Andrew Colvile, 8 September 1823, in Cline, *Ogden*, p. 42.

38. Glyndwr Williams, "Peter Skene Ogden," in *Dictionary of Canadian Biography* (1985) 8:660–61; Cline, "Ogden's Nevada," p. 4; Galbraith, *Imperial Factor*, p. 90.

39. Galbraith, *Imperial Factor*, p. 90; Patterson, Introduction to *Journal*, pp. lxi–lxii.

40. Simpson, *Character Book*, pp. 193–94.

41. Ibid., p. 194.

CHAPTER 4: WE HOLD THIS COUNTRY BY SO SLIGHT A TENURE

1. Williams, "Hudson's Bay Company," pp. 63–64.

2. Ogden, "Snake Country Report 1825/26," p. 262. "His definition is interesting because in it he reveals a strange picture of spatial relationships in which he revolved the true map ninety degrees counter clockwise. But it also explains why his travels, which took him far beyond the drainage basin of the Snake River, or the lands of the Snake people, are consistently described as travels in the Snake Country and part of the Snake Country command." Johansen, Introduction to Ogden, pp. xxvi–xxvii.

3. Ogden, "Snake Country Report 1825/26," p. 263.

4. Ibid., pp. 262, 263.

5. Ross, *Hunters*, p. 177.

6. Entry for 3 November 1824, Simpson, *Journal*, pp. 56–57. Fort George, the former Astoria, was near the mouth of the Columbia River.

7. Letter from George Simpson to Andrew Colvile, 9 August 1824, Innis, Introduction to *Minutes*, p. xxxiii; Williams, "Hudson's Bay Company," p. 64.

8. Letter from George Simpson to John McLoughlin, 10 July 1826, in Merk, Introduction, p. xxiii; letter from same to same, 15 March 1829, Simpson, *Journal*, p. 308.

9. Letter from Governor & Committee to Chief Factors Columbia Department, 27 July 1825, and letter from same to George Simpson, 12 March 1827, Merk, *Fur Trade and Empire*, pp. 252, 286; Williams, "Hudson's Bay Company," p. 56; Mattes, *Fur Traders*, p. 11.

10. Lamb, Introduction to McLoughlin *Letters*, p. lxi; "Ogden's Report," p. 118.

11. Simpson's Report, 1828, in *Minutes of Northern Department*, p. 230, n. 1; Barker, Book Review, p. 44; Lamb, Introduction to McLoughlin *Letters*, p. xiii. Also, see Rich, *Fur Trade*, p. 272. Part of the plan was to station a Hudson's Bay vessel on the coast to hinder American maritime traders. Williams, "Hudson's Bay Company," p. 63.

12. Barker, Book Review, p. 44; Haines, Introduction to Work, p. xvii; Carey, *General History*, p. 105; Letter from John McLoughlin to Governor and Committee, 16 November 1836, *Letters of McLoughlin—First Series*, pp. 172–73.

13. Letter from James Douglas to Governor and Committee, 18 October 1838, *Letters of McLoughlin—First Series*, p. 242. Also, see Holmes, "James Douglas," pp. 144–45.

14. McLean, *Notes of Service*, p. 351 (lay waste); Clokey, *Ashley*, p. 155 (*cordon sanitaire*); Josephy, *Nez Perce*, p. 71 (buffer wasteland); Morgan, *Jedediah Smith*, p. 132 (fur desert); Warner, "Peter Skene Ogden," p. 213 (fur desert); Howay, Sage, and Angus, *British Columbia*, p. 63 (fur desert); Galbraith, "British-American Competition," pp. 246–47 (fur desert); Innis, Introduction to *Minutes*, p. lxviii (fire guard); Williams, "Hudson's Bay Company," p. 63 (scorched-earth); Miller and Miller, Introduction to Ogden, p. xiv (scorched stream).

15. Galbraith, *Imperial Factor*, p. 89.

16. Letter from Governor and Committee to George Simpson, 12 March 1827, in Merk, *Fur Trade and Empire*, p. 286; letter from Committee to George Simpson, 23 February 1826, Innis, Introduction to *Minutes*, p. lxxiv.

17. Entry for 9 June 1826, Ogden, *First Snake Journals*, p. 181; entry for 29 April 1829, Ogden, *Fourth Snake Journal*, p. 145; Miller and Miller, Introduction to Ogden, pp. xiv–xv, lxvi. Similarly, see Entry for 2 October 1826, in Ogden, *Second Snake Journal*, pp. 8–9.

18. Council of 26 June 1826 and Standing Rules and Regulations (1828–1835), *Minutes of Northern Department*, pp. 168–70, 229.

19. Resolve #109, Minutes of Council 1825 Abridged, p. 316; letter from George Simpson to John Stuart, 2 August 1826, *Minutes of Northern Department*, p. 170, n. 2; Morton, *Canadian West*, p. 697; Merk, Introduction, p. xxiii.

20. Innis, Introduction to *Minutes*, pp. lix–lx; Smyth, "Piegan Trade," p. 8. "The sedentariness of the beaver, which made trapping easy, and the relatively low rate of natural increase (when compared, for example, to the muskrat) leaves the beaver vulnerable to depletion." Wishart, *Fur Trade*, p. 30. Also, see *Thompson's Narrative*, p. 94.

21. Minutes of the Council of the Northern District of Rupert's Land, 14 June 1841 and 10 June 1843, in *Canadian North-West*, 2: 832–33, 865–66; Ray, *Indians in Fur Trade*, pp. 198–99.

22. Standing Rules and Regulations (1828–1835), *Minutes of Northern Department*, p. 229.

23. Standing Rules and Regulations (1836), *Canadian North-West*, 2:754–55; Ray, *Indians in Fur Trade*, p. 199. For an American trader's summary of the HBC's "nursing" system, see Wishart, *Fur Trade*, p. 32.

24. Standing Rules and Regulations (1828–1835), *Minutes of Northern Department*, p. 230; ibid., p. 170, n. 1.

25. Letter from Governor and Committee to George Simpson, 16 January 1828, *Simpson's 1828 Journey*, p. 157; letter from John McLoughlin to Finan McDonald, 17 August 1825, in Ogden, "Snake Country Report 1825/26," pp. 258–59.

26. Letter from John McLoughlin to George Simpson, 7 April 1841, *Letters of McLoughlin—Second Series*, p. 258; Lamb, Third Introduction, pp. xxvii–xxviii. Also, see Douthit, "Hudson's Bay," pp. 30–31.

27. Letter from George Simpson to Governor and Committee, 25 November 1841, *Simpson London Letters*, p. 55. For Simpson's plan for New Caledonia, see Lavender, "Thomas McKay," p. 267.

28. Letter from John McLoughlin to George Simpson, 20 March 1827, Merk, *Fur Trade and Empire*, p. 289; entries for 16 November 1822 and 8 January 1823, Anon., *Bow River Journal*; Morgan, *Jedediah Smith*, p. 273.

29. Letter from William Clark to Lewis Cass, 20 November 1831, Fur Trade 1831 Letter; letter from William H. Ashley to Governor John Miller, 26 December 1828, William H. Ashley Papers. Also, see Wishart, *Fur Trade*, p. 32.

30. Letter from William Gordon to Lewis Cass, 3 October 1831, in *Chardon's Journal*, p. 348.

31. John McLoughlin, "Remarks upon Mr. Cushing's Report," *Letters of McLoughlin—Third Series*, pp. 271–72 (quoting William A. Slacum).

32. Letter from John McLoughlin to Governor and Committee, 17 June 1836, *Letters of McLoughlin—First Series*, p. 150; letter from George Simpson to the Governor and Committee, 25 November 1841, *Simpson London Letters*, p. 53.

33. Letters from George Simpson to Governor and Committee, 25 November and 20 June 1841, *Simpson London Letters*, pp. 56–57, 33. Ogden sometimes blamed American trappers for taking all the beaver. Entry for 8 May 1825, in Ogden, *First Snake Journals*, p. 45; entry for 20 October 1827, Ogden, *Third Snake Journal*, p. 17.

34. Morgan, *Jedediah Smith*, p. 272; Graham and Smith, "Report," p. 49; Galbraith, *Imperial Factor*, p. 95; Miller and Miller, Introduction to Ogden, pp. xxxv–xxxvi. But see Wishart, *Fur Trade*, p. 31.

35. Merk, Introduction, p. xxvi.

36. Barker, Book Review, pp. 44–45; Barker, Introduction to Ogden, pp. xliii–xliv; Merk, Introduction, p. lvi.

CHAPTER 5: THEY ARE TOO LAZY TO COME IN WITH THEIR FURS

1. Entries for 26, 27 November 1827, Ross, *Flathead Journal*.

2. Entry for 20 December 1824, Kittson, *Snake Country Journal*, pp. 209–10; entry for 20 December 1824, Ross, *Flathead Journal*. Ross counted seventy-one men. Entry for 20 December 1824, Ross, Snake Country 1824 Journal, p. 388. Simpson wrote that there were twenty-five *engagés* and thirty-five freemen. Entry for 28 October 1824, Simpson, *Journal*, p. 47. A biographer says that there were fifty-eight men. Cline, *Ogden*, p. 52.

3. Ross would write that the trappers on his own expedition had been "badly provided with traps having only, on an average, five each, when they ought to have had double that number on such long journeys." Ross, *Fur Hunters*, 2:146.

4. Entry for 19 December 1824, Ross, *Flathead Journal*.

5. Entry for 20 December 1824, Kittson, *Snake Country Journal*, p. 210; entry for 20 December 1824, Ross, *Flathead Journal*.

6. Jackson, "Charles McKay," p. 253; Howay, Sage, and Angus, *British Columbia*, p. 37 (quoting Ramsay Crooks).

7. Ross, *Fur Hunters*, 2:141.

8. Wells, "Ignace Hatchiorauquasha (John Grey)."

9. Entry for 7 December 1824, Ross, *Flathead Journal*.

10. Entry for 20 December 1824, Kittson, *Snake Country Journal*, p. 209; Merk, *Oregon Question*, p. 76; Barker, Introduction to Ogden, p. xlvii.

11. McGregor, "Old Whitehead," p. 172; Galbraith, *Imperial Factor*, p. 82; Williams, "Hudson's Bay Company," p. 51.

12. Barker, Introduction to Ogden, p. xlvii.

13. Minutes of the Council of the Northern Department of Rupert's Land, 20 August 1822, *Canadian North-West*, 1: 640–41.

14. Ross, *Hunters*, p. 192.

15. He wrote that "there is something depraved in the word freedom." He urged Hudson's Bay not to hire them. Ross, *Fur Hunters*, 2:145.

16. Van Kirk, *Many Tender Ties*, p. 48. Ross Cox, Ross's colleague in the Pacific Fur and North West companies, said that these men "have generally Indian families." White, Introduction to Thompson, pp. 65–66, n. 25 (quoting Cox). There is little evidence supporting the claim that "[s]ome of these men were fugitives from justice, hardened and reckless of human life." Barker, Introduction to Ogden, p. lxxiii.

17. Nicks, "The Iroquois," pp. 91–92; Irving, *Astoria*, p. 81; McLeod, Notes, p. 54; Merk, *Oregon Question*, p. 76; Merk, "Snake Country Expedition," p. 98; Merk, *Fur Trade and Empire*, p. 20, n. 44.

18. Letter of H.B.C. Employee, 27 February 1822, in Innis, *Fur Trade*, p. 288.

19. Wells, "Michel Bourdon," p. 58; Kennedy, *Spokane Report*.

20. Letter from Alexander Kennedy to George Simpson, 12 April 1823, in Merk, *Fur Trade and Empire*, p. 193.

21. Kennedy, *Spokane Report*.

22. Letter from Alexander Kennedy to George Simpson, 12 April 1823, Merk, *Fur Trade and Empire*, p. 194.

23. Wells, "Michel Bourdon," p. 58.

24. Entries for 27 October and 28 December 1827, Ogden, *Third Snake Journal*, pp. 19, 41.

25. Entry for 14 March 1827, Ogden, *Second Snake Journal*, p. 94. Also, see entry for 10 February 1828, Ogden, *Third Snake Journal*, pp. 60–61; entry for 11 November 1826, Ogden, *Second Snake Journal*, p. 24; Johansen, Introduction to Ogden, pp. lxvi–lxvii; Ormsby, Book Review, pp. 231–32.

26. Entry for 6 December 1824, Ross, *Flathead Journal*; Ross, *Hunters*, p. 195.

27. Haines, "François Payette," pp. 15–16.

28. Entry for 12 January 1823, Pruden, *Seventh Carlton Journal*.

CHAPTER 6: NO MONEY WOULD INDUCE ME TO RISK AGAIN

1. Entry for 3 August 1812, Luttig, *Journal*, p. 64; Irving, *Bonneville*, p. 47.

2. Ball, *Autobiography*, p. 79. It appears that the American Fur Company called a man "free" if his contract had expired. Letter from J. Archibald Hamilton to Kenneth McKenzie, 15 November 1834, in Swagerty, "View from Bottom," pp. 28–29.

3. "We Americans were all private adventurers, each on his own hook, and were led into the enterprise by the promises of the Company, who agreed to subsist us to the trapping grounds, we helping to navigate the boats, and on

our arrival they were to furnish us each with a rifle and sufficient ammunition, six good beaver traps, and also four men of their hired French, to be under our individual commands for a period of three years." James, *Three Years*, p. 9.

4. *Narrative of Robert Campbell*, p. 12; Irving, *Bonneville*, p. 47 (quoting Benjamin Bonneville).

5. Irving, *Bonneville*, p. 47 (quoting Benjamin Bonneville).

6. Entry for 1 June 1834, Townsend, *Narrative*, p. 181. Also, see DeVoto, *Across Missouri*, pp. 160–61.

7. Irving, *Bonneville*, p, 47.

8. Dale, *Ashley-Smith Explorations*, p. 93.

9. *Letters of McLoughlin—Second Series*, p. 2, n. 1.

10. Letters from James Douglas to Governor and Committee, 16 October 1838 and John McLoughlin to same, 8 July 1839, ibid., pp. 1–2.

11. Letters from Governor and Committee to James Douglas, 15 November 1837 and same to John McLoughlin, 9 August 1840, ibid., p. 2, n. 1. The punishment suggested, dismissal without receiving transportation out of the country, seems to have been practiced. In the isolation of Carlton House, in Saskatchewan department, a man was discharged "from the employment of Cook & Servant" for breaking and entering. It seems that he was turned out of the post. Entry for 1 April 1829, Pruden, *Eleventh Carlton Journal*.

12. Letter from Governor and Committee to John McLoughlin, 27 September 1843, *Letters of McLoughlin—Second Series*, p. 308; Loo, *Making Law*, pp. 23–24.

13. Letter from Humphrey Martin to William Tomison, 11 September 1777, in Tomison, *Second Cumberland Journal*, p. 226 ; entry for 8 January 1821, Simpson, *Athabaska Journal*, pp. 212–13. Also, see Memorandum to Mr. Ross, [1829], *Letters of John McLoughlin*, p. 7 ("writes he has fined Delonnais half his years wages"); entry for 8 April 1820, Fidler, *Dauphin Journal* ("I particularly warned him of the consequences in refusing to do his duty. That he should be put off duty & receive no wages for the future. [T]o all this he paid not the least attention, so from this day he will not be intitled to receive any wages").

14. Glover, Introduction to Second Cumberland, p. lii (also quoting Umfreville, *Present State of Hudson's Bay*, p. 213).

15. Entry for 30 May 1813, Bird, *Seventh Edmonton Journal*. Pruden may have appealed to Bird because masters of trading houses had to rely on higher authority then their own when applying fines. For example, the master of Cumberland House stated the offenses of two men and then wrote in his journal, "I have nominated a fine of five pounds on John Brough and two pounds ten shillings on Thomas Souttit, at the same time I leave it to your Honours to be the best Judges, whether these men ought not to be punished." Entry for 5 March 1803, Tomison, *Fourteenth Cumberland Journal*. John Sutherland complained to Bird that one of his officers "has been guilty of drunkenness and other misdemeanors degrading in an officer," and recommended a fine of

£60. "Called in Mr St Germain in the presence of Messers Robertson, Suther-land, Logan & McLeod, explained to him the charges laid against him, and as he could by no means vindicate his conduct . . . I told him that he would be fined to the amount mentioned in Mr. Sutherland's note." Letter from John Sutherland to James Bird, 7 August 1816 and entry for 7 August 1816, Bird, *Tenth Edmonton Journal.* For a fine of half a man's wages, see Loo, *Making Law,* p. 24.

16. Entry for 25 November 1833, Anon., *Edmonton Journal;* entries for 12 April 1825 and 27 March 1825, Simpson, *Journal,* pp. 127, 137 (it is not certain whether Simpson is speaking of one man, or two). For the case of a cook being "bound hand and foot" and sent out of New Caledonia, see Loo, *Making Law,* p. 24.

17. Morton, *Canadian West,* pp. 629–30.

18. Entry for 21 September 1824, Simpson, *Journal,* pp. 21–22.

19. Entry for 11 October 1824, ibid., p. 31.

20. Entry for 6 December 1826, Ogden, *Second Snake Journal,* p. 37.

21. For American fur men, restrictions on sales and purchases sounded in contract; it was not an issue of legislative grant. When they did not receive furs to which they felt themselves entitled, they thought of fraud, not of crime. For example, one American trapper wrote to his partner from the mountains of eight or ten packs of fur: "we have lost by the rascality of a few men, who were largely indebted to us and who traded their fall's hunt with other companies during the winter as it happened they did not winter near any of our parties. I am in hopes that it will not happen in the future as I have so arranged that it will be hard for any of them to defraud us hereafter." Letter from Lucien Fontenelle to Pierre Chouteau, 17 September 1834, Chittenden, *Fur Trade,* 1: 374–75.

22. Kennedy, *Spokane Report* (1823).

23. Simpson attempted to discipline Indians by closing posts. Entry for 22 April 1825, Simpson, *Journal,* p. 142.

24. Entry for 5 September 1825, Work, 1825–26 Journal, p. 115.

25. Entry for 20 December 1825, ibid., p. 261.

26. Entries for 23, 26 November 1824, Stuart, *Carlton Journal.*

27. Ross, *Hunters,* p. 64.

28. Entries for 26 January and 20 May 1833, Small, *Edmonton Journal.*

29. Entry for 20 August 1824, Ross, *Snake Country Journal.*

30. "[B]ut Mr. Dease directed them to get a little in case they delivered in their furs." Entry for 20 December 1825, Work, 1825–26 Journal, p. 261.

31. Entry for 22 April 1825, Simpson, *Journal,* p. 143.

32. Letter from John McLoughlin to Governor and Committee, 18 Novem-ber 1843, *Letters of McLoughlin—Second Series,* p. 156; Nunis, "Michel Laframboise," p. 168 (quoting a letter from McLoughlin to Simpson).

33. Johanson, Introduction to Ogden, p. xxi n. 3.

34. Morgan, *Jedediah Smith*, p. 152.

35. Letter from Peter Skene Ogden to George Simpson, the Chief Factors, and Chief Traders, 10 July 1825, Merk, "Snake Country Expedition," p. 113.

CHAPTER 7: LET RULES BE MADE THEY WILL SOON BE BROKEN

1. Entry for 20 December 1824, Kittson, *Snake Country Journal*, p. 209; entry for 21 December 1824, Ross, *Flathead Journal*.

2. Entry for 20 December 1824, Ogden, *First Snake Journals*, p. 5; entry for 21 December 1824, Ross, *Flathead Journal*.

3. Entry for 20 December 1824, Ogden, *First Snake Journals*, p. 5.

4. For "Article 112," restricting trade by *engagés*, see Swagerty and Wilson, "Faithful Service," p. 247; for an order to an officer to restrict freemen, see Minutes of the Council of the Northern Department of Rupert's Land, 20 August 1822, *Canadian North-West*, 1: 640–41.

5. Agreement of 12 October 1820, Heron, *Third Edmonton Journal*.

6. Entries for 1, 2, 6 March 1825, Ross, *Flathead Journal*.

7. Entry for 12 February 1825, ibid.

8. Entry for 8 March 1825, ibid.; entry for 12 June 1825, Ogden, *First Snake Journals*, pp. 59–60.

9. Entry for 28 October 1824, Simpson, *Journal*, pp. 46–47; letter from George Simpson to Peter Skene Ogden, 10 January 1825, in Kittson, *Snake Country Journal*, p. 250.

10. Entry for 3 November 1824, Simpson, *Journal*, p. 56.

11. Letters from George Simpson to Peter Skene Ogden, 10 January, 14 March, and 10 April 1824, in Kittson, *Snake Country Journal*, pp. 251, 253, 254.

12. Merk, "Snake Country Expedition," p. 101.

13. Letter from George Simpson to Peter Skene Ogden, 10 April 1825, in Kittson, *Snake Country Journal*, p. 255.

14. Jackson, "Charles McKay," pp. 253–54; Miller and Miller, Introduction to Ogden, p. xiv.

15. Entry for 21 December 1824, Ogden *First Snake Journals*, p. 6; entry for 22 December 1824, Kittson, *Snake Country Journal*, p. 210; entry for 22 December 1824, Ogden, *First Snake Journals*, p. 6.

16. Entry for 26 December 1824, Ogden, *First Snake Journals*, p. 7.

17. Entries for 23, 24 February 1825, in Kittson, *Snake Country Journal*, p. 219.

18. Entries for 27, 28 February 1825, ibid., p. 219.

19. Entry for 31 January 1825, Ogden, *First Snake Journals*, p. 19.

20. Entry for 1 February, 23 April 1825, ibid., pp. 19, 39; entry for 22 [23] April 1825, Kittson, *Snake Country Journal*, p. 229.

21. Letter from Peter Skene Ogden to the Governor, et al., 10 July 1825, in Merk, "Snake Country Expedition," p. 108.

22. Entry for 8, 10 April 1825, Ogden, *First Snake Journals*, p. 34; letter from Peter Skene Ogden to Governor, et al., 10 July 1825, in Merk, "Snake Country Expedition," p. 108.

23. Entry for 13 April 1825, Ogden, *First Snake Journals*, p. 36.

24. Entries for 17, 18, 19, 20 April 1825, Kittson, *Snake Country Journal*, p. 228.

CHAPTER 8: WE MUST ENDEAVOR TO ANNOY THEM

1. Entry for 2 January 1825, Ogden, *First Snake Journals*, p. 10; entry for 18 March 1825, Kittson, *Snake Country Journal*, pp. 221–22.

2. Entry for 26 December 1824, Ogden, *First Snake Journals*, p. 7. Kittson did record the reasons: "From the ill state of health of one of the Freemen's wives we had to remain in the same encampment. An encrease has taken place in our number from the birth of a child." Entry for 26 December 1824, Kittson, *Snake Country Journal*, p. 210.

3. Entry for 29 December 1824, Kittson, *Snake Country Journal*, p. 211; Howay, Sage, and Angus, *British Columbia*, p. 50.

4. Entry for 14 October 1824, Ross, Snake Country 1824 Journal, p. 385; entries of 14 October, 25 October, and 2 November 1824, Ross, *Snake Country Journal*.

5. Lewis and Phillips, Introduction, at 44, n. 80; Cline, *Ogden*, p. 49.

6. Entry for 14 October 1824, Ross, *Snake Country Journal*.

7. Entry for 12 December 1824, Ross, *Flathead Journal*.

8. Entry for 18 March 1825, Kittson, *Snake Country Journal*, p. 221.

9. They recrossed the Divide on 11 February.

10. Entry for 19 March 1825, Kittson, *Snake Country Journal*, p. 221. Ogden made no mention of the Americans on that day.

11. Entries for 16, 17, 18, 19 March 1825, Ogden, *First Snake Journals*, pp. 27–28.

12. Entry for 19 March 1825, Kittson, *Snake Country Journal*, pp. 221–22; Barker, Introduction to Ogden, p. xlviii; Wishart, *Fur Trade*, p. 124.

13. Entry for 21 March 1825, Kittson, *Snake Country Journal*, p. 223.

14. Entry for 24 March 1825, ibid.

15. Entries of 30 March and 7 April 1825, ibid., pp. 224, 225.

16. Entry for 8 April 1825, Ogden, *First Snake Journals*, p. 33.

17. Entry for 8 April 1825, Kittson, *Snake Country Journal*, p. 226.

18. Entry for 11 April 1825, ibid., p. 227; entry for 10 April 1825, Ogden, *First Snake Journals*, p. 35.

19. Entry for 16 April 1825, ibid.

20. Entry for 17 April 1825, ibid.

21. Entries for 18, 19, 20 April 1825, ibid., pp. 38–39; entry for 20 April 1825, Kittson, *Snake Country Journal*, p. 228.

22. Entry for 26 April 1825, Kittson, ibid., pp. 229–30; entry for 26 April 1825, Ogden, *First Snake Journals*, p. 40.

23. Entry for 4 May 1825, Ogden, ibid., p. 43. The Snakes "wore their war garments": entry for 3 May 1825, Kittson, *Snake Country Journal*, p. 231.

24. Cline, *Ogden*, p. 56.

25. Entry for 8 May 1825, Ogden, *First Snake Journals*, p. 45.

26. Entry for 9, 11 May 1825, ibid., pp. 45–46.

27. Entry for 12 May 1825, ibid., p. 46.

28. Entry for 13 May 1825, ibid., p. 46; entry for 13 May 1825, Kittson, *Snake Country Journal*, p. 232.

29. Entries for 16 May 1825, Ogden, *First Snake Journals*, p. 47.

30. Entries for 19, 18 May 1825, ibid., p. 48.

31. Entry for 16 May 1825, Kittson, *Snake Country Journal*, p. 232; entry for 21 May 1825, Ogden, *First Snake Journals*, pp. 48–49.

CHAPTER 9: DO YOU KNOW IN WHOSE COUNTRY YOU ARE?

1. Letter from Peter Skene Ogden to Governor, Chief Factors, and Chief Traders, 27 July 1825, *Letters of McLoughlin—First Series*, p. 296.

2. Letter from P. S. Ogden to the Governor, et al., 10 July 1825, Merk, "Snake Country Expedition," p. 108.

3. Entry for 22 May 1825, Kittson, *Snake Country Journal*, p. 233.

4. Entry for 22 May 1825, Ogden, *First Snake Journals*, pp. 49–50. Etienne Provost, whom Ogden would meet the next day, had sent some of his men to Taos, apparently for supplies. Weber, *Taos Trappers*, p. 76.

5. Entry for 23 May 1825, Kittson, *Snake Country Journal*, p. 233; Clokey, *Ashley*, pp. 156–57; Goetzmann, *New Lands*, p. 142; Wishart, *Fur Trade*, p. 128. Concerning whether Jackson was with Weber, see Talbot, *David E. Jackson*, pp. 47–52.

6. Irving, *Bonneville*, p. 11. "Provost had come from the southeast, up from Taos with his band; Ogden had travelled from the northwest, from the Columbia River, with his Snake River brigade; and Ashley's men had flooded in from the east, the upper Missouri and up the Platte to the Green River valley and beyond." Hafen, "Brief History," p. 80.

7. Entry for 23 May 1825, Kittson, *Snake Country Journal*, p. 233; entry for 23 May 1825, Ogden, *First Snake Journals*, p. 51.

8. "Articles of Agreement," 5 July 1832, Chouteau Collection; Galbraith, *Imperial Factor*, p. 91.

9. Barker, Introduction to Ogden, p. xlix (put out feelers); Morgan, *Jedediah Smith*, pp. 148–49.

10. Letter from William H. Ashley, *Missouri Observer*, 31 October 1827, in *West of Ashley*, pp. 176–77; Utley, *Life Wild and Perilous*, pp. 75–76.

11. Entry for 23 May 1825, Ogden, *First Snake Journals*, p. 51; entry for 23 May 1825, Kittson, *Snake Country Journal*, pp. 233–34.

12. Entry for 23 May 1825, Ogden, *First Snake Journals*, p. 51; letter from P. S. Ogden to Governor, et al., 10 July 1825, Merk, "Snake Country Expedition," pp. 109–10. "[N]ight coming on, no more was said. Strict watch set for the night." Entry for 23 May 1825, Kittson, *Snake Country Journal*, p. 234.

13. Entry for 24 May 1825, Ogden, *First Snake Journals*, p. 51.

14. Entry for 18 May 1825, ibid., p. 48.

15. Article 3, Adams-Onis Treaty, in Brooks, *Diplomacy and Borderlands*, p. 206.

16. That Ogden wrote "neighbours" does not indicate he was using the plural and referring to both Mexico and Great Britain. In his usage, "neighbours" more often meant "neighbor's" than "neighbors."

17. Entry for 23 [24] May 1825, Kittson, *Snake Country Journal*, p. 234.

18. Letter from John McLoughlin to Governor and Committee, 6 October 1825, *Letters of McLoughlin—First Series*, p. 9.

19. "Gardner probably knew this, but was merely using this bluff as an attempt to justify his actions at the time." David E. Miller, Notes to Odgen, Utah Journal, p. 182, n. 90. John Jacob Astor, the most prominent American in the fur trade, may have influenced Adams. See Brooks, *Diplomacy and Borderlands*, pp. 150–54.

20. Quoted in Barker, Introduction to Ogden, p. liii.

21. Letter from John McLoughlin to John Work, 10 August 1825, in *Letters of McLoughlin—First Series*, p. 301.

22. Letter from John McLoughlin to Chief Factors and Chief Traders, 10 August 1825, ibid., p. 302.

CHAPTER 10: GO WE WILL WHERE WE SHALL BE PAID

1. Entry for 19 March 1824, Ross, *Snake Country Journal*; Morgan, *Jedediah Smith*, p. 149. Two days out from Flathead Post, "John Grey returned to the Fort for his wife and Children." Entry for 22 December 1824, Kittson, *Snake Country Journal*, p. 210.

2. Letter from P. S. Ogden to Governor, et al., 10 July 1825, Merk, "Snake Country Expedition," p 110. In a companion letter, Ogden blamed the fact that the Iroquois were prepared to desert him on Jedediah Smith. He quoted Grey: "all the Iroquois as well as myself have long wished for an opportunity to join the Americans, and if we did not sooner it was entirely owing to our bad luck our not meeting with them, but this year we had taken our precautions, alluding to the 7 Americans who had wintered and left us in April and again joined here, but now we go and all you can say or do cannot or will not prevent us from going." Letter from Peter Skene Ogden to Governor, Chief Factors, and Chief Traders, 27 June 1825, *Letters of McLoughlin—First Series*, p. 297. When he mentioned "five years," Grey was referring to their period of working for the Hudson's Bay Company. He and most of the other freemen

had been on the Columbia for more years than five, previously working for the North West Company.

3. Galbraith, *Imperial Factor*, p. 91.

4. Letter from Peter Skene Ogden to Governor, Chief Factors, and Chief Traders, 27 June 1825, *Letters of McLoughlin—First Series*, p. 297. There does not seem to be evidence supporting the claim made by some recent observers that Gardner told the freemen that their debts with Hudson's Bay were annulled or that they were now free to break their agreements with the company. Karamanski, "Iroquois and the Fur Trade," p. 10; Wells, "Ignace Hatchiorauquasha (John Grey)," p. 167.

5. Lamb, Introduction to McLoughlin *Letters*, p. lxii.

6. Wells, "Ignace Hatchiorauquasha (John Grey)," pp. 161–75.

7. Lavender, "American Characteristics," p. 184; entry for 29 November 1804, François-Antoine Larocque, "Missouri Journal," p. 140.

8. Fitzgerald, *Hudson's Bay*, pp. 64–65; Merk, Introduction, pp. xiii.

9. Galbraith, *Imperial Factor*, p. 178.

10. Williams, "Hudson's Bay Company," pp. 78–79.

11. Letter from J. H. Pelly to Lords of the Committee of the Privy Council for Trade, 7 February 1838, Simpson, *Journal*, pp. 341–42. The company also claimed it was not a monopoly because it had to compete against the Russians and Americans in the London fur market. Fitzgerald, *Hudson's Bay*, p. 62. Monopoly was also said "to guard against any encroachments of the United States on the line of the Boundary." Letter from Benjamin and Joseph Frobisher to General Haldimand, 4 October 1784, in Wallace, *Documents*, p. 71.

12. Rich, Robertson Introduction, p. cix. Some historical contentions justifying monopoly as humane are simply wrong: "Monopoly in itself was a support to humane councils, providing a permanent stake in the Indian country as compared with the transitory interest of American trappers, and justifying as a matter of enlightened self–interest a policy of conserving and strengthening Indian life." Merk, Introduction, pp. lviii–lix.

13. Wells, "Ignace Hatchiorauquash (John Grey)," p. 162.

14. Entry for 24 May 1825, Ogden, *First Snake Journals*, p. 52.

15. Ross, *Hunters*, pp. 135–36.

16. Entry for 24 May 1825, Ogden, *First Snake Journals*, p. 52.

17. See Chapter 6, p. 84.

18. Letter from Peter Skene Ogden to Governor, Chief Factors, and Chief Traders, 27 June 1825, *Letters of McLoughlin—First Series*, p. 298. Also, see letter from same to Governor, et al., 10 July 1825, in Merk, "Snake Country Expedition," p. 112.

19. Miller, "Ogden Discovered Indians." This was the only explosive confrontation between any of Ogden's expeditions and rival American trappers, at which time the 'cold' fur war almost boiled over into a 'hot' war" (p. 140).

20. Williams, Appendix A, to Ogden, *Fourth Snake Journal*, p. 170.

21. Elliott, "Peter Skene Ogden," p. 248. Similarly, see Wallace, "Strategy of Fur Traders," p. 16.

22. Miller and Miller, Introduction to Ogden, p. xxiv.

23. That is how one of McLoughlin's editors described the removal of beaver to the American camp. Lamb, Introduction to McLoughlin *Letters*, p. lxxvi.

24. Haines, "Johnson Gardner," pp. 157–58; Merk, "Snake Country Expedition," p. 101.

25. Letter from Peter Skene Ogden to Governor, Chief Factors, and Chief Traders, 27 June 1825, *Letters of McLoughlin—First Series*, p. 298.

26. Cline, *Ogden*, pp. 60–61; Letter from P. S. Ogden to Governor et al., 10 July 1825, Merk, "Snake Country Expedition," p. 112. Also, see letter from Peter Skene Ogden to Governor, Chief Factors, and Chief Traders, 27 June 1825, *Letters of McLoughlin—First Series*, p. 298.

27. Entry for 8 June 1825, Ogden, *First Snake Journals*, p. 58; Weber, *Taos Trappers*, pp. 76– 77; Hafen, "Etienne Provost," pp. 372–74.

28. *Patterns of Vengeance*, pp. 55–56, 75–84, 206–8.

29. The next day, as they started the trip back to the Columbia, Kittson noted: "Our party is now reduced to the number of 22 Freemen, 11 Engages and 6 Boys besides Mr. Ogden and I." Entry for 25 May 1825, Kittson, *Snake Country Journal*, p. 235.

30. Letter from John McLoughlin to Chief Factors and Chief Traders, 10 August 1825, *Letters of McLoughlin—First Series*, p. 302.

31. For example, entries for 7 and 23 May 1827, Ogden, *Second Snake Journal*, pp. 113, 119; entry for 2 April 1829, Ogden, *Fourth Snake Journal*, p. 138.

32. Letter from John McLoughlin to Chief Factors and Chief Traders, 10 August 1825, *Letters of McLoughlin—First Series*, p. 303.

33. Entry for 23 [24] May 1825, Kittson, *Snake Country Journal*, p. 235.

> In the evening Alexander Carson [a freeman and deserter] came back and warned me to be on my guard as a plot was forming amongst the Iroquois and some of the Americans to pillage me in the night as I had refused to sell them Tabacco, I then conversed with some of the most trusty Freemen and engaged Men to know if they would assist in defending the Companys property in case of attack and they said we will, we then made every preparation and kept double guard during the night.

Letter from P. S. Ogden to Governor, et al., 10 July 1825, Merk, "Snake Country Expedition," p. 111.

34. There was also a confrontation between Gardner and Kittson during which Kittson challenged Gardner to "do your worse and make it a point of dispute between our two Governments." There is, however, no mention of weapons. Entry for 25 May 1825, Kittson, *Snake Country Journal*, p. 235.

35. Merk, "Snake Country Expedition," p. 101; letter from John McLoughlin to Governor and Committee, 6 July 1827, *Letters of McLoughlin—First Series,* p. 40.

36. Merk, "Snake Country Expedition," p. 109; letter from Governor and Committee to John McLoughlin, 20 September 1826, ibid., p. 119. Gardner's biographer, for example, also using the word *despoiling,* calls the event "a thinly-veiled robbery." Haines, "Johnson Gardner," p. 157. For the interpretation of a historian who was both a lawyer and judge, see Carey, *General History,* p. 228.

37. Letter from John McLoughlin to Chief Factors and Chief Traders, 10 August 1825, *Letters of McLoughlin—First Series,* p. 302.

38. Letter from P. S. Ogden to Governor, et al., 10 July 1825, Merk, "Snake Country Expedition," p. 111. "Duford, Perrault and Kanota escaped with their Furs in fact some of them conveyed theirs in the night to the American Camp." Entry for 24 May 1825, Ogden, *First Snake Journals,* p. 53.

39. On Ogden's third expedition meat was sold "at the rate of a Beaver Skin per Deer." The sales occurred in the Oregon country, not Rupert's Land, and were not illegal under parliament's legislation, but may have been against company rules. Ogden tried to stop the practice by furnishing food to the needy when he was able. Entry for 29 January 1827, Ogden, *Second Snake Journal,* p. 61.

40. Barker, Introduction to Ogden, p. xli.

41. See Chapter 9, p. 102.

42. Entry for 23 [24] May 1825, Kittson, p. 234.

43. Entry for 23 [24] May 1825, Ibid. When Ogden prevented Old Pierre from taking two horses with him when he deserted, the Iroquois bought one of them. On other expeditions, trappers deserting to the Americans paid their debts. E.g., entry for 16 January 1833, Work, *California Journal,* p. 27.

44. Entries for 9, 10 April 1826, Ogden, *First Snake Journals,* p. 154.

45. However, one scholar has concluded: "[B]y some advantage held over them (the full nature of which is not yet understood) the deserters of the previous year were compelled to pay their debts to the H. B. Co. by turning in over four hundred dollars' worth of beaver." T. C. Elliott, Editorial Notes, p. 335. The fact is, as both Ogden and Kittson wrote, Montour, for one, tried to pay his debts that day on the Weber.

46. Entry for 11 April 1826, *First Snake Journals,* p. 155; entry for 25 October 1827, Ogden, *Third Snake Journal,* p. 19.

47. Entry for 17 February 1828, *Third Snake Journal,* p. 63.

48. Wallace, Introduction to *Simpson's 1828 Journey,* p. xlii.

49. Entry for 25 May 1825, Ogden, *First Snake Journals,* p. 54.

CHAPTER 11: THEY ARE NOW TO BE FOUND IN ALL PARTS OF THE SNAKE COUNTRY

1. Entry for 25 May 1825, Ogden, *First Snake Journals,* p. 54.

2. Letter from P. S. Ogden to the Governor, et al., 10 July 1825, Merk, "Snake Country Expedition," p. 109.

3. Entry for 25 May 1825, Ogden, *First Snake Journals*, pp. 54–55.

4. Ibid., p. 55.

5. Letter from Peter Skene Ogden to Governor, Chief Factors, and Chief Traders, 27 June 1825, *Letters of McLoughlin—First Series*, p. 298.

6. Entry for 25 May 1825, Kittson, *Snake Country Journal*, p. 235; letter from P. S. Ogden to Governor, et al., 10 July 1825, Merk, "Snake Country Expedition," p. 111.

7. "Mr. Montour . . . had seven thousand five hundred and sixty two livres when he went free in 1821 and since put to his credit one hundred and Seventy two Livres and ten Sols. But we do not know whether he has drawn any of this Money or not, however he desired Prudhomme's and his advances to be paid out of it." Letter of 6 October 1825, *Letters of McLoughlin—First Series*, p. 8.

8. Entry for 10 April 1826, Ogden, *First Snake Journals*, p. 154; Barker, Introduction to Ogden, p. lviii.

9. Entry for 7 November 1826, Rowand, *Second Edmonton Journal* (reporting receipt of a letter from Mr. Fisher at Rocky Mountain House to whom Montour had written on 18 April 1826 from the Blackfoot River).

10. Letter from P. S. Ogden to Governor, et al., 10 July 1825, Merk, "Snake Country Expedition," pp. 111–12; entry for 25 May 1825, Kittson, *Snake Country Journal*, p. 235.

11. Entry for 25 May 1825, Ogden, *First Snake Journals*, p. 54; Letter from P. S. Ogden to Governor, et al., 10 July 1825, Merk, "Snake Country Expedition," p. 112.

12. Entry for 25 May 1825, Kittson, *Snake Country Journal*, p. 235. Ogden had been waiting for the absent men on the Weber. He said there were six, Kittson said five.

13. Entries for 26, 27 May 1825, Ogden, *First Snake Journals*, p. 55; entries for 26, 27 May 1825, Kittson, *Snake Country Journal*, pp. 235–36.

14. Entry for 28 May 1825, Ogden, *First Snake Journals*, p. 55; entries for 28, 29 May 1825, Kittson, *Snake Country Journal*, p. 236.

15. Entry for 29 May 1825, Ogden, *First Snake Journals*, p. 56.

16. Entry for 7 June 1825, ibid., pp. 57–58; Josephy, *Nez Perce*, p. 64.

17. Entry for 8 June 1825, Ogden, *First Snake Journals*, p. 58. "On raising camp this morning I percieved [*sic*] 3 young half Breeds were remaining behind for the purpose of proceeding down the Snake River and try to steal horses from the Snakes, knowing the bad consequences of such a step I persuaded them to join the Camp which they did." Entry for 8 June 1825, Kittson, *Snake Country Journal*, p. 237.

18. Hafen, "Etienne Provost," pp. 372–74; Weber, *Taos Trappers*, pp. 76–77; Hafen, "Provost," p. 102. For the legal principles generally, see *Patterns of Vengeance*.

19. Letter from P. S. Ogden to Governor, et al., 10 July 1825, Merk, "Snake Country Expedition," p. 114; entry for 21 June 1825, Ogden, *First Snake Journals*, p. 62.

20. Letter from P. S. Ogden to Governor, et al., 10 July 1825, Merk, "Snake Country Expedition," p. 114.

21. Letter from Peter Skene Ogden to the Governor, Chief Factors, and Chief Traders, 27 July 1825, *Letters of McLoughlin—First Series*, p. 299.

22. Entry for 20 June 1825, Ashley, 1825 Diary, p. 282.

23. "We . . . proceeded . . . up the river to a point where the Canadians and [Iroquois] Indians had engaged to meet him with their peltry. The general [Ashley] appointed me captain of a party to meet the Canadians, and escort them to the rendezvous which he had proposed to them, while he and some few others remained to bring up the goods." Jim Beckwourth quoted in Morgan, Ashley, 1825 Diary, p. 285, n. 141.

24. "The Ashley Narrative," *West of Ashley*, p. 118; Ashley, 1825 Diary, p. 285; Auerbach, "Old Trails," pp. 49–50.

25. Noting that Ashley was a militia general, Simpson described him as a man "who notwithstanding his dignified title has had a number of ups and downs in life having been a Farmer[,] a Shopkeeper, a Miner and latterly an Indian Trader." *Simpson's 1828 Journey*, pp. 53–54.

26. Letter from George Simpson to Governor and Committee, 1 March 1829, *Frontier Experience*, p. 66; Merk, *Oregon Question*, p. 81; Clokey, *Ashley*, p. 158. Nathaniel Wyeth said the skins were worth $75,000, a sum he surely was told by McLoughlin. Letter from Nathaniel J. Wyeth to Henry Hall, et al., 8 November 1833, Wyeth, *Correspondence and Journals*, p. 74. Ashley indulged in similar exaggerations, saying of Hudson's Bay hunts "made upon our Territory west of the Rocky mountains, [that] they had taken about eighty-five thousand beaver, say 150,000 pounds." Letter from William H. Ashley to William Orr, 31 October 1827 *Missouri Observer*, in *West of Ashley*, p. 177. For Dale Morgan's discussion of Ashley's exaggerations, see *West of Ashley*, p. 288, n. 211.

27. Entry for 5 January 1828, Ogden, *Third Snake Journal*, p. 45.

28. Wishart, *Fur Trade*, p. 131 (quoting Ogden).

29. Entry for 5 January 1828, Ogden, *Third Snake Journal*, pp. 45–46.

30. Entry for 16 July 1825, Kittson, *Snake Country Journal*, p. 243. Kittson gave another indication that the fur belonged to the freemen when he said: "Several of the Freemen have given up their Beaver for me to take along." Entry for 15 July 1825, ibid., p. 243.

31. Entry for 26 August 1825, Kittson, *Snake Country Journal*, pp. 249–50.

32. McGregor, "Old Whitehead," p. 178; Galbraith, *Imperial Factor*, p. 92; Lamb, Introduction to McLoughlin *Letters*, p. lxiv; letter of 7 October 1825, *Letters of McLoughlin—First Series*, p. 24. The officer in charge of the Thompson River post at Kamloops may have summed up the conclusion reached by most officers: "The affairs of the Columbia, in general, seem to be promising and

but for the disasters which befell Mr. Ogden at the hands of the Americans, they would have been prosperous indeed." Letter to Robert Miles, 14 March 1826, McDonald, *Letters of Ermatinger*, p. 63.

33. Letter from P. S. Ogden to George Simpson, 12 November 1825, Kittson, *Snake Country Journal*, pp. 255–56.

CHAPTER 12: THE CHEAPEST SHOP WILL CARRY THE DAY

1. Letter from John McLoughlin to Governor, Chief Factors, and Chief Traders, 10 August 1825, Merk, *Fur Trade and Empire*, pp. 253–54; *Simpson's 1828 Journey*, p. 70; letter of 6 October 1825, *Letters of McLoughlin—First Series*, p. 9.

2. Letter of 6 October 1825, *Letters of McLoughlin—First Series*, p. 10.

3. Letter of 6 July 1827, ibid., p. 48; letter from John McLoughlin to George Simpson, 20 March 1827, Merk, *Fur Trade and Empire*, p. 290–91.

4. Letter from John McLoughlin to London Committee, 1 September 1826, Miller and Miller, Introduction to Ogden, p. xxvi.

5. Letter from P. S. Ogden to Governor, Chief Factors, and Chief Traders, 10 October 1826, Merk, *Fur Trade and Empire*, pp. 283–84.

6. Lamb, Introduction to McLoughlin *Letters*, p. lxv.

7. Letter of 6 July 1827, *Letters of McLoughlin—First Series*, p. 40; letter from John McLoughlin to George Simpson, 20 March 1827, Merk, *Fur Trade and Empire*, p. 290.

8. Letter from John McLoughlin to George Simpson, 20 March 1846 [1826], Merk, "Snake Country Expedition," p. 121.

9. Letter of 1 September 1826, *Letters of McLoughlin—First Series*, p. 34.

10. Ibid.; letter to Simpson, in Lamb, Introduction to McLoughlin *Letters*, p. lxv.

11. Letter from John McLoughlin to George Simpson, 20 March 1827, Innis, Introduction to *Minutes*, p. lxvii.

12. Baker, Introduction to Ogden, p. lxv.

13. Letter from George Simpson to Governor and Committee, 20 August 1826, *Simpson's 1828 Journey*, p. 153.

14. Letter from George Simpson to John McLoughlin, 9 July 1827, ibid., p. 156.

15. Letter from Governor and Committee to George Simpson, 12 March 1827, ibid., pp. 154–55.

16. Letter of 6 July 1827, *Letters of McLoughlin—First Series*, p. 41.

17. Letter from P. S. Ogden to the Governor, Chief Factors, and Chief Traders, 10 October 1826, Merk, *Fur Trade and Empire*, p. 284.

18. Entry for 5 January 1828, Ogden, *Third Snake Journal*, p. 45.

19. Galbraith, *Imperial Factor*, pp. 92–93; Morgan, *Jedediah Smith*, pp. 231–32.

20. Wishart, *Fur Trade*, p. 131.

21. Letter from Governor and Committee to John McLoughlin, 20 September 1826, Merk, *Oregon Question*, p. 95; *Letters of McLoughlin—First Series*, p. 9, n. 2.

22. Letter to George Simpson, 2 June 1826, quoted in Barker, Introduction to Ogden, p. liii.

23. Ogden, *First Snake Journals*, p. 66, n. 2.

24. Letter from Governor and Committee to John McLoughlin, 20 September 1826, Merk, *Oregon Question*, p. 95; letter from Governor and Committee to George Simpson, 12 March 1827, *Simpson's 1828 Journey*, p. 155.

25. Letter of 6 October 1825, *Letters of McLoughlin—First Series*, p. 9.

26. Letter from John McLoughlin to George Simpson, 20 March 1828, Galbraith, *Imperial Factor*, p. 92.

27. Letter of 7 October 1825, *Letters of McLoughlin—First Series*, p. 24.

28. Letter from P. S. Ogden to George Simpson, 12 November 1825, Barker, Introduction to Ogden, pp. 255–56; introductory entry and entries for 10, 15 October 1825, in Anon., *Bow River Journal*.

29. Or that is a good guess. Unfortunately, the best authority is Frederick Merk, who guessed at much: "The highest field officers of the Hudson's Bay Company, Governor Simpson and Dr. McLoughlin, sanctioned Ogden's trespass into the Missouri Valley. They ordered it, in fact. They laid out the outward route of march, and five weeks after Ogden started, he was writing the governor of his operations from the 'Sources of the Missouri,' a letter which the governor read with every indication of approval." Merk, *Oregon Question*, p. 82.

30. Letter from George Simpson to Joshua Pilcher, 18 February 1829, Merk, *Fur Trade and Empire*, pp. 307–8; Sunder, *Pilcher*, pp. 69–71.

31. Letter to George Simpson, 16 March 1831, *Letters of McLoughlin—First Series*, pp. 227–28.

CHAPTER 13: IT IS A LOTTERY WITH ALL EXPEDITIONS

1. Instructions from John McLoughlin to P. S. Ogden, 20 June 1825, *Letters of McLoughlin—First Series*, p. 295; letter from John McLoughlin to the Governor, et al., 5 November 1826, in Galbraith, "Note on Trade," p. 254, n. 2.

2. Howay, Sage, and Angus, *British Columbia*, p. 56; Barker, Introduction to Ogden, p. lvi.

3. Letter from Peter Skene Ogden to Governor, Chief Factors, and Chief Traders, 2 February 1826, Ogden, "Snake Country Report 1825/26," p. 261.

4. Miller and Miller, Introduction to Ogden, p. xxvi. "Mr. Ogden's Men are all Freemen and engaged Trappers, the last on the same terms as last year, say their wages £17—all the expenses of the hunt charged at Inventory prices to be paid in Beaver at the rate of 4/p Skin, the half of the remainder to go to the Concern and the Servant to be paid the other half at the rate 4/ per made Beaver." Letter from John McLoughlin to George Simpson, 20 March 1827, in Ogden, *Second Snake Journal*, p. 4, n. 1.

5. Entries for 12, 20 March 1826, Ogden, *First Snake Journals*, pp. 141, 143–44; Barker, Introduction to Ogden, p. lvii. The man killed was Antoine Benoit.

6. Entries for 20, 24 March 1826, Ogden, *First Snake Journals*, pp. 144, 146. The Snake camp held the band that had killed the American trappers led by Etienne Provost.

7. Entry for 9 April 1826, ibid., p. 154; Barker, Introduction to Ogden, p. lvii, n. 1.

8. Entry for 10 April 1826, Ogden, *First Snake Journals*, p. 154.

9. See Chapter 10, pp. 131–32 and Chapter 11, p. 138.

10. Letter from P. S. Ogden to the Governor, Chief Factors, and Chief Traders, 10 October 1826, Merk, *Fur Trade and Empire*, p. 282.

11. Entry for 11 April 1826, Ogden, *First Snake Journals*, pp. 154–55.

12. Entry for 11 April 1826, ibid., p. 155.

13. Entry for 10 April 1826, ibid., p. 154.

14. Entry for 10 April 1826, ibid.

15. Letter from P. S. Ogden to Governor, Chief Factors, and Chief Traders, 10 October 1826, Merk, *Fur Trade and Empire*, p. 283.

16. Letter from P. S. Ogden to George Simpson, 1 July 1826, ibid., pp. 276, 275.

17. "Ogden's Report," p. 118; Galbraith, *Imperial Factor*, p. 86.

18. Letter from P. S. Ogden to George Simpson, 1 July 1826, Merk, *Fur Trade and Empire*, p. 275.

19. Letter from P. S. Ogden to Governor, Chief Factors, and Chief Traders, 10 October 1826, ibid., p. 285.

20. Letter from P. S. Ogden to George Simpson, 1 July 1826, ibid., pp. 275, 277.

21. Entry for 18 May 1827, Ogden, *Second Snake Journal*, p. 117.

CHAPTER 14: OUR OWN PEOPLE ARE NOW PERFECTLY SATISFIED

1. Letter from Governor and Committee to George Simpson, 12 March 1827, *Simpson's 1828 Journey*, p. 155; Merk, *Fur Trade and Empire*, pp. 286–87.

2. Letter from P. S. Ogden to Governor, Chief Factors, and Chief Traders, 10 October 1826, Merk, *Fur Trade and Empire*, pp. 284–85.

3. Letter from P. S. Ogden to Governor, Chief Factors, and Chief Traders, 10 October 1826, ibid., p. 285; letter from George Simpson to John McLoughlin, 9 July 1827, Innis, Introduction to *Minutes*, p. lxviii.

4. Entries for 15, 26 September 1827, Ogden, *Third Snake Journal*, pp. 6, 10.

5. Entries for 27, 28, 29 September 1827, ibid., pp. 10–12.

6. Barker, Introduction to Ogden, p. lx; entry for 22 October 1827, Ogden, *Third Snake Journal*, p. 18.

7. Entries for 6, 7, 11 October 1827, Ogden, *Third Snake Journal*, pp. 14, 15; Miller and Miller, Introduction to Ogden, p. xxviii; Warner, "Peter Skene Ogden," p. 224.

8. Entries for 18, 20 October 1827, Ogden, *Third Snake Journal*, p. 17.

9. Entry for 25 October 1827, ibid., p. 19; Miller and Miller, Introduction to Ogden, p. xxviii.

10. Entries for 1, 10 November 1827, Ogden, *Third Snake Journal*, pp. 21–22, 24.

11. Entry for 30 November 1827, ibid., pp. 29–30; Barker, Introduction to Ogden, p. lx.

12. Entry for 20 December 1827, Ogden, *Third Snake Journal*, p. 38.

13. Ibid.

14. Entry for 24 December 1827, ibid., pp. 39–40; Morgan, *Jedediah Smith*, p. 292.

15. Letter from William H. Ashley to Thomas H. Benton, 11 January 1829, *West of Ashley*, p. 184. It is reasonable to suggest that Ashley deliberately exaggerated the number of Ogden's men as being sixty.

16. Fragment of letter from William H. Ashley to (apparently) Thomas H. Benton, January 1829, Ashley Papers.

17. Letter from William H. Ashley to Thomas H. Benton, 11 January 1829, *West of Ashley*, p. 184. In the apparent earlier draft, Ashley's figures were different: "Mr Sublette informs me that the traders of this company have recently sold goods to Indians (who are friendly to our traders and confine their trade principally to them) for not much more than the probable cost of the articles, & not more than one sixth or ninth part of the price they had previously been in the habit of selling them for." Fragment of letter from William H. Ashley to (apparently) Thomas H. Benton, January 1829, Ashley Papers.

18. Fragment of letter from William H. Ashley to (apparently) Thomas H. Benton, January 1829, Ashley Papers. The tone and boldness of Ashley's implications against the Hudson Bay Company may be judged by the following:

> The Hudson Bay Compy employ a great proportion of their men, of mixed blood, many of whom possess as much of the savage Character as any Indians whatever & indeed I should apprehend more danger from them—They are paid by the company a certain price for Each skin they deliver, whether the same be plundered, purchased of Indians, or taken by themselves, I presume is a matter not Enquired into by the compy—The circumstances herein stated are but few, of many, Equally strong, which govern my opinion, that our difficulties with the Indians west of the Mountains, are mainly produced by foreigners who are allowed a free trade & Entercourse in that country.

Letter from William H. Ashley to Thomas H. Benton, 11 January 1829, *West of Ashley*, p. 184. Ashley's arguments helped keep Benton a defender of the American fur trade. But on the Oregon question his moderation was instrumental in ratifying the final resolution, avoiding war. Jones and Rakestraw, *Prologue to Destiny*, pp. 252, 261–62.

19. Entries for 28 December 1827 and 5 January 1828, Ogden, *Third Snake Journal*, pp. 41, 45–46.

20. Entry for 25 January 1828, ibid., pp. 54–55.

21. Entries of 16, 18 January 1828, ibid., pp. 49, 50.

22. Entry for 20 January 1828, ibid., p. 50.

23. Entry for 23 January 1828, ibid., p. 53.

24. Entries for 24, 25 January 1828, ibid., pp. 53–54.

25. Entries for 27, 28 January 1828, ibid., pp. 56, 57.

26. Entry for 4 February 1828, ibid., p. 59.

27. Entry for 17 February 1828, ibid., pp. 63–64.

28. Old Goddin's son had left the expedition that fall promising to return. Here Ogden surely is referring not to him but to Thiery Goddin, the father, who deserted in 1825.

29. Entry for 18 February 1828, Ogden, *Third Snake Journal*, p. 64. Interestingly, Ogden did not ask how American trappers managed to retain their money. Campbell's men sold his people eight packs of playing cards. "I am glad however they do not gamble high, far different I am informed is the case in the American camp, some of the trappers have already lost upwards of four hundred dollars equal to two hundred beaver with us." *Third Snake Journal*, p. 64.

30. P. 174.

31. Entry for 20 February 1828, Ogden, *Third Snake Journal*, pp. 64–65.

32. Entry for 19 February 1828, ibid., p. 65.

33. Entries for 21, 22 February 1828, ibid., p. 65.

34. Entry for 3 March 1828, ibid., p. 68. Payette provides another example of the changes that were occurring. He insisted on being a freeman because he thought that now, under the reformed prices, he could do financially better in that status than as an engaged servant. Haines, "Francois Payette," pp. 15–16.

35. Entry for 3 March 1828, Ogden, *Third Snake Journal*, p. 68.

36. Entry for 17 March 1828, Ogden, *Third Snake Journal*, p. 70. There were only five Americans because Campbell had taken some of the men with him and others had started for Bear River.

37. Entry for 26 March 1828, ibid., p. 72.

38. Letter from William H. Ashley to Thomas H. Benton, 11 January 1829, *West of Ashley*, p. 184; Morgan, *Jedediah Smith*, p. 294. "Some information subsequent to this attack induces Mr [William] Sublette to believe that the Indians who committed this outrage were our old enemies the Blackfoot." Fragment of letter from William H. Ashley to (apparently) Thomas H. Benton, January 1829, Ashley Papers.

39. Sunder, "Sublette," p. 346.

40. Letter from William H. Ashley to Thomas H. Benton, 11 January 1829, *West of Ashley*, p. 184. "I do not believe from the idea I have of the character of

Mr. Ogden, that he would dictate such conduct to Indians." Fragment of letter from William H. Ashley to (apparently) Thomas H. Benton, January 1829, Ashley Papers.

41. Entries for 25 January and 10 May 1828, Ogden, *Third Snake Journal*, pp. 54, 81–82.

42. Entry for 11 May 1828, ibid., p. 82.

43. After Tulloch he had one more meeting with three Americans who came to his camp to trade. Entry for 28 March 1828, ibid., p. 73.

44. *Simpson's 1828 Journey*, pp. 48–49. Also, see Lamb, Introduction to McLoughlin *Letters*, p. lxvii; Miller and Miller, Introduction to Ogden, p. xxx; Barker, Introduction to Ogden, p. lxxx.

45. Lamb, Introduction to McLoughlin *Letters*, p. xcv; Innis, Introduction to *Minutes*, p. lxviii.

CHAPTER 15: THE COUNTRY VIRTUALLY FALLS INTO OUR KEEPING

1. Wishart, *Fur Trade*, p. 131; letters from John McLoughlin to Governor and Committee, 10 July 1828, from George Simpson to Governor and Committee, 18 July 1828, and John McLoughlin to John Work, in Miller and Miller, Introduction to Ogden, pp. xxxvi–xxxvii.

2. Entry for 2 June 1826, Ogden, *First Snake Journals*, p. 174; Morgan, *Jedediah Smith*, p. 186.

3. Entry for 5 October 1828, Ogden, *Fourth Snake Journal*, p. 99.

4. Entry for 18 May 1829, ibid., p. 150. Besides Payette, who separated near the mouth of Burnt River on 5 October, he had detached a "forking party" under Charles Plante when still in today's Utah. Entry for 30 March 1829, ibid., pp. 136–37.

5. Letter of 5 August 1829, *Letters of McLoughlin—First Series*, pp. 74–75.

6. Utley, *Life Wild and Perilous*, pp. 96, 337, n. 30.

7. Which sent an expedition to investigate and avenge the attack. *Patterns of Vengeance*, pp. 174–82; "Restraints of Vengeance," pp. 71–85.

8. "Ogden's Report," p. 120.

9. Letter from George Simpson to Governor and Committee, 10 July 1831, in Miller and Miller, Introduction to Ogden, pp. xxxv–xxxvi.

10. Letter from George Simpson to John McLoughlin, 15 March 1829, Merk, *Fur Trade and Empire*, p. 309.

11. On one occasion, like Ogden before him, he had difficulty giving an American trapping party the slip. The American trappers succeeded in following him. Entry for 12 October 1830, Work, *Field Journal*, pp. 32–33.

12. Entry for 16 April 1831, ibid., pp. 94–95.

13. Entry for 16 April 1831, ibid., p. 95.

14. Entry for 17 April 1831, ibid., pp. 95–97. Dumais remained with Work and went on the expedition of the next year, drowning on the way home in the Snake River. Entry for 19 July 1832, *John Work Journal*, p. 174.

15. Entry for 30 December 1831, ibid., p. 119.

16. Innis, Introduction to *Minutes*, p. lxix.

17. Letter from Kenneth McKenzie to Pierre Chouteau, Jr., 7 July 1829, Chouteau Collection.

18. Letter from George Simpson to London Officers, 1 March 1829, in Russell, "Trapper Trails," pp. 95–96.

19. Chance, *Influences of HBC*, p. 30; Dee, "Irishman," p. 251; Merk, *Oregon Question*, p. 251.

20. Entry for 30 January 1832, and letter from John Work to Edward Ermatinger, 5 August 1832, *John Work Journal*, pp. 127–28, 180, 179.

21. See Work, *California Journal.*

22. Letter from Governor and Committee to John McLoughlin, 4 December 1833, in Phillips, *Fur Trade*, 2: 457–58.

23. Letter from James Douglas to Governor and Committee, 18 October 1838, *Letters of McLoughlin—First Series*, p. 255.

24. Letter from James Douglas to Governor and Committee, 14 October 1839, *Letters of McLoughlin—Second Series*, p. 225.

25. Sunder, "Sublette," p. 348.

26. Letter of 6 February 1840, McDonald, *Letters of Ermatinger*, p. 225.

27. Mattes, *Fur Traders*, p. 5. In a book published by a university press, it was said of Hudson's Bay trappers competing against Americans: "The Rocky Mountain men paid the Indians double the Hudson's Bay Company's prices for furs and, defying the laws of their Government, they opened a fountain of ruin in the wilderness in their effort to starve Ogden off the ground. They lay in wait for the H.B. C. brigades or set the Indians on to attack them, and pirated their furs. It was war to the knife." Skinner, *Adventurers of Oregon*, p. 225.

28. For a short discussion of the horse raids and the recovery of the horses, see "Beaver's Law in Elephant's Country," pp. 198–200.

29. Johansen Notes, p. 48, n. 52; *Newell's Memoranda*, p. 39.

30. W. J. Ghent, "Joseph L. Meek," *Dictionary of American Biography* (1961) 6:494–95, p. 494 (referring both to Newell and to Joe Meek, who joined him).

31. Hafen, "Robert Newell," in *Mountain Men*, 8:272–73.

32. Wallace, Introduction to *Simpson's 1828 Journey*, p. xliv.

33. Elliott, "Robert Newell," pp. 181, 184.

34. Utley, *Life Wild and Perilous*, pp. 207–9, 212–16.

Short Title List

Anon., *Bow River Journal*
Anonymous, *Journal of Occurrences Connected with the Bow River Expedition from its departure from YF 21 July 1822, until its return from there on 30th June 1823* (Hudson's Bay Company MS B. 34/a/4).

Anon., *Edmonton Journal*
Anonymous, *Journal of Occurrences at Edmonton Commencing 20th May, 1833* (Hudson's Bay Company MS B. 60/a/28).

Ashley, 1825 Diary
Ashley, William Henry. "Diary." In "The Diary of William H. Ashley, March 25—June 27, 1825: A Record of Exploration West Across the Continental Divide Down the Green River and into the Great Basin." Dale L. Morgan, ed. *Bulletin of the Missouri Historical Society* 11 (October 1954, January–April 1955): 9–40, 158–86, 279–302.

"Ashley Narrative"
"Ashley Narrative." In *West of Ashley*, pp. 93–125.

Ashley Papers
Ashley, Willian H. Papers. MS, Missouri Historical Society, St. Louis.

Auerbach, "Old Trails"
Auerbach, Herbert S. "Old Trails, Old Forts, Old Trappers and Traders." *Utah Historical Quarterly* 9 (January–April 1941): 13–63.

Ball, *Autobiography*
Ball, John. *Autobiography of John Ball.* Kate Ball Powers, Flora Ball Hopkins, and Lucy Ball, eds. Grand Rapids, Mich.: Dean-Hicks Company, 1925.

Barker, Book Review
Barker, Burt Brown. Review of *Simpson's 1828 Journey to The Columbia. British Columbia Historical Quarterly* 13 (January 1949): 43–46.

Barker, Introduction to Ogden
———. Introduction to Ogden, *First Snake Journals*, pp. xi–lxxix.

"Beaver's Law in Elephant Country"
Reid, John Phillip. "The Beaver's Law in the Elephant's Country: An Excursion into Transboundary Legal History." *Western Legal History* 4, no. 2 (Summer–Fall 1991): 149–201.

Binns, *Ogden*
  Binns, Archie. *Peter Skene Ogden: Fur Trader.* Portland, Ore.: Binfords & Mort, Publishers, 1967.

Bird, *Edmonton Report*
  Bird, James. *Edmonton Report 1815* (Hudson's Bay Company MS B. 60/e/1).

Bird, *Fourth Carlton Journal*
  ———. *Journal by James Bird Carlton 1816/17* (Hudson's Bay Company MS B. 27/a/6).

Bird, *Ninth Edmonton Journal*
  ———. *A Sketch of the Principal Occurrences &c. at Edmonton House Commencing 19th July 1814 Ending 19 June 1815* (Hudson's Bay Company Ms B. 60/a/13).

Bird, *Seventh Edmonton Journal*
  ———. *A Sketch of the Principal Transactions and Occurrences at Saskatchewan Factory and on a Voyage to and from York Factory* (Hudson's Bay Company MS B. 60/a/11).

Bird, *Tenth Edmonton Journal*
  ———. *A Sketch of the Principal Transactions and Occurrences at Edmonton House, and on the passage to and from York Factory* (Hudson's Bay Company MS B. 60/a/15).

Brooks, *Diplomacy and Borderlands*
  Brooks, Philip Coolidge. *Diplomacy and the Borderlands: The Adams-Onis Treaty of 1819.* University of California Publications in History. Vol. 24. Berkeley: University of California Press, 1939.

Bruff, *Journals*
  Gold Rush: The Journals, Drawings, and Other Papers of J. Goldsborough Bruff, Captain, Washington City and California Mining Association, April 2, 1849–July 20, 1851. Georgia Willis Read and Ruth Gaines, eds. New York: Columbia University Press, 1944.

Campbell, *North West Company*
  Campbell, Marjorie Wilkins. *The North West Company.* Toronto: Macmillan Company of Canada Limited, 1956.

Canadian North-West
  The Canadian North-West: Its Early Development and Legislative Records—Minutes of the Councils of the Red River Colony and the Northern Department of Rupert's Land. E. H. Oliver, ed. 2 vols. Ottawa: Government Printing Bureau, 1914.

Carey, *General History*
  Carey, Charles H. *General History of Oregon through Early Statehood.* Portland, Ore.: Binfords & Mort, Publishers, 1971.

Chance, *Influences of HBC*
  Chance, David H. *Influences of the Hudson's Bay Company on the Native Cultures of the Colvile District.* Moscow, Id.: Published as Northwest Anthropological Research Notes, vol. 7, no. 1, pt. 2, 1973.

Chardon's Journal
> *Chardon's Journal at Fort Clark 1834–1839: Descriptive of Life on the Upper Missouri; of a Fur Trader's Experiences Among the Mandans, Gros Ventres, and their Neighbors; of the Ravages of the Small-Pox Epidemic of 1837.* Annie Heloise Abel, ed. Freeport, N.Y.: Books for Libraries Press, 1970.

Chittenden, *Fur Trade*
> Chittenden, Hiram Martin. *The American Fur Trade of the Far West: A History of Pioneer Trading Posts & Early Fur Companies of the Missouri Valley & Rocky Mountains & of the Overland Commerce with Sante Fé.* Stallo Vinton, ed. 2 vols. Lincoln: University of Nebraska Press, 1986.

Chouteau Collection
> Chouteau Collection, Missouri Historical Society Archives, St. Louis.

Cline, *Ogden*
> Cline, Gloria Griffen. *Peter Skene Ogden and the Hudson's Bay Company.* Norman: University of Oklahoma Press, 1974.

Cline, "Ogden's Nevada"
> ———. "Peter Skene Ogden's Nevada Explorations." *Nevada Historical Society Quarterly* 3, no. 3 (July–September, 1960): 3–11.

Clokey, *Ashley*
> Clokey, Richard M. *William H. Ashley: Enterprise and Politics in the Trans-Mississippi West.* Norman: University of Oklahoma Press, 1980.

Conyers, "Diary"
> "Diary of E. W. Conyers, a Pioneer of 1852." *Transactions of the Thirty-Third Annual Reunion of the Oregon Pioneer Association, June 15, 1905.* Portland: Peaslee Bros., 1906, pp. 423–512.

Cox, *Columbia River*
> Cox, Ross. *The Columbia River: Or Scenes and Adventures During a Residence of Six Years on the Western Side of the Rocky Mountains among various Tribes of Indians hitherto Unknown; together with "A Journey Across the American Continent."* Edgar I. Stewart and Jane R. Stewart, eds. Norman: University of Oklahoma Press, 1957.

Cumberland House Journals—First Series
> *Cumberland House Journals and Inland Journals 1775–1782: First Series 1775–79.* E. E. Rich, ed. The Hudson's Bay Record Society, 1951.

Cumberland House Journals—Second Series
> *Cumberland House Journals and Inland Journals 1775–82: Second Series, 1779–82.* E. E. Rich, ed. London: The Hudson's Bay Record Society, 1952.

Dale, *Ashley-Smith Explorations*
> Dale, Harrison Clifford. *The Ashley-Smith Explorations and the Discovery of a Central Route to the Pacific 1822–1829.* Cleveland, Ohio: Arthur H. Clark Company, 1941.

Dee, "Irishman"
> Dee, Henry Drummond. "An Irishman in the Fur Trade: The Life and Journals of John Work." *British Columbia Historical Quarterly* 7, no. 4 (October 1943): 229–70.

DeVoto, *Across Missouri*
  DeVoto, Bernard. *Across the Wide Missouri*. Boston: Houghton Mifflin Company, 1947.

Documents of 1817
  Informations, Complaints, Agreements, and other Documents (Hudson's Bay Company MS B. 27/a/7).

Douthit, "Hudson's Bay"
  Douthit, Nathan. "The Hudson's Bay Company and the Indians of Southern Oregon." *Oregon Historical Quarterly* 93 (Spring 1992): 25–64.

Early Fur Trade on the Northern Plains
  Early Fur Trade on the Northern Plains: Canadian Traders among the Mandan and Hidatsa Indians 1738–1818—The Narratives of John Macdonnell, David Thompson, Francois-Antoine Larocque, and Charles McKenzie. W. Raymond Wood and Thomas D. Thiesson, eds. Norman: University of Oklahoma Press, 1985.

Early Western Travels
  Early Western Travels 1748–1846. Vol. 2. Reuben Gold Thwaites, ed. Cleveland, Ohio: Arthur H. Clark Company, 1905, pp. 111–369.

Elliott, Editorial Notes
  Elliott, T. C. Editorial Notes to Ogden, "Snake Journal 1825." *Quarterly of the Oregon Historical Society* 10 (December 1909): 331–65.

Elliott, "Peter Skene Ogden"
  ———. "Peter Skene Ogden, Fur Trader." *Quarterly of the Oregon Historical Society* 11 (September 1910): 229–78.

Elliott, "Robert Newell"
  ———. "'Doctor' Robert Newell, Mountain Man." *Washington Historical Quarterly* 18 (July 1927): 181–86.

Essays American West
  Essays on the American West No. 3. Thomas G. Alexander, ed. Provo, Utah: Brigham Young University Press, 1974, pp. 137–66.

Fidler, *Dauphin Journal*
  Fidler, Peter. *Journal &c. at Fort Dauphin 1820* (Hudson's Bay Company MS B. 51/a/2).

Fitzgerald, *Hudson's Bay*
  Fitzgerald, James Edward. *An Examination of the Charter and Proceedings of the Hudson's Bay Company, with Reference to the Grant of Vancouver's Island*. London: Trelawney Saunders, 1849.

Frontier Experience
  The Frontier Experience: Readings in the Trans-Mississippi West. Robert V. Hine and Edwin R. Bingham, eds. Belmont, Calif.: Wadsworth Publishing Company, 1996

Fur Trade 1831 Letter
    Letter from Superintendant of Indian Affairs William Clark to Secretary of
        War Lewis Cass, 20 November 1831 (photostat, from Office of Indian
        Affairs, United States Department of the Interior, Missouri Historical
        Society, St. Louis).

Fur Trade Revisited
    *The Fur Trade Revisited: Selected Papers of the Sixth North American Fur Trade Con-
        ference, Mackinac Island, Michigan, 1991.* Jennifer S. H. Brown, W. J. Eccles,
        and Donald P. Heldman, eds. East Lansing and Mackinac Island, Mich.:
        Michigan State University Press and Mackinac State Historic Park, 1994.

Galbraith, "British-American Competition"
    Galbraith, John S. "British-American Competition in the Border Fur Trade
        of the 1820s." *Minnesota History* 36 (September 1959): 241–49.

Galbraith, *Imperial Factor*
    ———. *The Hudson's Bay Company as an Imperial Factor 1821–1869.* Berkeley:
        University of California Press, 1957.

Galbraith, "Note on Trade"
    ———. "A Note on the British Fur Trade in California, 1821–1846." *Pacific
        Historical Review* 24 (1955): 253–60.

Glover, Introduction to Second Cumberland
    Glover, Richard Glover. Introduction and Notes to *Cumberland Journals—Sec-
        ond Series,* pp. xiii–lxii.

Goetzmann, *New Lands*
    Goetzmann, William H. *New Lands, New Men: America and the Second Great
        Age of Discovery.* New York: Viking Penguin Inc., 1986.

Graham and Smith, "Report"
    Graham, Lieutenant Richard Hill, and Lieutenant Sidney Smith. "Report of
        Journey to Rocky Mountains," 12 November 1843. John F. Sunder, ed.
        Bulletin of the Missouri Historical Society 11 (October 1954): 41–53.

Hafen, "Brief History"
    Hafen, LeRoy R. "A Brief History of the Fur Trade in the Far West." In *Moun-
        tain Men,* 1:21–76.

Hafen, "Etienne Provost"
    ———. "Etienne Provost." In *Mountain Men,* 6: 371–85.

Hafen, "Provost"
    ———. "Etienne Provost, Mountain Man and Utah Pioneer." *Utah Histori-
        cal Quarterly* 36 (Spring 1968): 99–112.

Hafen, "Robert Newell"
    ———. "Robert Newell." In *Mountain Men,* 8:272–73.

Haines, "François Payette"
    Haines, Francis Jr. "François Payette." *Idaho Yesterdays* 8, no. 4 (Winter
        1964–65): 12–20.

Haines, Introduction to Work
————. Editor's Introduction to Work, *Field Journal,* pp. xv–xxvii.

Haines, "Johnson Gardner"
Haines, Aubrey L. "Johnson Gardner." In *Mountain Men,* 2: 157–59.

Harmon, *Journal*
Harmon, Daniel W. *A Journal of Voyages and Travels in the interior of North America between the 47th and 58th degree of North latitude, extending from Montreal nearly to the Pacific Ocean, a distance of about 5000 miles, including an Account of the Principal Occurrences during a residence of nearly nineteen years in different parts of that Country.* Daniel Haskel, ed. New York: Allerton Book Co., 1905.

Heron, *Third Edmonton Journal*
Heron, Francis. *Journal of Occurrences at Edmonton House from [7th October] 1820 Until May 1821* (Hudson's Bay Company MS B. 60/a/19).

Holmes, "James Douglas"
Holmes, Kenneth L. "James Douglas." In *Mountain Men,* 9:139–46.

Hoover, *Diary*
Hoover, Vincent A. *Diary of Journey from Mobile, Ala. . . by Way of the Oregon Trail to Salt Lake City and Southward through Utah & Nevada to Los Angeles . . . (1849)* (MS, in 3 vols., HM27628, Huntington Library).

Hoover, *Revised Journal*
————. *Journal* (MS, HM 27628, Huntington Library).

Howay, Sage, and Angus, *British Columbia*
Howay, F. W., W. N. Sage, and H. F. Angus. *British Columbia and the United States: The North Pacific Slope from Fur Trade to Aviation.* H. F. Angus, ed. New York: Russell & Russell, 1942.

Hudson's Bay Miscellany
Hudson's Bay Miscellany 1670–1870. Glyndwr Williams, ed. Winnipeg: The Hudson's Bay Record Society, 1975, pp. 151–236.

Innis, *Fur Trade*
Innis, Harold A. *The Fur Trade in Canada: An Introduction to Canadian Economic History.* Toronto: University of Toronto Press, 1956. Rev. ed. New Haven: Yale University Press, 1930.

Innis, Introduction to *Minutes*
————. Introduction to *Minutes of Northern Department,* pp. xi–lxxvii.

Irving, *Astoria*
Irving, Washington. *Astoria, or Anecdotes of an Enterprize Beyond the Rocky Mountains.* Richard Dilworth Rust, ed. Boston: Twayne Publishers, 1976.

Irving, *Bonneville*
————. *The Adventures of Captain Bonneville.* Robert A. Rees and Alan Sandy, eds. Boston: Twayne Publishers, 1977.

Jackson, "Charles McKay"
Jackson, John C. "Charles McKay." In *Mountain Men,* 9: 251–58.

James, *Three Years*
> James, Thomas. *Three Years among the Indians and Mexicans*. Milo Milton Quaife, ed. New York: Citadel Press, 1966.

Johansen, Introduction to Ogden
> Johansen, Dorothy O. Introduction and Notes to Ogden, *Second Snake Journal*, pp. xiii–lxxii.

Johansen, "Notes"
> ———. Notes to *Newell's Memoranda*.

John Work Journal
> *The Journal of John Work: A Chief-Trader of the Hudson's Bay Co. During his Expedition from Vancouver to the Flatheads and Blackfeet of the Pacific Northwest*. William S. Lewis and Paul C. Phillips, eds. Cleveland: Arthur H. Clark Company, 1923.

Jones and Rakestraw, *Prologue to Destiny*
> Jones, Howard, and Donald A. Rakestraw. *Prologue to Manifest Destiny: Anglo-American Relations in the 1840s*. Wilmington, Del.: Scholarly Resources Inc., 1997.

Josephy, *Nez Perce*
> Josephy, Alvin M., Jr. *The Nez Perce Indians and the Opening of the Northwest*. New Haven, Conn.: Yale University Press, 1965.

Karamanski, Book Review
> Karamanski, Theodore J. Review of John C. Jackson's *Shadow of the Tetons: David E. Jackson and the Claiming of the American West* (1993). *Journal of American History* 81 (1995): 1706–7.

Karamanski, "Iroquois and Fur Trade"
> ———. "The Iroquois and the Fur Trade of the Far West." *The Beaver* (Spring 1982): 5–13.

Kennedy, *Spokane Report*
> Kennedy, Alexander. *Spokane Report, 1822–23* (Hudson's Bay Company MS B. 208/e/1).

Kittson, *Snake Country Journal*
> Kittson, William. *Journal of Occurrences in a Trapping Expedition to and from the Snake Country in the Year 1824 and (25) Kept by William Kittson*. In Appendix A to Ogden, *First Snake Journals*, pp. 209–57.

Lamb, Introduction to McLoughlin *Letters*
> Lamb, W. Kaye. Introduction to *Letters of McLoughlin—First Series*, pp. xi–cxxviii.

Lamb, Third Introduction
> ———. Introduction to *Letters of McLoughlin—Third Series*, pp. xi–lxiii.

Larocque, "Missouri Journal"
> Larocque, François-Antoine. "Missouri Journal." In *Early Fur Trade on the Northern Plains*, pp. 129–55.

Lavender, "American Characteristics"
    Lavender, David. "Some American Characteristics of the American Fur Company." *Minnesota History* 40, no. 4 (Winter 1966): 178–87.

Lavender, "Thomas McKay"
    ———. "Thomas McKay." In *Mountain Men*, 6: 259–77.

Law for the Elephant
    John Phillip Reid, *Law for the Elephant: Property and Social Behavior on the Overland Trail.* San Marino, Calif.: The Huntington Library, 1980.

Letters of Francis Ermatinger
    See McDonald, *Letters of Ermatinger*

Letters of John McLoughlin
    Letters of Dr. John McLoughlin Written at Fort Vancouver 1829–1832. Burt Brown Barker, ed. Portland, Ore.: Binfords & Mort, Publishers, 1948.

Letters of McLoughlin—First Series
    The Letters of John McLoughlin from Fort Vancouver to the Governor and Committee: First Series, 1825–38. E. E. Rich, ed. Toronto: The Champlain Society, 1941.

Letters of McLoughlin—Second Series
    The Letters of John McLoughlin from Fort Vancouver to the Governor and Committee: Second Series, 1839–44. E. E. Rich, ed. Toronto: The Champlain Society, 1943.

Letters of McLoughlin—Third Series
    The Letters of John McLoughlin from Fort Vancouver to the Governor and Committee: Third Series, 1844–46. E. E. Rich, ed. Toronto: The Champlain Society, 1944.

Lewis and Phillips, Introduction
    Lewis, William S., and Paul C. Phillips, Introduction and Notes to *John Work Journal*, pp.15–69.

Loo, *Making Law*
    Loo, Tina. *Making Law, Order, and Authority in British Columbia, 1821–1871.* Toronto: University of Toronto Press, 1994.

Luttig, *Journal*
    Luttig, John C. *Journal of a Fur-Trading Expedition on the Upper Missouri 1812–1813.* Stella M. Drumm, ed. New York: Argosy Antiquarian Ltd., 1964.

McDonald, *Letters of Ermatinger*
    McDonald, Lois Halliday. *Fur Trade Letters of Francis Ermatinger Written to his brother Edward during his service with the Hudson's Bay Company 1818–1853.* Glendale, Calif.: Arthur H. Clark Company, 1980.

McDonald, *Peace River*
    McDonald, Archibald. *Peace River. A Canoe Voyage from Hudson's Bay to Pacific by the late Sir George Simpson, in 1828.* Malcolm McLeod, ed. Ottawa: J. Durie & Son, 1872.

[McGillivray,] *On the Origin*
   [McGillivray, Duncan]. *On the Origin and Progress of the North-West Company of
      Canada, with a History of the Fur Trade, as Connected with that Concern; and
      Observations on the Political Importance of the Company's Intercourse with and
      Influence over the Indians or Savage Nations of the Interior and on the Necessity
      of Maintaining and Supporting the System from which that Influence Arises, and
      by which it can be preserved.* London: Printed by Cox, Son, and Baylis, 1811.

McGregor, "Old Whitehead"
   McGregor, D. A. "'Old Whitehead'—Peter Skene Ogden." *British Columbia
      Historical Quarterly* 17, nos. 3–4 (July–October 1953): 161–95.

McLean, *Notes of Service*
   [McLean, John]. *John McLean's Notes of a Twenty-Five Year's Service in the Hud-
      son's Bay Territory.* W. S. Wallace, ed. Toronto: The Champlain Society, 1932.

McLeod, Notes
   McLeod, Malcolm. Notes to McDonald, *Peace River,* pp. 39–119.

Mattes, *Fur Traders*
   Mattes, Merrill J. *Fur Traders and Trappers of the Old West.* Yellowstone Library
      and Museum Association and the Grand Teton National Association,
      1944. Reprint, 1947.

Merk, *Fur Trade and Empire*
   Merk, Frederick. *Fur Trade and Empire: George Simpson's Journal Entitled
      Remarks Connected with the Fur Trade in the Course of Voyage from York Factory
      to Fort George and back to York Factory 1824–1825, with Related Documents.*
      Cambridge, Mass.: Harvard University Press, 1931. Rev. ed. 1968.

Merk, Introduction
   ———. Introduction to the Revised Edition: "The Strategy of Monopoly"
      and Introduction to the First Edition to Merk, *Fur Trade and Empire,*
      pp. xi–lxii.

Merk, *Oregon Question*
   ———. *The Oregon Question: Essays in Anglo-American Diplomacy and Politics.*
      Cambridge, Mass.: Harvard University Press, 1967.

Merk, "Snake Country Expedition"
   ———. "Snake Country Expedition, 1824–25: An Episode of Fur Trade and
      Empire." *Oregon Historical Quarterly* 35, no. 2 (June 1934): 93–122.

Miller, Notes
   Miller, David E. Notes, to Ogden, "Utah Journal."

Miller, "Ogden Discovered Indians"
   ———. "Peter Skene Ogden Discovered Indians." In *Essays on the American
      West,* pp. 137–66.

Miller and Miller, Introduction to Ogden
   Miller, David E., and David H. Miller, Introduction to Ogden, *Fourth Snake
      Journal,* pp.xiii–lxx.

"Minutes of Council 1825 Abridged"
  "Minutes of Council 1825 Abridged," *Canadian Historical Review* 7 (1926):
  304–20.

Minutes of Northern Department
  Minutes of Council Northern Department of Rupert Land, 1821–31. R. Harvey
  Fleming, ed. Toronto: The Champlain Society, 1940.

Morgan, "Ashey's Diary"
  Morgan, Dale L. Introduction and Footnotes in Ashley, "1825 Diary."

Morgan, *Jedediah Smith*
  ———. *Jedediah Smith and the Opening of the West.* Lincoln: University of
  Nebraska Press, 1964.

Morton, *Canadian West*
  Morton, Arthur S. *A History of the Canadian West to 1870–71 Being a History
  of Rupert's Land (the Hudson's Bay Company's Territory) and of the North-West
  Territory (including the Pacific Slope).* 2d ed. Lewis G. Thomas, ed. Toronto:
  University of Toronto Press, 1973.

Morton, "Jurisdiction Act"
  Morton, A. S. "The Canada Jurisdiction Act (1803) and the North West,"
  *Proceedings and Transactions of the Royal Society of Canada—Third Series—Vol.
  XXXII—Meeting of May 1938: Transactions Section II* (1938): 121–37.

Mountain Men
  *The Mountain Men and the Fur Trade of the Far West: Biographical Sketches of
  the Participants by Scholars of the Subject and with Introductions by the Editor.*
  LeRoy R. Hafen, ed. 10 vols. Glendale, Calif.: Arthur H. Clark Company,
  1965–1972.

Narrative of Robert Campbell
  *A Narrative of Col. Robert Campbell's Experiences in the Rocky Mountain Fur Trade
  from 1825–1835,* dictated to William Fayel in 1870 (TS, Campbell Family
  Papers, Missouri Historical Society, St. Louis).

Newell's Memoranda
  *Robert Newell's Memoranda: Travles in the Territory of Missourie; Travle to the
  Kayuse War; together with a Report on the Indians South of the Columbia River.*
  Dorothy O. Johansen, ed. Portland, Ore.: Champoeg Press, 1959.

Nicks, "The Iroquois"
  Nicks, Trudy. "The Iroquois and the Fur Trade in Western Canada." In *Old
  Trails.* pp. 85–101.

Nunis, "Michel Laframboise"
  Nunis, Doyce B. Jr., "Michel Laframboise." In *Mountain Men,* 5:145–70.

Ogden, *First Snake Journals*
  Ogden, Peter Skene. *Peter Skene Ogden's Snake Country Journals 1824–25 and
  1825–26.* E. E. Rich and A. M. Johnson, eds. London: Hudson's Bay Record
  Society, 1950.

Ogden, *Fourth Snake Journal*
——. *Peter Skene Ogden's Snake Country Journals 1827–28 and 1828–29.* Gyndwr Williams, ed. London: Hudson's Bay Record Society, 1971, pp. 97–166.

"Ogden's Report"
——. "Ogden's Report of His 1829–1830 Expedition," John Scaglione, ed. *California Historical Society Quarterly* 28 (June 1949): 117–24.

Ogden, *Second Snake Journal*
——. *Peter Skene Ogden's Snake Country Journal 1826–27.* K. G. Davies and A. M. Johnson, eds. London: Hudson's Bay Record Society, 1961.

Ogden, "Snake Country Report 1825/26"
——. "Snake Country Report 1825/26." In Appendix B in Ogden, *First Snake Journals*, pp. 258–66.

Ogden, "Snake Journal, 1825"
——. "The Peter Skene Ogden Journals," T. C. Elliott, ed. *Quarterly of the Oregon Historical Society* 10 (December 1909): 331–65.

Ogden, *Third Snake Journal*
——. *Peter Skene Ogden's Snake Country Journals 1827–28 and 1828–29.* Glyndwr Williams, ed. London: Hudson's Bay Record Society, 1971, pp. 1–94.

Ogden, *Utah Journal*
——. "Peter Skene Ogden's Journal of His Expedition to Utah, 1825." David E. Miller, ed. *Utah Historical Quarterly* 20 (April 1952): 159–86.

Old Trails
Old Trails and New Directions: Papers of the Third North American Fur Trade Conference. Carol M. Judd and Arthur J. Ray, eds. Toronto: University of Toronto Press, 1980.

Ormsby, Book Review
Ormsby, Margaret A. Book Review. *British Columbia Historical Quarterly* 15 (July–October 1951): 229–32.

Patterns of Vengeance
Reid, John Phillip. *Patterns of Vengeance: Crosscultural Homicide in the North American Fur Trade.* Pasadena: Calif.: Ninth Circuit Historical Society, 1999.

Patterson, Introduction to *Journal*
Patterson, R. M. Introduction and Appendix to *A Journal of a Voyage from Rocky Mountain Portage in Peace River to the Sources of Finlays Branch and North West Ward in Summer 1824.* E. E. Rich, ed. London: Hudson's Bay Record Society, 1955, pp. xiii–c, 215–46.

Phillips, *Fur Trade*
Phillips, Paul Chrisler. *The Fur Trade.* 2 vols. Norman: University of Oklahoma Press, 1961.

Pruden, *Eleventh Carlton Journal*
Pruden, John Peter. *Journal of Transactions & Occurrences at Carlton Commencing 29th May 1828* (Hudson's Bay Company MS B. 27/a/17).

Pruden, *Seventh Carlton Journal*
———. *Journal of Transactions in Carlton District 1822 & 1823* (Hudson's Bay Company MS B. 27/a/12).

Ray, *Indians in Fur Trade*
Ray, Arthur J. *Indians in the Fur Trade: Their Role as Trappers, Hunters, and Middlemen in the Lands Southwest of Hudson Bay 1660–1870.* Toronto: University of Toronto Press, 1974.

"Restraints of Vengeance"
Reid, John Phillip. "Restraints of Vengeance: Retaliation-in-kind and the Use of Indian Law in the Old Oregon Country." *Oregon Historical Quarterly* 95 (Spring 1994): 48–92.

Rich, *Fur Trade*
Rich, E. E. *The Fur Trade and the Northwest to 1857.* Toronto: McClelland and Stewart Limited, 1967.

Rich, "Robertson Appendix"
———. Appendix A to *Robertson's Correspondence*, pp. 203–45.

Rich, "Robertson Introduction"
———. Introduction to *Robertson's Correspondence*, pp. xiii–cxxxi.

Robertson's Correspondence
Colin Robertson's Correspondence Book, September 1817 to September 1822. E. E. Rich, ed. Toronto: The Champlain Society, 1939.

Ronda, *Astoria*
Ronda, James P. *Astoria and Empire.* Lincoln: University of Nebraska Press, 1990.

Ross, *Flathead Journal*
Ross, Alexander. *Journal Kept at Flathead Post during the Winter 1824–25* (Hudson's Bay Company MS B. 69/a/1).

Ross, *Fur Hunters*
Ross, Alexander. *The Fur Hunters of the Far West: A Narrative of Adventures in the Oregon and Rocky Mountains.* 2 vols. London: Smith, Elder and Co., 1855.

Ross, *Hunters*
———. *The Fur Hunters of the Far West.* Kenneth A. Spaulding, ed. Norman: University of Oklahoma Press, 1956.

Ross, *Snake Country Journal*
———. *Journal of Occurrences Kept during a Voyage to the Snake Country by Alexander Ross Commencing on T[h]ursday the 10th day of February 1824* (Hudson's Bay Company MS B. 202/a/1).

Ross, Snake Country 1824 Journal
———. "Journal of Alexander Ross—Snake Country Expedition, 1824." T. C. Elliott, ed. *Quarterly of the Oregon Historical Society* 14 (December 1913): 366–88.

Rowand, *Second Edmonton Journal*
Rowand, John. *Diary of Occurrences transpiring at Edmonton House, Fall 1826 and continued by John Rowand Chief Factor* (Hudson's Bay Company MS B. 60/a/24).

Rowand, *Second Edmonton Report*
————. *Edmonton Report 1823–24* (Hudson's Bay Company MS B. 60/e/6).

Russell, "Trapper Trails"
Russell, Carl P. "Trapper Trails to the Sisk-ke-dee." *Annals of Wyoming* 17 (July 1945): 88–105.

Simpson, *Athabasca Journal*
[Simpson, George]. *Journal of Occurrences in the Athabasca Department by George Simpson, 1820 and 1821, and Report.* E. E. Rich, ed. Toronto: The Champlain Society, 1938, pp. 1– 474.

Simpson, *Character Book*
[————]. *The "Character Book" of Governor George Simpson* (1832). In *Hudson's Bay Miscellany*, pp. 151–236.

Simpson's 1828 Journey
[————]. *Part of Dispatch from George Simpson Esqr. Governor of Ruperts Land to the Governor & Committee of the Hudson's Bay Company London: March 1, 1829. Continued and Completed March 24 and June 5, 1829.* E. E. Rich, ed.. Toronto: The Champlain Society, 1947.

Simpson, *Journal*
[————]. *George Simpson's Journals Entitled Remarks Connected with the Fur Trade in the Course of a Voyage from York Factory to Fort George and Back to York Factory 1824–1825.* In Merk, *Fur Trade and Empire*, pp. 3–174.

Simpson London Letters
[————]. *London Correspondence Inward from Sir George Simpson 1841–42.* Glyndwr Williams, ed. London: The Hudson's Bay Record Society, 1973.

Skinner, *Adventurers of Oregon*
Skinner, Constance L. *Adventurers of Oregon: A Chronicle of the Fur Trade.* Vol. 22. New Haven: Yale University Press, 1921.

Small, *Edmonton Journal*
Small, Patrick. *Journal of Occurrences at Fort Sanspariel From 23rd May 1832 . . . * (Hudson's Bay Company MS B. 60/a/27).

Smyth, "Piegan Trade"
Smyth, David. "The Struggle for the Piegan Trade: The Saskatchewan vs. the Missouri," *Montana: The Magazine of Western History* 34, no. 2 (Spring 1984): 2–15.

Stuart, *Carlton Journal*
Stuart, John. *Summary Journal from York Factory Hudsons Bay towards the Sascatchewan 1824* (Hudson's Bay Company MS B. 27/a/14).

Sunder, *Pilcher*
> Sunder, John E. *Joshua Pilcher Fur Trader and Indian Agent.* Norman: University of Oklahoma Press, 1968.

Sunder, "Sublette"
> ————. "William Lewis Sublette." In *Mountain Men,* 5: 347–59.

Swagerty, "View from Bottom"
> Swagerty, William R. "A View from the Bottom Up: The Work Force of the American Fur Company on the Upper Missouri in the 1830s," *Montana: The Magazine of Western History* 43, no. 1 (Winter 1993): 18–33.

Swagerty and Wilson, "Faithful Service"
> Swagerty, William R., and Dick A. Wilson, "Faithful Service under Different Flags: A Socioeconomic Portrait of the Columbia District, Hudson's Bay Company and the Upper Missouri Outfit, American Fur Company, 1825–1835. In *Fur Trade Revisited,* pp. 243–67.

Talbot, *David E. Jackson*
> Talbot, Vivian Linford. *David E. Jackson: Field Captain of the Rocky Mountain Fur Trade.* Jackson, Wyo.: Jackson Hole Historical Society and Museum, 1996.

Thompson, *Journals Relating to Montana*
> [Thompson, David]. *David Thompson's Journals Relating to Montana and Adjacent Regions 1808–1812.* M. Catherine White, ed. Missoula: Montana State University Press, 1950.

Thompson's Narrative
> [————]. *David Thompson's Narrative of his Explorations in Western America 1784–1812.* J. B. Tyrrell, ed. Toronto: The Champlain Society, 1916.

Tomison, *Fourteenth Cumberland Journal*
> Tomison, William. *A Diary of Occurrences kept at Cumberland House by Mr. William Tomison Chief Factory [sic] for and on account of the Hon. Hudson's Bay Company Commencing June 8th, 1802 and Ending July the 13, 1803* (Hudson's Bay Company MS B. 49/a/32a).

Tomison, *Second Cumberland Journal*
> ————. *A Journal of the most remarkable Transactions and Occurrences at Cumberland House from 5 July 1777 to 1st July 1778.* In *Cumberland House Journals—First Series,* pp. 225–45.

Townsend, *Narrative*
> Townsend, John K. *Narrative of a Journey Across the Rocky Mountains, to the Columbia River, and a Visit to the Sandwich Islands, Chili &c.* Philadelphia: 1839. In *Early Western Travels,* 21:111–369.

Tyrrell, "Peter Fidler"
> Tyrrell, J. B. "Peter Fidler, Trader and Surveyor. 1769 to 1822." *Proceedings and Transactions of the Royal Society of Canada. Third Series–Vol. VII. Transactions Section II* (1913): 117–27.

Umfreville, *Present State of Hudson's Bay*
    Umfreville, Edward. *The Present State of Hudson's Bay: Containing a Full Descrip-
    tion of that Settlement, and the Adjacent Country; and Likewise of the Fur Trade,
    with Hints for Its Improvement, &c. &c.* London: 1790. Reprint Toronto:
    Ryerson Press, 1954, edited with notes by W. Stuart Wallace.

Utley, *Life Wild and Perilous*
    Utley, Robert M. *A Life Wild and Perilous: Mountain Men and the Paths to the
    Pacific.* New York: Henry Holt and Company, 1997.

Van Kirk, *Many Tender Ties*
    Van Kirk, Sylvia . *Many Tender Ties: Women in Fur-Trade Society, 1670–1870.*
    Norman: University of Oklahoma Press, 1980.

Wallace, *Documents*
    Documents Relating to the North West Company. W. Stewart Wallace, ed. Toronto:
    The Champlain Society, 1934.

Wallace, "Explorer of Finlay River"
    Wallace, J. N. "The Explorer of Finlay River in 1824," *Canadian Historical
    Review* 9 (March 1928): 25–31.

Wallace, Introduction
    Wallace, W. Stewart. Introduction to *Simpson's 1828 Journey*, pp. xi–lii.

Wallace, "Strategy of Fur Traders"
    Wallace, Gerald R. "The Strategy of the Fur Traders in the Snake River Val-
    ley, 1824 to 1846." TS, Master's thesis, University of California, n.d.

Warner, "Peter Skene Ogden"
    Warner, Ted J. "Peter Skene Ogden." In *Mountain Men*, 3: 213–38.

Weber, *Taos Trappers*
    Weber, David J. *The Taos Trappers: The Fur Trade in the Far Southwest,
    1540–1846.* New ed. Norman: University of Oklahoma Press, 1971.

Wells, "Ignace Hatchiorauquasha (John Grey)"
    Wells, Merle. "Ignace Hatchiorauquasha (John Grey)." In *Mountain Men*,
    7:161–75.

Wells, "Michel Bourdon"
    ———. "Michel Bourdon." In *Mountain Men*, 3:55–60.

West of Ashley
    *The West of William H. Ashley: The international struggle for the fur trade of the Mis-
    souri, the Rocky Mountains, and the Columbia, with explorations beyond the Con-
    tinental Divide, recorded in the diaries and letters of William H. Ashley and his
    contemporaries 1822–1838.* Dale L. Morgan, ed. Denver: Old West Publish-
    ing Company, 1964.

White, Introduction to Thompson
    White, M. Catherine. Introduction and Footnotes to Thompson, *Journals
    Relating to Montana*, pp. xix–clxi.

William H. Ashley Papers
    See Ashley Papers

Williams, Appendix A
    Williams, Glyndwr. Appendix A to Ogden, *Fourth Snake Journal,* pp. 169–72.

Williams, "Hudson's Bay Company"
    ————. "The Hudson's Bay Company and the Fur Trade 1670–1870," *The Beaver* (Autumn 1983): 4–82.

Wishart, *Fur Trade*
    Wishart, David J. *The Fur Trade of the American West 1807–1840: A Geographical Synthesis.* Lincoln: University of Nebraska Press, 1979.

Work, *California Journal*
    [Work, John]. *Fur Brigade to the Bonaventura: John Work's California Expedition 1832–1833 for the Hudson's Bay Company.* Alice Bay Maloney, ed. San Francisco: California Historical Society, 1945.

Work, *Field Journal*
    [————]. *The Snake Country Expedition of 1830–1831: John Work's Field Journal.* Francis D. Haines, Jr., ed. Norman: University of Oklahoma Press, 1971.

Work, 1825–26 Journal
    "Journal of John Work" (for June–October 1825, September–December 1825, and December 15th, 1825, to June 12th, 1826). T. C. Elliott, ed. *Washington Historical Quarterly* 5 (1914): 83–115, 163–91, 258–87.

Wyeth, *Correspondence and Journals*
[Wyeth, Nathaniel J.]. *The Correspondence and Journals of Captain Nathaniel J. Wyeth 1831–6.* F. G. Young., ed. Sources of the History of Oregon, Vol. 1, Pts. 3 to 6. Eugene, Ore.: University Press, 1899.

Acknowledgments

Leave from teaching responsibilities at New York University School of Law was provided by the Filomen D'Agostino Greenberg and Max E. Greenberg Faculty Research Fund at New York University School of Law, and by John Sexton, dean of the School of Law. Research was made both easier and more pleasant by the professional competence, help, and good cheer of the staff of the Huntington Library in San Marino, California, and of the Missouri Historical Society, St. Louis. A special debt of gratitude is also owed to Gretchen Feltes, Conservation Librarian and Carol Alpert, Multimedia Librarian at the New York University School of Law, Ann Morton, Research and Reference Librarian, Hudson's Bay Company Archives, Provincial Archives of Manitoba, Martha Clevenger, Archivist, Missouri Historical Society, and to Robert Ritchie, Director of Research at the Huntington Library.

It is not very likely, but in some inexplicable manner this study may have profited by being read, discussed, and commented on by the most distinguished gathering of legal historians in the world, the members of the New York University School of Law colloquium in legal history: Catherine McCauliff, Dan Hulsebosch, Louise Halper, Gerald Giannattasio, R. B. Bernstein, William Edward Nelson, and Howard Venable. It benefitted much more from the citation and substance checking and indexing by Barbara Wilcie Kern of East Ninth Street.

Finally, very special acknowledgments must be given to Martin Ridge and William P. LaPiana. For some reason that he never explained to me, Professor Ridge of the Huntington Library decided that this book needed an introduction and volunteered to write it. It was Professor LaPiana of New York Law School who found in the archives of the *Society for the Preservation of the Beaver* the original letter written by Franklin

Pierce proving that it was Pierce, then a congressman, and not James K. Polk, who wrote the *Society*: "I don't care if the Brits denude the Snake country, as long as they know when to leave."

Index